THE IMPACT OF DEVOLUTION ON SOCIAL POLICY

Derek Birrell

This edition published in Great Britain in 2009 by

The Policy Press
University of Bristol
Fourth Floor
Beacon House
Queen's Road
Bristol BS8 1QU
UK

tel +44 (0)117 331 4054
fax +44 (0)117 331 4093
email tpp-info@bristol.ac.uk
www.policypress.co.uk

North American office:
The Policy Press
c/o International Specialized Books Services
920 NE 58th Avenue, Suite 300
Portland, OR 97213-3786, USA
tel +1 503 287 3093
fax +1 503 280 8832
email info@isbs.com

British Library Cataloguing in Publication Data
A catalogue record for this book is available from the British Library.

Library of Congress Cataloging-in-Publication Data
A catalog record for this book has been requested.

ISBN 978 1 84742 225 5 paperback
ISBN 978 1 84742 226 2 hardcover

Cover design by Robin Hawes
Front cover: image kindly supplied by www.alamy.com
Printed and bound in Great Britain by MPG Books Group

For Emma, David and Ian

Contents

Detailed contents

List of tables

List of abbreviations

ALMOs	arm's-length management organisations
AME	annually managed expenditure
BIC	British-Irish Council
CAMHS	Child and Adolescent Mental Health Services
CHCs	community health councils
COSLA	Convention of Scottish Local Authorities
CSR	comprehensive spending review
DEL	departmental expenditure limit
DH	Department of Health
DWP	Department for Work and Pensions
EHRC	Equality and Human Rights Commission
ERDF	European Regional Development Fund
ESF	European Social Fund
EU	European Union
FPNC	free personal and nursing care
HMRC	Her Majesty's Revenue & Customs
JMC	joint ministerial committee
Lib-Dem	Liberal Democrat
LINks	local involvement networks
NAW	National Assembly for Wales
NHS	National Health Service
NIA	Northern Ireland Assembly
NIAO	Northern Ireland Audit Office
NICE	National Institute for Health and Clinical Excellence
NIE	Northern Ireland Executive
NIHE	Northern Ireland Housing Executive
NIO	Northern Ireland Office
NPHS	National Public Health Service
NSF	National Service Framework
OFMDFM	Office of the First Minister and Deputy First Minister
PFI	private finance initiative
PPP	public–private partnership
RPA	Review of Public Administration (Northern Ireland)
RSL	registered social landlord
SDLP	Social Democratic and Labour Party
SMC	Scottish Medicines Consortium
SNP	Scottish National Party
SOA	single outcome agreement
SSAC	Social Security Advisory Committee

TSN	targeting social need
UK	United Kingdom
UNCRC	United Nations Convention on the Rights of the Child
WAG	Welsh Assembly Government
WLGA	Welsh Local Government Association

Acknowledgements

Many thanks to everyone who provided support to make this book possible. I would like to express my appreciation to several colleagues and former colleagues at the University of Ulster who commented on various chapters. I would also like to thank, in particular, Emily Watt for her guidance and support and also Jessica Hughes and Laura Greaves for their assistance (all at The Policy Press). Thanks also to the anonymous referees for both their encouragement and constructive criticism. I would also mention Saul Becker for his advice on the original idea and structure of the text and also Richard Parry for his always valuable comments on devolution. Finally, I am very grateful to Gerry Hasson for his diligence in providing support for production of the text and also Colleen McDaid for her help.

ONE

Introduction

As devolution in the United Kingdom moves into its second decade and is fully operational in Scotland, Wales and Northern Ireland it is an appropriate time to undertake a comprehensive analysis of the impact of devolution on social policy, based on the experience of all three countries.[1] Earlier perspectives emphasised the importance of the relationship between devolution and social policy. The view was extensively promulgated that social policy formed the core of devolved powers and even that the devolved parliament and assemblies could best be regarded as social policy parliaments. Social policy has a key role in the powers devolved to Scotland, Wales and Northern Ireland and social welfare services have been a major component of policies emerging from devolved administrations. Just how significant social policy is for the devolution enterprise has been the subject of some debate with the view widely expressed that the social policies are a dominant or at least a very significant feature. Looking ahead, Parry (1997) suggested that the ability to take distinctive action on social policy was one of the main justifications for a Scottish assembly or parliament. Subsequently Scott and Mooney (2005) suggested that a strong argument could be made for social policy being a key driver of the Scottish Parliament and Stewart (2004a) noted that in a very real sense devolution is about welfare and indeed social welfare constitutes the bulk of its remit. Chaney and Drakeford (2004) went as far as terming the Welsh Assembly a social policy assembly for Wales and a similar assessment has been made that the Scottish Parliament is largely concerned with welfare and/or social policy (Mooney et al, 2006).

Such evaluations were largely based on the original nature of devolved powers, public expectations and the early policy outputs of the devolved administrations. The operation of devolution tended to be dominated by the major social services areas of health, social care, education and housing and by major social policy themes and contemporary agendas: child poverty, children's services, social exclusion, equality, the regeneration of local communities and fuel poverty.

Significant changes have since taken place in the overall context of devolution. The major change has been the coming into office of new governments, following the 2007 elections, with the Scottish National Party (SNP) forming the government in Scotland for the first time and with a new Labour–Plaid Cymru coalition in government in Wales for the first time. In Northern Ireland devolution was restored after suspension with a new four party coalition (although it is best described as an involuntary coalition). Constitutional change and a shift in political power also took place. The review of Welsh devolution and the resultant 2006 Government of Wales Act created a separation of the Assembly and Executive, but, importantly for social policy, provided Wales with a new form of legislative power to increase its policy-making capacity. The 2006 St Andrews Agreement paved the way for the constitutional settlement in Northern Ireland to get back on track with an attempt to remove some of the destabilising problems that had previously disrupted devolution. When the SNP came into power in Scotland this also had constitutional implications as they regarded devolution as an interim arrangement that could lead to complete independence for Scotland. The changes in government also carried the potential for an alternative relationship with the UK Government. It brought to an end Labour Party dominance in government in England, Scotland and Wales, a change that had the potential to influence policy outcomes in Scotland and Wales.

With devolution well established social policy has continued to play an important role. Determining whether social policy has a dominant role requires a consideration of the scope and significance of policies, decisions and actions relating to the main areas of social policy (health, social care, education, housing and income distribution and social security as well as aspects of treatment of offenders, planning, energy and community services). Policy making by the devolved administrations in social policy areas covers a wide range of formats. These include primary legislation that has been extensive in Scotland, limited in Wales because of the legislative restrictions on Welsh devolution and less extensive also in Northern Ireland, because of political disruption to the operation of the institutions. It is sometimes overlooked that in all three countries a substantial amount of secondary legislation, mainly regulations dealing with the detail of policy and provision, has been passed. A major format useful for evaluating the predominance or otherwise of social policy is the programmes of government that the devolved governments have all published. Much of the social policy output of the devolved administrations is in the form of strategy documents and consultation papers that include a discussion of policy issues and the working out of evaluations, public representations and government positions. Strategy documents may be accompanied by detailed action plans setting out the implementation of policies, changes in provision and delivery structures. Action plans can also be complementary to budget statements and statements of priorities in expenditure. An overall comparison, inevitably, has to mainly take a broad-brush approach that may not get into the detailed nuances of difference.

Academic analysis of social policy and devolution, and to a large extent political and media analysis, have tended to focus on the differential impact of devolution on major social policies and welfare provision. Academic studies have focused on the divergence–convergence theme in discussing the impact of devolution, usually from a one-country basis, that is, in practice usually comparing Scotland with England or Wales with England (Chaney and Drakeford 2004; Stewart, 2004a; Scott and Mooney, 2005; Drakeford 2006; Mooney and Williams, 2006). Comparing the impact of devolution on social policy across the three countries can assist our understanding of both the operation and consequences of devolution and our understanding of the nature of social policy in the UK. Comparing differences in social policy and the provision of services can be a complex exercise, requiring in the first instance the identification of the nature of differences. Evaluating the evidence for a Scottish social policy or a Welsh social policy or a Northern Irish social policy is also important. It is not possible to analyse the impact of devolution on social policy in Scotland, Wales and Northern Ireland without including references to England and the UK context. Former or existing UK policy and provision is in many areas the benchmark for determining the degree of change that devolution has produced. It is also important to take into account the extent to which the policy or provision already differed from England under territorial governance arrangements for Scotland, Wales and Northern Ireland prior to 1999. Once differences are identified in social policies, legislation, strategies, action plans and provision, it is a further task to evaluate the significance of their impact. Identifiable differences can range from clear-cut and important differences that may be unique policies or new and innovative activities through to what can be judged as partially different, or as displaying more minor differences. For the purposes of analysis and clarification this book uses a typology of difference, based on a broad threefold categorisation between innovative and distinctive policies, significantly different policies and more low-level incremental differences arising through the implementation of broadly similar policies.

The widespread interest and focus on differences and divergent policies from England is understandable. If devolution does not produce policy differences it would raise questions about the value and need for the system in the first place. This focus has had major consequences for the study of social policy. Williams and Mooney (2008) use the phrase 'decentring social policy' to mean that it is no longer appropriate or valid to write of one British social policy or the UK welfare system or UK social citizenship. Such perspectives give rise to the possible identification of four distinct systems of social policy in the UK. However, the focus on differences should not detract from the need to take a more balanced view of the impact of devolution on social policy as there are other important considerations. It is necessary to consider the continued significance of convergence or actual parity in social policy throughout the four countries of the UK and the reasons for this. Aspects of social policy that have remained as reserved or non-devolved responsibilities of the UK Government are of obvious importance in ensuring convergence. A range of other influences comes into play in promoting convergence in social policies and provision. Some of these are external to devolution such as European Union (EU) requirements; others are internal such as the process of policy transfer and copying. Another important area of consideration is the scope and effects of interfaces and overlaps between devolved and non-devolved policies and services. This has been a somewhat neglected topic but has become a more salient issue, developing a number of dimensions and requiring forms of cooperation between the devolved administrations and the UK Government.

While the main focus of this study is on the analysis of trends in policy and comparisons of policy it is also relevant to consider available statistical and other evidence that may facilitate an assessment of policy outputs. It is possible, with caution, to make comparisons relevant to provision using data distinguishing between Scotland, Wales, Northern Ireland and England. A range of socio-economic indicators gives at least a snapshot of social need and the Treasury annually publishes a comparison of public expenditure between the four countries, broken down by expenditure per capita on the major public services. Evidence pertaining to the measurement of performance and comparison of performance between the four countries is more fragmented but exists for some services and is also available over a time period, so covering the whole period of devolution. This evidence can be supplemented by evaluations of provision and performance produced by the devolved administrations and by the respective Audit Offices for Scotland, Wales and Northern Ireland. Devolved government and Audit Office reports tend to be based on a mix of statistical and qualitative analysis and often include recommendations for future changes in policy or service implementation. Comparative research studies or research reports are still quite rare but the findings of a few studies are available.

A set of background factors determine the capacity of the devolved administrations to formulate social policy: the nature of legislative powers, the capacity of the devolved bureaucracies, the administrative structure and efficacy of public bodies and local authorities and the availability of financial resources (one could also add here the ability of politicians). These factors clearly affect the degree of differences in policy and provision. However, the key to understanding distinctive social policies, strategies, delivery structures, patterns of provision and public responsiveness lies more in the influence of ideas, principles and values. It is necessary to discern and analyse the underpinning values and ideology for the social policies and approaches that the respective devolved governments have adopted. General assessments of the impact of devolution on social policy range from cautious overall conclusions to more specific assessments of individual countries or specific evaluations of individual services.

This book attempts to provide a comprehensive assessment and a comparative framework for a general analysis of the impact of devolution on social policy, using as examples major initiatives and the most recent social policy developments. The book chapters are organised in such a way as to provide both a comprehensive analysis of the impact of devolution on social policy in Scotland, Wales and Northern Ireland and a comparative description and overview. The main themes are presented through an integrated approach. This begins in Chapter Two with a comparison of the scope of devolved powers over social policy in Scotland, Wales and Northern Ireland and an assessment of the role and importance of social policy in each country in addition to comments on the administrative and financial resources and capacity of each country to formulate and deliver social policies. Chapters Three to Five cover the core theme of comparing the social policies and strategies of the devolved administrations with appropriate references to England. These chapters explore the differences in social policy and provision using a threefold typology of difference ranging from innovative and distinctive differences through significant divergence to more low-level incremental differences. After this, Chapter Six assesses the scope and significance of continuing convergence in social policy throughout the four countries of the UK and highlights the main factors promoting convergence. Chapter Seven examines in some detail the important area of interfaces and overlaps in policy and provision which have developed with the interaction of both devolved and non-devolved powers between Scotland, Wales, Northern Ireland and the UK Government. Chapter Eight addresses a key issue of explaining and comparing the approaches of the devolved administrations to social policy development through an analysis of underlying values and principles. While the book mainly examines the content of policies, Chapter Nine looks at some of the available evidence for comparing social need and the outcome of provision and expenditure since devolution. Finally, in Chapter Ten, an assessment of the impact of devolution is made using a number of dimensions.

Note
[1] The term 'country' is used to describe Scotland, Wales, and Northern Ireland and England rather than other possible terms such as territory, region, nation, jurisdiction, sub-state or sub-national unit. The term 'United Kingdom' refers to all four countries and the term 'Great Britain' to England, Scotland and Wales.

TWO

The salience of social policy in devolved policy, governance and expenditure

The significance of social policy for the operation of devolution can be assessed by examining the nature and scope of devolved powers, the substance of programmes for government and the content of legislation, and also by considering to what extent the implementation and delivery capacity of the devolved administrations is configured around social policy. The key elements of the mechanisms for delivering social policy are described as the central bureaucracy in Edinburgh, Cardiff and Belfast; the contribution of quangos and local government. The capacity to deliver social policies is also determined by availability of financial resources and expenditure allocations.

Social policy powers

The legislation that established devolution for Scotland and Northern Ireland adopted the same principle for the division of powers between the UK Parliament and the devolved bodies that had been used historically in setting up devolution for Northern Ireland in the 1920 and 1973 legislation. The powers that were retained by Westminster were listed in the legislation and every matter that was not listed became a devolved matter.

The list of matters reserved to Westminster in the 1998 Scotland Act included some social policy matters, specifically: social security, employment, equality legislation, regulation of professions, immigration, abortion and human fertilisation. Even with these exceptions the majority of devolved matters largely fell into the social policy category, including health, social care, education and training and housing (see Table 2.1). The remainder of devolved matters outside social policy mainly related to: the environment, agriculture, economic development, transport, sport and the arts.

Similarly the 1998 Northern Ireland Act defined as transferred (that is, devolved) all those matters not listed as retained to Westminster, which consisted of two categories. The first was reserved matters (which included some social policy-related matters, for example, criminal justice, human fertilisation and the National Minimum Wage), which might at some stage pass to the Northern Ireland Assembly (NIA) or could be legislated on with the Secretary of State's consent. The second was excepted matters (which included the Northern Ireland National Insurance Fund and immigration), which would remain permanently the responsibility of the UK Parliament and Government. All the main social services areas are formally devolved to Northern Ireland: health and social care, housing, education and training and also legally, if not in practice, social security (see also Chapter Six for discussion).

The 1998 legislation meant that the Scottish Parliament and the NIA could pass primary and secondary legislation for devolved matters, including the main areas of social policy.

The original devolution settlement for Wales did not devolve similar primary legislative powers but only executive powers, and these to the Assembly as a corporate entity with no distinction between an Assembly and the Executive. The Welsh Assembly was empowered to develop secondary or subordinate legislation, allowing it to make rules and regulations, to set standards and to issue guidance in 18 fields of competence as well as to exercise executive functions. This principle of allocation of functions was different from Scotland and Northern Ireland as only matters specifically listed as transferred to the Welsh Assembly were devolved. Of the fields covered some were highly relevant to social policy (such as health, social services, education and training, planning and local government) while others had some relevance (the Welsh language and economic development).

Responsibility for primary legislation for all social policies remained at Westminster, which meant that the Welsh Assembly Government (WAG) had to persuade Westminster to approve Wales-only bills or Wales-only clauses in UK legislation and also overcome the Westminster legislative logjam. Control over subordinate legislation allowed WAG to alter the level of prescription charges, student support and standards for care homes. However, the operation of this more limited form of devolution attracted much criticism, leading to a commission of inquiry (the Richard Commission) into the depth and breadth of devolved powers (Richard, 2004). The Commission noted the frustrations and delay with the current system and recommended that Wales should have more independence over legislation and also a separate legislature and executive. This was followed by a UK Government White Paper *Better government for Wales* (Wales Office, 2005), which agreed on a separate legislature and executive but proposed a gradual move to greater legislative powers. Subsequent legislation, the 2006 Government of Wales Act, separated the legislature and executive but the devolution of primary legislative powers was to be delayed and only introduced following a referendum.

Under a new interim arrangement Wales has been given enhanced legislative powers. This process involves the Westminster Parliament passing an order-in-council to devolve the power to make laws through Welsh Assembly measures on specifically listed matters within 20 devolved broad policy areas called 'fields' and set out in Schedule 5 of the 2006 Government of Wales Act. A legislative competence order can be initiated by the Welsh Assembly, reducing the dependence on finding a suitable Westminster bill (NAW, 2008a). The 20 fields are only a slight extension to the 18 fields in the 1998 Act and list core areas of social policy: health and health services, social welfare, education and training and housing, as well as others with relevance to social policy (see Table 2.1). Thus each Welsh Assembly measure adds a list of matters to the field, for example, the field of education and training includes 16 matters such as admission of pupils and the school curriculum. The executive actions and subordinate legislation of the Assembly also cover the same 20 subjects as the 'fields'. Schedule 7 of the 2006 Government of Wales Act gives a detailed list of the future subjects of devolved primary legislation, similar to the fields, but lists exceptions, for example abortion and the regulation of health professions are exceptions under health and health services. In practice, Schedule 7 supplies a list of devolved and non-devolved topics within the 20 policy areas.

Within each country there has been a movement towards the extension of devolved powers and also a continuing demand for a greater extension of powers. Such changes would mean further development in the importance of social policy areas. In Wales the new legislative competence process means that there will be an accumulation of new matters in each of the 20 fields, and by 2009 there was a total of 30 matters. The time it takes for the legislative competence process to be completed is lengthy, about 10 months, and cumbersome. It is likely that there will be support for a referendum on conferring full law-making powers on the Assembly. An All Wales Convention has been established to explore fully people's views on the issue of full law-making powers and will report to WAG on whether Wales is ready for a referendum.

The St Andrews Agreement in Northern Ireland envisaged the transfer of criminal justice, policing and treatment of offenders to the devolved administration within a year or so of the restoration of devolution in 2007. The Northern Ireland Office (NIO) (2006) wished to see the transfer of all the functions as a coherent whole, requiring a new devolved department and minister. A difference of opinion between the unionist and nationalist politicians on the timing of the transfer meant a delay of the remaining element of the powers that would be devolved to Stormont. This has made integrated working with some devolved areas of community-based social policies more difficult, for example, community safety and probation.

In Scotland there has been a limited process of extending functions. Some amendments have been made to the executive functions of Scottish ministers because of the administrative coherence of them having these powers, even though the subject matter is reserved (for example, financial assistance to transport in rural areas and food safety). Additions to the legislative competence of the Scottish Parliament have been relatively rare, with railways being the main example. The SNP Government's election in 2007 has led to a renewed consideration of the Scottish Parliament's powers – they have established a *National Conversation* on Scotland's future that will explore the possibility of Scotland becoming a fully independent country, with, by implication, full control over social policy, or instead of independence extending devolved responsibilities in areas identified during the *Conversation* (Scottish Executive, 2007a). The background paper *Choosing Scotland's Future* specifically identified (apart from greater devolution of taxation and spending) some further areas of social policy for possible devolution). Furthermore, an independent commission, the Commission on Scottish Devolution, was established (Calman, 2008), supported by the Scottish parties (except the SNP) and by the UK Government, to review the workings of devolution within the context of the United Kingdom. The major focus has tended to be on tax raising powers and more fiscal autonomy for Scotland but it has considered the distribution of functions.

Programmes for government

The programmes for government, produced by the devolved administrations, indicate the significance of social policy. In Wales the first programme produced in 2000 (WAG, 2000), *A better Wales*, was a 10-year plan which had three elements: new and improved services in health, social services, education and transport; reducing inequalities of all kinds; and sharing prosperity and a new direction for Wales in workforce skills and economic growth. Programmes for government have often been developed into detailed lists of targets or commitments – the first Welsh programme set out more than 100 targets and actions for achievement, 50 of which could be termed as falling within social policy. Targets included: the number of infant classes with more than

Table 2.1: Social policy areas: devolved legislative powers

Fully devolved		
Scotland	**Northern Ireland**	**Wales Fields (subjects)**
Health	Health	Health and health service
Social care	Social care	Social welfare
Education and training	Education and training	Education and training
Housing	Housing	Housing
Planning	Social security	Town and country planning
Finance	Finance	Finance
EU funding administration	Planning	Economic devolution
Criminal Justice	EU funding administration	Local government
Local government	Local government	Public administration
Administrative structures	Administrative structures	Welsh language

Sources: Scotland Act 1998, Northern Ireland Act 1998, Government of Wales Act 2006

30 pupils, fewer than one third of pupils leaving school without a qualification and better management of hospital waiting times. The agenda of the 2003 strategy, *Wales: A better country* (WAG, 2003a), provided the top 10 commitments to address fundamental issues around health, communities, skills and jobs:

• abolish prescription charges
• reduced and free bus travel
• school breakfasts
• a crime fighting fund
• top-up fees
• knowledge bank
• safer routes to school
• free swimming for young and old
• scrap home care charges for people with disabilities
• invest in schools, GP surgeries and hospitals

Nine of these top 10 commitments can clearly be defined as social policies. Of all the detailed 2003 commitments, over half related to education, health and social care services and local communities. In examining these many plans Rawlings (2003) identified three overarching themes of sustainable development, social inclusion and equality of opportunity. In 2007 the *One Wales* document was the foundation stone of the new coalition partnership and was described as a 'progressive agenda' based on the principles of shared values, common goals and joint aspirations (WAG, 2007a). The programme envisaged the use of the new Welsh legislative competences and the key policies were presented under an eight-heading framework:

- A strong and confident nation — governance
- A healthy future — health and social care
- A prosperous society — jobs and skills
- Living communities — housing and transport
- Learning for life — education and children
- A fair and just society — equality, rights, child poverty and youth justice
- A sustainable environment — environment
- A rich and diverse culture — language and the arts

Five headings of the framework can be firmly located in social policy: a healthy future, a prosperous society, living communities, learning for life, and a fair and just society. Looking at this in more detail, *One Wales* actually gives 228 specific commitments, with over half falling within social policy areas.

Northern Ireland's new devolved government produced a substantial programme for government (NIE, 2001). This programme marked a consensus between the coalition parties and took a five-themed framework, as outlined below:

- Growing as a community — equality, rights, tackling poverty, housing and community relations
- Working for a healthier people — health
- Investing in education and skills — education, skills and lifelong learning
- Securing a competitive economy — economic development, growth, regeneration and environment
- Developing north/south/east/ west relations — intergovernmental cooperation

Three of the five main themes relate almost exclusively to social policy, and a substantial element of cross-border cooperation also falls into this category. The programme for government of the restored executive in

2007-08 was a much briefer document, written in very general terms, and reflected the difficulty of the new four party coalition in reaching a consensus (NIE, 2008a). Five priority and key areas were identified:

- growing the economy
- promoting tolerance, inclusion and health
- protecting the environment
- building the infrastructure
- delivering high-quality services

Of 38 key goals listed under these five priorities, 17 fell into the social policy category. These priorities were set out in a framework of 23 public service agreements and of these only one third clearly came within social policy, but when broken down into more detailed objectives, 44 out of 95 can be categorised as social policy (NIE, 2008b, Annex I). Despite a change of emphasis in this second programme for government, with greater priority for the economy and infrastructure, social policy topics still had a significant role.

The first programme for the new Scottish Government, *Making it work together* (Scottish Executive, 1999a), the product of a partnership between the Labour Party and the Liberal Democrat (Lib-Dem) Party, contained the commitment to make a real difference for Scotland. The document led with listing 12 policy areas, eight of which were social policy areas, giving an early evidence base for the notion of a social policy parliament in Scotland. The substance of the document selected seven areas for a detailed action plan and specified targets, for example, additional teachers, nursing places, a carers strategy and an end to rough sleeping. These seven general areas related to health, children, poverty, a fairer, safer Scotland, enhancing rural Scotland, a successful and prosperous Scotland including education, and transport and the environment. Only this latter area had few social policy implications. In 2003 the programme for government, *A partnership for a better Scotland* (Scottish Executive, 2003a), represented a combination of the Labour and Lib-Dem manifestos. The document set out a number of areas of policy initiatives which, in terms of their relationship to social policy, can be categorised as:

- Social policy — health, education, children and youth work, and social services, including housing
- Related to social policy — rural development and improving public services
- Other — growing the economy, transport, sport and culture

This still represented a majority of activity orientated towards social policy. Each policy area contained a narrative of high-level commitments as well as a listing of supportive activity, for example, reducing the number of people who are in hospital longer than they should be. Of a total of 39 specified supportive activities, 26 fall clearly into social policy. The programmes for government produced by the SNP Government have displayed some differences of emphasis but largely in terms of the narrative, claiming a fresh approach to government. A new overall context was presented in the shape of the overarching issue of how Scotland is to be governed in the future and an underlying presentation of a positive case for independence. The big issues identified for the future of Scotland were: the 'economy, justice and home affairs, social policy, energy and the environment' (Scottish Government, 2008a, Section 1). The new Scottish Government has produced annual revised programmes but the main narrative has contained the same five strategic objectives, presented concisely as:

- wealthier and fairer
- smarter
- healthier
- safer and stronger
- greener

There is something of a shift of emphasis to 'a more successful country' flourishing through increasing sustainable economic growth, with a strong emphasis as well on the environment and climate change and on criminal justice. Health and education and children are identified as two of the five strategic areas. While this might indicate overall rather less emphasis on social policy, the position of social policy is accorded a greater role in the listing of detailed priority agendas. In the 2007-08 *Principles and priorities* programme (Scottish Government, 2007a), social policy actions comprised 25 out of the 39 actions described and in the 2008-09 programme, *Moving Scotland forward* (Scottish Government, 2008a), forty-four out of 90 measures identified fell into the social policy category. In both programmes health with education and children account for nearly half of all the priorities, needs and actions identified.

Content of legislation

The subject matter of legislative action by the devolved parliament, assemblies and executives may also be an indicator of the significance of social policy within devolution. Scotland provides the clearest evidence of a full legislative programme (see Table 2.2), with Wales having only imitated primary legislative activity through legislative competence orders in 2008 and Northern Ireland having a disrupted record of legislative action (see Table 2.3).

Acts of the Scottish Parliament have the same status as Acts of the Westminster Parliament. In practice, the Scottish Parliament has enacted a considerable volume of legislation, greater than the number of Scottish Acts Westminster might have been expected to pass in the absence of devolution (Page, 2005).

Table 2.2: Content of Scottish legislation

	First session 1999–2003	Second session 2003–07	Third session 2008 (Bills)	Total
Total acts	62	65	5 (7)	132
Identified as social policy	22	24	2 (3)	48
Finance	6	5	1	12

Source: OPSI (2008a)

Identifying social policy legislation is not a precise exercise and Table 2.2 notes separately budget and financial legislation that has an impact on social policy. Social policy legislation comprises just over one third of the legislation and this seems a consistent proportion, indicating that social policy does not actually dominate the legislative programme. In 2008 the Scottish Government listed its legislative priorities for 2008-09 – of the 15 priorities five could be defined as social policy and three others included aspects of social policy. McGarvey and Cairney (2008) warn that other measures than legislation may be just as important in policy developments. In practice the Scottish Parliament is also responsible for another category of devolved legislation – it can approve a motion to allow Westminster legislation to cover a devolved matter in Scotland. These 'Sewel' motions (originally named after a Scotland Office minister, Lord Sewel) are initiated by the Scottish Executive which invites the Scottish Parliament to give consent to the provisions being dealt with by Westminster legislation. Sewel motions became much more common than anticipated, with 86 approved between 1999 and 2008. An analysis of these motions, now called legislative consent motions, shows that 30% (such as the 2006 Health and Social Care Bill and the Housing and Regeneration Bill 2008) fell into social policy areas. A further 21% fell into the area of criminal justice, some of which have social policy implications. A relevant Scottish parliamentary committee considers a memorandum about the UK bill and the motion is put to Parliament as a whole, so the use of legislative consent motions represents the considered view of the Scottish Executive and Parliament.

Northern Ireland preserved a more limited scenario post-1999 of the use of devolved legislative powers. In the brief period from 1999 to 2002 the NIA passed 36 primary legislative acts and a further 22 bills were in the pipeline at the time of the suspension of the Stormont Assembly in 2002. These were subsequently passed relatively unchanged through Westminster Parliament and included the Commissioner for Children and Young People Order. It has been suggested that this was a fairly high rate of legislative activity, given the circumstances (Anthony and Morison, 2005). An analysis of the nature of legislation to date on a similar basis to Scottish legislation is shown in Table 2.3.

Table 2.3: Content of Northern Ireland legislation

	1999-2002	Enacted later	2007-08	Total
Identified as social policy	15	10	9	34
Finance	6	4	3	13
Other	15	8	3	26
Total	36	22	15	73

Source: OPSI (2008b)

The period since the restoration of devolution has seen a small legislative programme to produce agreed legislation, in the context of difficulties with the functioning of the Executive. However, it is clear that social policy areas have dominated, with the introduction of public health and child protection acts, although some acts were social security legislation maintaining parity with Great Britain.

The Welsh legislative process presents a complex picture for identifying the significance of social policy legislation, but it is possible to make a limited assessment. Originally, the Welsh Assembly could request Wales-only legislation from Westminster through the Secretary of State for Wales, and between 2001 and 2006 eight bids were successful. This mechanism proved a limited and difficult vehicle for WAG influence but it can be noted that four of the eight related to health or children. Some Westminster legislation contained substantially different provisions for Wales, and between 1999 and 2004 Patchett (2005) identified 17 such acts, with 10 covering social policy topics. WAG enacted subordinate legislation and although some of these statutory instruments can be technical or very detailed it also gives some indication of the legislative concerns and competencies in Wales. There are 200-300 statutory instruments per annum which have tended to be dominated by agriculture but this is followed by education and children and then health and social care. However, it has been noted that in the context of limited Welsh competence Westminster made more statutory instruments for health and education in Wales than the Welsh Assembly (Navarro and Lambert, 2005). The enhanced powers for Wales since 2006 means that the Assembly is given legislative competence by order-in-council at Westminster to make laws in the devolved fields. As discussed above, these legislative competence orders insert specific matters into one or more of the 20 fields, in which the Assembly can pass legislation known as Assembly measures. It was anticipated that there might be only four or five legislative competence orders per year (Welsh Affairs Committee, 2008a) and to date there have been four legislative competence orders completed relating to education and training, affordable housing, domiciliary care, and children and families, with a further six in progress, including orders covering mental health and carers. The first actual Welsh Assembly measure to be enacted concerned National Health Service (NHS) redress. Subsequently, a further education measure was passed, and four of the measures in progress also relate to education. The legislative competence orders and measures developed to date are strongly orientated towards social policy topics. Thus the enhanced legislative progress has enabled Wales to engage more fully and significantly with social policy issues.

A further indication of the role of social policy is given, particularly in Scotland and Wales, in the way that the devolved administrations have presented their work. In 2008 both governments presented their work under a topic index (Table 2.4).

While the Northern Ireland Government does not present its work under topics, the main categories of public service agreements used to present the implementation of the programme for government in the budget provide an interesting comparison. It is striking that more social policy topics are put forward in Wales than Scotland but the other way around for economic activity. The Northern Ireland material is more evenly divided, but social policy forms the largest category in both Wales and Northern Ireland.

Table 2.4: Government topics

	Scotland	Wales	Northern Ireland
Social policy	3	7	8
Business/economy	7	3	6
Environment	3	2	4
Government	4	3	2
Other	3	4	3
Total	20	19	23

Source: Analysis of data on devolved government websites

Central bureaucracies

Devolution required an expanded structure of central administration in Scotland and Wales. The main model following devolution was of government departments, in part influenced by existing territorial structures and Whitehall patterns of departments as well as by the programmes for government. One factor determining their establishment and operation was that all the staff remained as UK civil servants. A further unifying factor was the overarching position of one permanent secretary in Scotland and Wales and a management board for corporate development to deliver devolved policies.

Wales has kept to a traditional structure of 10 core government departments and four small support departments. Each main Welsh department has a director as the lead civil servant. The main departments are led politically by a minister but social justice, health and children and families also have departmental deputy ministers. Changes in the configuration of departments have reflected changes in government or changes in priorities and strategies. Following the 2007 election, the former departments of social justice and regeneration and local government and culture were restructured. As Table 2.5 indicates, eight of the 10 main departments relate strongly to social policies, whether wholly or in part.

Similarly in Scotland there is only one permanent secretary, which creates a unifying influence and strong leadership for administration and management functions. Directorates have replaced the traditional department structure with lead directors for each directorate and a director-general for each of the core government areas. The Scottish administration also has a strategic board consisting of the permanent secretary and the director-general and two external non-executive directors.

Northern Ireland presents a very different civil service set-up. Since 1921 Northern Ireland has maintained its own separate civil service and this continued under direct rule. Thus the Northern Ireland Civil Service and the devolved central administration has a structure which formally reflects a mini home civil service. There is a head of the Northern Ireland Civil Service but each department is headed by a permanent secretary. The overarching management mechanism is a permanent secretary group meeting, akin to the permanent secretaries management group in Whitehall.

Table 2.5: Social policy-related departments 2008

Wales	Northern Ireland	Scotland	(including)
Health and Social Services	Health and Social Services	Health	Public Health Communities
Children and Education	Education	Education	Children/Schools
Public Health and Professions	Employment and Learning		
Social Justice and Local Government	OFMDFM Social Development	Justice and Community	Community Safety
Finance	Finance and Personnel	Finance and Growth	Enterprise Transfer
Environment and Housing	Environment (Local Government)		
Consumer Affairs	Regional Development		
Equality and Communication			
Rural Affairs	Agriculture and Rural Development	Environment	Environment

For the first two periods of devolution until 2007, Scottish Executive departments reflected a more traditional approach, with six main service delivery departments covering: education, health, finance, justice, enterprise and lifelong learning and environment and rural affairs. Since 2007 there are cabinet secretaries (senior ministers), supported by deputy ministers, for finance, and sustainable growth, education and lifelong learning, health and well-being, justice and rural affairs and the environment. Also since 2007 the Scottish administration has been organised into 50 directorates for aspects of the five core strategic objectives and corresponding to five cabinet minister responsibilities. This reconfiguration has produced a concentration of social policy issues into two core strategic areas of health and education, with elements in the other areas relating to housing, community safety and rural issues. The restructuring in Scotland demonstrated the flexibility in devolution to move beyond traditional civil service department structures to mould central administration to core policy objectives and priorities. Scottish civil servants have been seen as crucial for the development and implementation of policy (McGarvey and Cairney, 2008, p 123).

When devolution was established in Northern Ireland in 1998, 11 government departments were created to administer devolved or transferred matters. These replaced six previous departments, largely in response to the political need to create more senior ministerial positions to be shared by the political parties in the coalition government. This meant an element of artificiality in dividing education into two and creating such groupings as housing and social security in a department for social development. The Office of the First Minister and Deputy First Minister (OFMDFM) takes responsibility for a range of cross-cutting policies and services including equality, economic policy and cross-border cooperation. The overall configuration, as Table 2.5 indicates, is not dissimilar from Wales and Scotland, with major elements representing social policy topics and only one or two departments not involving aspects of social policy. Largely for political reasons, the configuration and number of departments has remained unchanged since 1999 and agreement on change or less rigidity may be difficult. There have been problems operating joined-up government because ministers have tended to take a 'silo approach'. The configuration of departments does not reflect some more modern themes in social policy, with no linkage of schools with children's services and fragmented responsibilities between departments in dealing with policy areas such as fuel poverty and welfare to work.

The devolved central bureaucracies clearly provide an important mechanism and capacity for the formulation of devolved social policies, the implementation of policy, the delivery of services and monitoring the output. Scotland and Wales show how there can be a more integrated or joined-up central administration than the Whitehall or Northern Ireland traditional model of separate functional departments. The structures have proved capable, particularly in Scotland, of being used in a very flexible way and are easy to change. This has facilitated the political management of the system of central administration to reflect the aims and priorities of the Scottish and Welsh Governments. There have however been criticisms of the role and influence of the civil service, especially in relation to their policy capability. There were suggestions that departments in Wales were dependent on UK departments in London as a policy resource (Parry, 2005), and this was also the case in Scotland. The Northern Ireland Civil Service, while adhering to political impartiality, has not generated many innovations in social policy and there is a need for greater policy capacity (Carmichael and Osborne, 2003; Birrell, 2007a).

As part of the UK home civil service the Scottish and Welsh administrations can still readily access major policy networks. This has been an argument used against the creation of a separate and wholly devolved civil service for Scotland copying the Northern Ireland model, which has been the subject of discussion (Parry, 2007). There does not appear to be a difficulty with UK civil servants working totally for Scottish ministers and to a Scottish government and parliament. While it has been anticipated that Wales would build up its own cadre of civil servants with experience of the Welsh public sector and networks, and become more autonomous in policy making (Osmond, 2004), there has been more of a debate about the viability and value of a unified public service comprising all sectors in Wales.

Contribution of quangos

With the introduction of devolution the new administrations became responsible for large numbers of public bodies or quangos (quasi non-governmental organisations), when previously the sponsoring departments had been UK departments. Quangos carry out delivery, advisory and regulatory functions, many covering areas of social provision. The devolved administrations' relationship with quangos was to prove somewhat problematic. In all three countries there were initial government proposals to abolish or to reduce the number of quangos and/or to absorb these bodies into devolved administration. The Scottish Executive (2001d) announced its intention to abolish public bodies with a further 61 bodies to be reviewed. In Wales it was announced that three major executive quangos would be incorporated into Assembly government departments (Watkins and Pearce, 2004). A review in Northern Ireland, which was part of a wider review of devolved public administration, reflected the new Executive's wish to alter arrangements to suit devolution. The final outcome of the review (RPA, 2006), envisaged a streamlining of the number of quangos.

One of the main reasons for this action to 'cull' quangos related to the capacity and direct powers of devolved governments. Thus the Scottish Executive did not wish to impose an unnecessary barrier between ministers and those implementing functions (Scottish Executive, 2001d, p 6). A similar argument was used in Wales, that if public bodies were taking a lead role in key policies or policy delivery they should be merged with the administration (Thomas, 2004). Thus the takeover or absorption of public bodies could represent an enhancement of the policy tools available to the new devolved governments (Lloyd, 2000). Absorbing quangos would create more capacity at the centre of devolved government, make government bigger and increase the scope of policy making (Birrell, 2008). The other rationale for an anti-quango mood saw the position of unelected and unrepresentative bodies delivering services as incompatible with democratic devolution. In practice the total abolition of a quango, including its functions, proved to be rare. A small number were abolished, for example the Scottish Medical Practices Commission and the Northern Ireland Housing Council. There were amalgamations particularly of health bodies, with 43 separate board structures in Scotland rationalised into 15 new health boards as well as 32 boards, trusts and support bodies merged into 12.

The transfer of functions to devolved government departments was most significant in Wales. Three bodies were brought into WAG, including the National Training and Education Council. Also proposed for transfer were Health Professions Wales, the Curriculum and Assessment Authority and the Welsh Language Board.

There were fewer examples in Scotland but Scottish Homes was abolished and transferred to central government as a new executive agency, Communities Scotland, which later transferred into the Scottish Housing and Regeneration Directorate. Despite the emotive criticisms of quangos by politicians in all three countries significant numbers have remained in operation.

The devolved administrations accepted that there was a case for the retention of some quangos and arm's-length public bodies, whether for reasons of bringing professional expertise to the delivery of some services, having a specialist single purpose body, where quasi-judicial decisions had to be made, or where political impartiality was important and there was a need for some bodies to be independent of government, for example, consumer councils. Thus the proposal to abolish the Welsh Language Board was seen as politicising the language issue (MacLeavy and Gay, 2005). In practice there has actually been a growth in quango numbers as devolution developed. In Scotland between 2000 and 2006

13 regulatory and investigative bodies were created, eight of which fell into the quango board format, and five were single commissioner offices (Burnside and Dewar, 2006). These included the Scottish Commission for the Regulation of Care. Devolution itself produced the need for new quangos, for example, separate social care councils for Scotland, Wales and Northern Ireland. If the abolition or absorption of quangos was limited, the devolved administrations were able to increase their scrutiny over quangos to make them more clearly instruments of devolved governance and more subject to political control, with ministers setting targets, conducting periodic reviews and parliamentary or assembly committees also able to review their work. Devolution has also had some impact in the operation of UK-wide quangos in Scotland – the Scottish Parliament can request reports to be submitted from UK quangos that operate in Scotland.

With new governments in place since 2007, issues of abolition and absorption came into prominence again with the First Minister in Scotland announcing a 25% reduction in the 199 quangos (Salmond, 2008). Action has already been taken to merge a range of skills and career functions into Skills Development Scotland and it was planned to integrate the Building Standards Agency into Scottish Government; however, it was the proposal to create a new merged arts body, Creative Scotland, that produced the most controversy. This strategy was justified as simplifying and streamlining public bodies and reducing unnecessary bureaucracy and duplication in service planning and delivery. In Northern Ireland a limited streamlining of public bodies also continued despite some questioning by ministers after 2007 of proposed new 'super quangos' in health, education and the environment. The devolved administrations have laid down principles that question the role of quangos but this large area of delegated governance remains a major component in the delivery mechanisms for social services in all three countries.

Role of local government

In Scotland and Wales devolution was in a sense imposed on a large existing local government structure which had major responsibilities for delivering large areas of social welfare through Scotland's 32 and Wales' 22 unitary councils. There was some concern that the role of local government would be undermined as devolution meant that Scottish ministers and departments became responsible for local government and its functions. In practice the introduction of devolution has brought little change in the functions of local government. In Wales devolution legislation requires ministers, in exercising their functions, to promote local government. Local authorities continued in Scotland and Wales with responsibilities for planning, resourcing and the direct provision of a wide range of social services: social care, education, housing, planning, public protection, community services, emergency planning, environmental health and leisure. Local government in Scotland has been seen as pivotal to the delivery of social justice and key policies (McGarvey, 2002). Most of what local councils do is implementing policies, strategies and action plans set by the two devolved governments. It is an indication of the scale of services that local authorities in Wales are responsible for one third of the total Welsh budget. In total contrast, local government in Northern Ireland has a system of 26 district councils with very limited powers that lie outside the major social services, and are responsible for only 4% of public expenditure. The new Northern Ireland Executive (NIE) (2001, p 66) had envisaged developing local government as part of the wider review of public administration. However, the outcome, as determined by the UK Government in 2005-06, was a slight enhancement of functions to only seven new councils, functions that would include community planning, urban and rural regeneration, physical planning and some aspects of housing management (Birrell, 2007b). The revised proposals from NIA in 2008 were still limited despite local government demands and research evidence (Knox, 2008) and the new devolved minister's rhetoric of creating strong dynamic local government (Foster, 2008). The number of new councils was increased by the devolved administration to 11, but the functions to be transferred were actually reduced. This means that minimal local government continues in Northern Ireland, with no major direct social services role.

A number of local government reform measures have been introduced in Scotland and Wales during devolution, mainly directed at operational performance. Reforms included value for money, the adoption of proportional representation in local elections in Scotland (McConnell, 2004), improving service delivery, audit inspections and internal political management. A Welsh local government measure in 2008 enables Welsh ministers to support improvement and intervene where necessary with local service providers.

A similar functional development in each country has related to the community planning area. Since 2003 local authorities in Scotland have been the key agency in a community planning process. This was a strategy to promote council community and public engagement with other service delivery organisations and to improve connections between local and national priorities. Wales was covered by the same duties as England in the 2000 Local Government Act, requiring community strategic partnerships to provide overarching coordination for strategic aspects of health education and regeneration. Wales has moved on to build on these arrangements through local service boards following the 2006 Review of Local Service Delivery (Beecham, 2006). In Northern Ireland community planning has been promoted as one of the main mechanisms for enhancing local government, but this may prove ineffective given the limited direct delivery responsibilities of councils, the lack of specific finance and the absence of coterminosity of boundaries. Evaluations of community planning in Scotland have raised doubts about their effectiveness in benefiting local communities, improving services and integrating a wide range of policy areas (Audit Scotland, 2006), and there are difficulties with public participation and local authority leadership (Cowell, 2004; Sinclair, 2008). Community planning through local community strategic partnerships exists in England but has also experienced some difficulties in more joined-up service delivery. This major innovation strategy in local government has not really led to the devolved administrations using the opportunity to devise their own specific community planning arrangements at the local level (Pemberton and Lloyd, 2008).

It is the relationship between the devolved administrations and local government that has attracted most comment and focused attention on how the Scottish and Welsh Governments have used the local government capacity. It has been argued that the difference devolution brought was that central–local relations became more important in the service delivery agenda than in England (McGarvey, 2002, p 43). Shared responsibility and working together in partnership have been the key principles. Partnership working is highly formalised in Wales with a Statutory Partnership Council consisting of representatives from local government and Welsh ministers. Partnership is assisted by the devolved administration working with the two representative organisations, the Convention of Scottish Local Authorities (COSLA) and the Welsh Local Government Association (WLGA). The Welsh Partnership Council has discussed such issues as a social services strategy for Wales, child protection and national service frameworks for children, young people and maternity services. Although the levels of central control over local government passed to the devolved administrations, the Scottish and Welsh experience had not been one of either central command and control, or of conflict.

Jeffery (2006a) sees devolution as affording opportunities to reconnect with central government, but in practice partnership has been more a project about participation than policy formulation. However, Laffin

(2002), even at that time, thought the WLGA was able to influence the Assembly on significant issues. In practice the devolved institutions in all three countries have been more open and accessible to local government than the previous territorial offices. This has to be balanced with research by McAteer and Bennett (2005), which found a majority of councillors who felt that the creation of an executive in Scotland had increased interference in local government affairs while other research found that there had not been a shift in the balance of power towards the locality (McConnell, 2006). In 2007 the Scottish Government negotiated a 'concordat' with COSLA. This contained their commitment to no restructuring, to freezing council tax rates and more flexible funding arrangements in return for each council negotiating a single outcome agreement (SOA) on how it would deliver locally on national priorities. Financial restraints, however, made it difficult for councils to deliver on such outcomes as smaller class sizes and free school meals for primary Years 1-3 (Cairney, 2009).

Financial resources for social policy

The devolved administrations' budgets in all three countries are set within the framework of UK public expenditure and are determined as part of the UK spending review along with UK Government departments. The arrangements for the most part continue long-standing conventions for Scotland, Wales and Northern Ireland prior to devolution (HM Treasury, 2007). The Treasury budget for the devolved administrations comprises two separate categories of public expenditure. *Departmental expenditure limit* (DEL), set over three years, is part of the UK Government's comprehensive spending review (CSR). The bulk of DEL is an 'assigned' budget, meaning that the devolved ministers have full discretion over the expenditure. Some items can be classified as non-assigned and are ring-fenced and can only be used for specific purposes, but the EU peace funding for Northern Ireland is now the only UK example. The second category of public expenditure is *annually managed expenditure* (AME) which covers items that cannot be subject to close three-year control. This includes housing support, student loans, NHS and teachers' pensions and in Northern Ireland, social security benefits. The bulk of expenditure falls into the DEL category.

The allocation basis used by the UK Treasury consists of two main components: an inherited expenditure base including new functions and incremental expenditure changes as determined by the Barnett formula (see Table 2.6). It is the latter which has attracted most attention in discussing the financial resources of the devolved administrations. The Barnett formula, which is non-statutory, has operated since before devolution and provides that when changes in expenditure by UK departments apply to England there will be an allocation on comparative programmes in Scotland, Wales and Northern Ireland based on a population basis. The changes to the assigned DEL budget are based on the following calculation:

Table 2.6: Barnett formula

Change to UK government departments' DEL	X	Comparability percentage	x	Population proportion

Source: HM Treasury (2007)

The population proportion used is now adjusted annually. Thus for relevant increases in spending in 2007, Scotland, Wales and Northern Ireland received 10.08%, 5.84% and 3.43% respectively (HM Treasury, 2007, para 47). The comparability percentage is based on the extent to which services delivered by UK Government departments correspond to devolved services in each country, for example, the comparability percentage for health is 99.3% for all three countries. The Barnett formula determines changes in the block grant or block budget element of DEL but does not determine the allocation to individual services. One of its attractions for the devolved administrations is that they can spend this 'new' money according to their political preferences without regard to those services in England that have generated the formula consequences (Heald and McLeod, 2005), in recent years mainly increased expenditure in health and education in England.

The Barnett formula has given rise to criticisms and has been the centre of a wider discussion of the basis of the funding of devolution. It does not allocate budgets on the basis of relative need between the countries of the UK. The Northern Ireland finance minister in the first period of devolution called the Barnett formula 'a chain round our necks lacking a clear needs basis', and as minister in 2002 he had initiated a series of needs-based studies (Farren, 2004). The restored Assembly has not rushed to endorse this option (Pidgeon, 2009). However, Heald (2003) has argued that a formal needs assessment may not work to Northern Ireland's advantage or probably Scotland and Wales' advantage, as need would be defined according to England's structure of services. A more prevalent criticism is that the formula over-rewards Scotland, Wales and Northern Ireland at the expense of England. McLean et al (2008) report an analysis that suggests that the current distribution of spending is neither fair nor equitable, based on selected measures of need. To date, the UK Government has not shown any inclination to change the system. The Barnett formula removes the need for direct negotiating of the allocations between the Treasury minister, secretaries of state and devolved ministers and thus minimises conflict between governments. It also provides a strong degree of certainty and predictability of funding to the devolved administrations over each three-year spending cycle, with the UK Government meeting any shortfall in tax revenue. The Barnett formula effectively means that increases or decreases to devolved budgets are determined by decisions made by England. It has been argued that Barnett has a limiting influence on the latitude for policy divergence (Bell and Christie, 2005) and on matching need. The system still means that the devolved administrations have considerable discretion over expenditure. Aldridge (2008) describes the degree of spending autonomy as remarkable and unusual by international standards. Criticisms of the Barnett formula and the funding arrangements for devolution, particularly in relation to accountability and need, have led to a consideration of other options. An independent commission (the Holtham Commission), set up by WAG, is examining the pros and cons of the funding formula in giving Wales a fair share and also identifying alternative funding mechanisms. Evidence to the Holtham Commission has suggested that Wales seems to have been less well-resourced in finance capacity than either Scotland or Northern Ireland (Heald, 2008). In Scotland the viability and desirability of measures that would facilitate more fiscal autonomy are under active consideration. The Calman report (2009) has concentrated on financial accountability. The 1998 Scotland Act allows the Scottish Government to vary personal income tax by 3 pence in the pound but its introduction would prove an unpopular measure. Options for greater fiscal autonomy include assigning selected tax revenues, oil and gas revenues, Scotland having its own tax base, borrowing powers as well as the full fiscal independence scenario.

The devolved administrations have access to four other sources of finance and may fund services through: EU programme funds, private finance, local taxation and borrowing.

EU programme funds: During the period 2000-06 Scotland, Wales and Northern Ireland had access to EU structural funds. These programmes had two elements, the EU funding from the European Commission and national matching funding that member states are required to provide. The main programmes were the European Regional Development Fund (ERDF) and the European Social Fund (ESF), the latter being the main instrument of community social policy but largely employment-orientated. EU structural funds were worth £1,094 million to Scotland during 2000-06 (McIver, 2006). Northern Ireland also benefited from the EU special peace programme, for projects to promote peace and reconciliation and regeneration. With EU enlargement, the funding available will be reduced in the structural and cohesion funds 2007-17 but monies from the ERDF and ESF will still be available, for example, worth £1.5 billon to Wales (Stokes, 2008), with ESF funding related to access to employment and social inclusion.

Private finance: The main form of access to private finance is through public–private partnerships (PPPs) and private finance initiatives (PFIs), where policy is devolved to Scotland, Wales and Northern Ireland. England makes by far the greatest use of PFIs (see Table 2.7), although Scotland and England demonstrate comparable levels in the capital value per head of population. Wales and Northern Ireland have a similar proportion of projects but PFI in Wales has a much lower capital value.

Table 2.7: PPP and PFIs

	Number of projects	% projects	Capital value per head	% of projects in education and health
Scotland	107	13	1,001	67
Wales	35	4	205	74
Northern Ireland	41	5	602	51
England	602	75	990	59

Source: Roy (2008a)

A majority of projects in all countries that have drawn on private finance are in education and health and this is especially true in Scotland and Wales. The current Scottish Government has moved away from the use of PPPs, although the devolved Northern Ireland Government has continued its commitment.

Local taxation: Local taxation is a further source of revenue for funding social services and given the local government context, much of local taxation helps fund local social services. Local taxation is of importance as it became a wholly devolved responsibility in Scotland and Northern Ireland, and is partially devolved in Wales. Local taxation amounts to around £4 billion a year in Scotland. It provides some autonomy over revenue raising. The existing systems of local taxation before devolution displayed some territorial differences, most obviously with council tax in Scotland and Wales, but with the continuation of rates in Northern Ireland. There are also differences between Scotland

and Wales and England in relation to the values in the eight bands of council tax. Following devolution the existing systems became subject to separate reviews with different outcomes. The rating review in Northern Ireland was set up by the new devolved government with the aim of raising more revenue, partly to bring average payments into line with Great Britain and partly to fund borrowing from the Treasury for infrastructural investment. The review also sought to make the system more equitable. Reviews in Scotland and in England were also examining the regressive impact of council tax. The Northern Ireland rating review provided some major divergences from England, Scotland and Wales in proposing the use of individual capital values, no bands, no maximum cap, regular revaluations, no 25% discount for single adult occupiers, no disregards for other vulnerable occupiers under 75 and no discount on second homes (Birrell, 2007c). The proposals were approved by the direct rule administration but were to be slightly altered by the restored Executive and Assembly. In 2007, a maximum cap was imposed and some further rates reliefs were accompanied by a rate-freeze on the regional component of the rates for three years, all in response to a popular outcry. Overall there would be an increase in rate revenue available to the Northern Ireland administration that supports services such as health, education, housing and planning. There was no freeze on the component of rates going directly to local council services. The Scottish Review (Burt, 2006) replicated (although did not acknowledge) the Northern Ireland proposal for a more progressive local property tax based on the capital value of individual properties, a proposal immediately rejected by the Scottish Executive. It appeared that one third of households would have had to pay more. WAG had put forward ideas for the reform of council tax benefits and the feasibility of a local income tax. These were not matters within the powers of the devolved assembly but WAG did use its powers in 2005 to implement a revalidation and a revision of bands, involving one new band and a new maximum cap of £424,000. In England the Lyons Inquiry made a number of recommendations to improve the fairness of council tax, including a revaluation of domestic properties and new bands at the top and bottom of the band structure (Lyons, 2007), but the UK Government rejected both ideas. In 2007, the new Scottish Government also announced a freeze in council tax bills, and widened the debate by proposing to replace council tax with a local income tax, which was seen as fairer and which would give the devolved government more financial control over resources. Without a political consensus and in the critical fiscal environment, the Scottish Government was to shelve its local income tax plans in early 2009 but the council tax freeze continued. Non-domestic rate income varies slightly in Scotland and Wales and the income (equivalent to council tax income in Scotland) is pooled and distributed back to local authorities. Until 2005 Northern Ireland had industrial derating and although this was to be phased out by 2011 it was applied in 2007 at 30%. Scotland has had a small business rate relief scheme since 2003 and Wales introduced a variable scheme from England in 2007, funded by the Assembly Government. A similar scheme was introduced in Northern Ireland in 2008 and non-domestic rates frozen for 2009-10. If Scotland used the option of adding 3 pence in the pound to the basic rate of taxation, it could generate £1.4 billion (Calman, 2008, p 72). This option has not been introduced and would be highly unpopular.

Borrowing: The devolved governments in Scotland and Wales are not allowed to borrow on their own account which limits their spending power on capital projects. It has been suggested that the Treasury's determination to control government debt led to this restriction and to the devolved authorities' capital funding having to come from the current budget or PPPs (Bell and Christie, 2008). There are exceptions relating to Northern Ireland as it was allowed to fund a proportion of its capital expenditure through borrowing up to a maximum limit as part of the post conflict regeneration investment.

Expenditure on social policy

Four general points can be made about the financial resources for social policy under devolution. First, the main social services take up a very large proportion of the budget. The Scottish draft budget for 2008-09 showed the share of proposed expenditure for the areas of health at 40%, education at 9.2% and local government (including social care) at 32.7%, that is, 81% of the total budget (Scottish Government, 2008a). The Welsh budget is broken down into main expenditure groups, of which there are nine. Health, children and education and social justice and local government make up 78% of the draft allocations for 2009-10 (WAG, 2008a). The total allocation in the Northern Ireland budget 2008-11 for health and social services and education is 41%; along with housing and social security the total is 70%.

The second point is how the available financial allocations work out between the four different countries of the UK. The available Treasury data for total expenditure per capita is shown in Table 2.8. This shows that allocation of expenditure per capita puts each country in the same order between 1998 and 2007, that is, Northern Ireland the highest, then Scotland, followed by Wales and England. Expenditure increases by

Table 2.8: Public expenditure per capita by country

	1998–99 outcome (£)	2006–07 outcome (£)	2007–08 plans (£)	Increase 1998–2008 (£)
Scotland	4,993	8,544	9,174	+3,651
Wales	4,947	8,172	8,577	+3,225
Northern Ireland	5,750	8,990	9,789	+3,240
England	4,165	7,076	7,535	+3,370
Total	4,321	7,308	7,790	+3,987

Source: HM Treasury (2008)

a similar increment in most years and devolution has not really altered the distribution except in the case of Scotland. This suggests that the current system for financing devolution would not permit a very sharp increase in expenditure per capita in any country.

The third general point is that the UK Treasury virtually controls the fiscal and taxing system. To date, the allocations under Barnett have been relatively generous and stable but could be squeezed. There is little scope for devolved administrations to raise more income for services although the SNP wanted to widen the parameters, not just in relation to a local income tax but also to a greater attribution to Scotland of North Sea oil and gas revenues and to borrowing powers. In times of financial and economic crisis the overarching capacity and dominant position of the UK Government has been clearly demonstrated.

Fourth, it appears that the current system with the Barnett formula is firmly embedded and is likely to remain in place for some time as the mechanism for funding the devolved administrations and their social policy programmes.

Conclusion

The devolution settlements and their development have demonstrated the key role of social policy in the powers and strategic and legislative decisions of the devolved administrations. There has been a continuing process and discussion of enhancement of these powers. The devolved administrations have settled in with a civil service capacity to formulate policies and strategies as well as the capability and power to mould local government, public bodies and cross-cultural partnerships to suit the delivery of social policy objectives. Financial resources to date have been sufficient to fund devolution and many of the social policy priorities in each country, but with the background constraint of overall

Treasury fiscal control. It is with these resources that the social policies have been developed and implemented.

THREE

Innovations, flagship policies and distinctiveness

Much of the analysis of social policy in Scotland and Wales has been dominated by the identification of flagship policies. The term 'flagship' tends to cover a number of different policy characteristics:

- innovative, as policies that have not existed previously in the UK, at least in key respects, for example, children's commissioners;
- distinctive as universal provision or in not having been universally provided in recent times in the UK, for example, free personal and nursing care in Scotland;
- unique to Scotland or Wales or Northern Ireland, for example, Welsh voluntary sector scheme;
- self-identified as flagship policies by the devolved governments, for example, student fees in Scotland and Wales.

It is possible to consider examples of social policies in each of the four categories, describe their characteristics and discuss their formulation and operation.

Innovative policies that had not previously existed

'Innovative policies' refers to policies which are largely new and original in the UK. Such innovative policies have normally required new legislation and/or setting up new institutions.

Children's commissioners

The innovative policy of a children's commissioner was initiated in Wales, where it came into operation in 2002. This followed a report by the Welsh Assembly Health and Social Services Committee, and was influenced by the recommendations of a tribunal of inquiry into the abuse of children in residential homes in North Wales. There was therefore a strong focus on the oversight of services for children. The initial rationale for the policy was also based on the need for a complaints system, an advocacy body and as a means to introduce and promote the United Nations (UN) Convention on the Rights of the Child (UNCRC). The policy of appointing a children's commissioner was followed by Northern Ireland in 2003, and Scotland and eventually England as well in 2005 (see also Chapter Six).

The Scottish Executive had actually raised the issue in 2000, but it was 2002 before the Scottish Parliament's Education, Culture and Sport Committee made proposals for a bill.

In Northern Ireland legislation to establish a commissioner was one of the few innovative pieces of legislation introduced in the first period of devolution.

Table 3.1: Children's commissioners

Title	Year commenced
Children's Commissioner for Wales	2001
Northern Ireland Commissioner for Children and Young People	2003
Scottish Commissioner for Children and Young People	2004
Children's Commissioner for England	2005

The overall aims and objectives of the three devolved commissioners were somewhat similar: to safeguard and promote the rights of children and to review the adequacy of policy and the delivery of services to children. They were set up as independent bodies in Wales and Northern Ireland and in Scotland as a crown appointment on nomination by the Scottish Parliament; all were funded by the respective devolved administrations. When the UK Government also decided to set up a children's commissioner for England they were given a weaker role, to promote awareness of the views and interests of children rather than their rights; other areas were subject to approval by the Secretary of State. Thus it appears that without devolution there would not have been children's commissioners with such extensive powers or independence and, in fact, maybe no children's commissioners at all. A comparison of the powers of the four commissioners shows largely a similar range of powers with some exceptions. In Wales the office has a broad remit to investigate complaints if they are of general application, to require information from agencies and a specific power to make representations to the Welsh Assembly.

The Northern Ireland commissioner has the most extensive powers of all the commissioners, including the power to review services and to initiate legal proceedings. The Scottish commissioner was not given the power to carry out the investigation of individual complaints and instead takes action to help people take their issues to other authorities. They are able to carry out an investigation into the extent a service provider has had regard to the rights of children, if it is a matter of general significance. The Scottish commissioner is also the only commissioner without the formal power of entry into premises.

The commissioner in England does not have the power to deal with complaints from individual children, and the commissioner has identified this as a source of criticism and disappointment (Joint Committee on Human Rights, 2007).

The staffing and funding of the commissioners also demonstrates the different role and powers (see Table 3.2). The Northern Ireland commissioner seems much more generously funded, and the low funding in England reflects as well the absence of a role in investigating complaints.

Table 3.2: Funding and staffing of children's commissioners, 2006

	Funding	Staffing	Number of children
Scotland	£1.2 m	14	1,200,000
Wales	£1.5 m	30	666,000
Northern Ireland	£1.9 m	30	500,000
England	£3.0 m	29	11,800,000

Source: NIA (2008a)

The actual performance of the children's commissioners indicates some different achievements and innovations. The Welsh commissioner has conducted a major review of policy on bullying, has commented on child and adolescent mental health services, child poverty and safeguarding children, and has been involved in criticism of the youth justice system and the dependence of children of asylum seekers.

The Northern Ireland commissioner has drawn government attention to lack of adequate provision of speech and language therapy, mental health needs, vetting procedures, unallocated child protection cases and under-investment in children's services.

In Scotland, major concerns have been children of asylum seekers, moving and lifting children with disabilities, children leaving care, and more generally, family law reform and adoption.

A common focus of all the commissioners has been on the facilitation of participation by children and young people. They have all set up strategies and frameworks of participation including focus groups, youth panels, reference groups, advisory groups and email surveys. In Scotland it has been reported that one third of staff are involved in participation work (Joint Committee on Human Rights, 2006, Memorandum 3). The commissioners have been original and innovative in developing means of involving children and young people.

Complaints resolution has been a much-used service in Northern Ireland, with 627 complaints in the first two-and-a-half years, the majority related to special educational needs and/or disabilities. In a small number of cases the commissioner initiated legal action on behalf of children and young people.

There have also been country-specific issues, such as coping with the legacy of the conflict in Northern Ireland and issues relating to Welsh-speaking children. The operation of the commissioners has also tended to throw up ideas for further innovation, for example, there have been calls for investigative powers in Northern Ireland to be extended to include private bodies, including faith-based and voluntary organisations (Fitzpatrick, 2006). The Commissioner's Office in Scotland has advocated the introduction of a children's rights impact assessment and Wales wants to establish a national advocacy unit to extend advocacy services across health, social care and education.

Older People's Commissioner for Wales

A not dissimilar innovation has been a commissioner for older people in Wales. One of the major early strategy documents produced in Wales was a study by an advisory group on a strategy for older people. This produced extensive recommendations based on bringing new thinking to the increasingly important role older people will play in society (Jarrett, 2006) – by 2021 one in three Welsh households will have someone aged 65 or over. Among the recommendations was the appointment of an older people's commissioner. The importance of older people was demonstrated by the production of the *Strategy for older people in Wales* (WAG, 2003b), based in part on the UN Principles for Older Persons. This ambitious Welsh strategy established a broad framework to tackle discrimination, to empower older people, to facilitate their continuing contribution, to promote their well-being and to improve services, and was the first comprehensive strategy document of its type in the UK (Windle and Porter, 2008). Support for priorities for older people was also indicated by the appointment of a deputy minister in 2003 with special responsibility for older people. The advisory group returned to the issue to advocate the establishment of a commissioner to ensure older people's interests were taken into account and to champion their needs. The commissioner for older people was introduced through specific Wales-only legislation at Westminster, one of few such measures. When the introduction of the bill was announced in 2005 it was noted that this was not only the first such commissioner in the UK but that there was no comparable independent office relating to older people anywhere else in the world (Jarrett, 2006, p 14). The first commissioner, Ruth Marks, took up her post in 2008. The general functions of the commissioner are: to promote awareness of older people in Wales and of the need to safeguard those interests, to eliminate discrimination and to keep under review the effect that public bodies have on older people. The commissioner is also able to provide guidance on best practice for providers of regulated services including private provision, on issues such as elder abuse. Other powers include the investigation of cases involving individuals, giving rise to more general issues, helping individuals with information or in bringing a complaint, and producing reports and recommendations for changes to services. The powers of the commissioner are to a large extent similar to those of the children's commissioner, but the commissioner for older people acts generally as a champion and ambassador for older people. Initiatives for older people in Wales have also been strengthened by the renewal of the Welsh strategy (WAG, 2008b) for 2008-13, which emphasised its policy primacy and continued the vision of valuing older people, maintaining their engagement, economic status and contribution, well-being and independence.

This Welsh innovation was to be followed by a similar measure for Scotland, introduced in 2006 as a member's bill in the Scottish Parliament. The proposed commissioner's general function was to promote awareness, review the adequacy of law and highlight best practice in service commission (Smith, 2006). The bill lapsed at dissolution of the Scottish Parliament in 2007 and has not been reintroduced. This was mainly on the grounds of duplication and overlap with other ombudsman-style bodies, although the Welsh provision has working agreements with the Equality and Human Rights Commission and the Public Services Ombudsman to counter this. The argument in Wales stresses that nobody provides the advocacy and challenge role of the Welsh commissioner. In 2007, however, Scotland did produce a detailed strategy on ageing, *All our futures* (Scottish Government, 2007b), including a proposal for a national forum on ageing. Since devolution Scotland has had what has been called 'an active approach' to ageing issues in contrast to Northern Ireland's 'disjointed and limited approach' (Trench and Jeffery, 2007).

The new devolved Assembly in Northern Ireland was to take a somewhat different but cautious approach in deciding to introduce an interim older people's advocate. This was to provide a focus for older people to highlight issues, to bring issues to the attention of ministers and to report on the views of the voluntary and community sector, and it was also to facilitate consultation on the role, remit and powers of an older people's commissioner. A commissioner post would require legislation and the advocate would cover the interim period. England, in this case, did not follow the Welsh model, but in 2008 appointed Dame Joan Bakewell as a champion of older people and an independent advocate.

Equality of opportunity in Northern Ireland

Innovative policies on equality of opportunity played a major role in the political negotiations leading to the Good Friday Agreement and the establishment of devolution in Northern Ireland. The Agreement included measures on furthering employment equality and covering the extension and strengthening of anti-discrimination legislation (UK Government, 1998, p 19). The 1998 Northern Ireland Act subsequently contained sections imposing a statutory equality of opportunity duty on public authorities and on anti-discrimination. These equality provisions were more detailed than provisions in the Scotland Act and the Government of Wales Act. The statutory equality duty on the public sector and the appointment of an equality commission were made the responsibility of the Secretary of State, although the Assembly would be able to legislate on these issues with the Secretary of State's consent. The existing provisions on fair employment, sex equality, race relations and disability were devolved matters for which the Assembly would have legislative responsibility. The first devolved programme for government noted that the provisions on equality of opportunity and human rights were central to the Agreement and contained a number of commitments to actions to take forward what became known as 'the equality agenda'.

Northern Ireland has had innovative and unique fair employment legislation since 1976, introduced and revised by successive British governments. Fair employment legislation was introduced to counter discrimination on religious and political grounds. It covered both public and private sector employers and introduced a range of innovative measures, including: annual returns of mandatory religious monitoring for employers with more then 10 employees; a complaints process; contract compliance; goals and timetables set for fair participation; and affirmative action programmes (Osborne, 2007). In the first programme for government the devolved administration was committed to continue to promote equality of opportunity in the workplace and progress continued with a significant drop in the differences in labour force participation and unemployment between the two communities, with the marked improvement of the position of Catholics in employment (Dickson and Osborne, 2007). The Northern Ireland fair employment policy has been seen as imposing duties on employers in a way that has never been seen before in the UK (Edwards, 1995; McLaughlin, 2007). It can be noted that when anti-discrimination law and equality provision were reviewed for Great Britain ahead of a single equality act, no recommendation was made for employment monitoring for the private and voluntary sector, and nor did the review link monitoring equality outcomes to positive action provisions. Surprisingly there was no attempt to evaluate the relevance or effectiveness of the innovative Northern Ireland fair employment model (Osborne, 2008).

The introduction of devolution saw two further significant innovations. The 1998 Act made provision for the amalgamation of the existing separate equality commissions for gender, disability, race and fair employment. A new Northern Ireland Equality Commission came into operation in 2000 and the transition to one equality body progressed smoothly without the marginalisation of any interest (Meehan, 2006). It was not until 2007 that the equivalent equality bodies in Britain were unified in the Equality and Human Rights Commission. The second major innovation with devolution was the mainstreaming equality provision of the devolution legislation. Section 75 of the 1998 Northern Ireland Act required all public bodies to have regard to: the need to promote equality of opportunity between 'persons of different religious belief, political opinion, racial group, age, material status, or sexual orientation; men and women generally; persons with a disability and persons without and between persons with dependents and persons without' (NIO, 1998). Each public body has to produce an equality scheme outlining how they will implement Section 75. There was also an obligation to consult the community and to carry out equality impact assessments on new and existing policies. The Equality Commission has a central role in enforcement through its monitoring and approval of the equality schemes. The equality duty, as it is known, came into operation in 2000. A preliminary assessment (McCrudden, 2001) suggested the potential of the innovative provisions for significant change. Section 75 continued to operate during the suspension of the devolved institutions and the issue received only a brief reference in the programme for government of the restored administration. Section 75 has been identified as an innovative policy through the statutory duty to promote and mainstream equality of opportunity (Harvey, 2001). However, its actual impact has been questioned. Osborne (2003) has pointed out that the process is intensely bureaucratic rather than outcome-orientated, even diverting resources from front-line services. The overall approach has been described as diligent but unimaginative (Dickson and Osborne, 2007) and resulting in 'tick box' practices (McLaughlin, 2007, p 119). A review by the Equality Commission claimed that Section 75 had changed how policy is made, but admitted that there was less evidence that the legislation had the intended impacts and outcomes for individuals (Equality Commission for Northern Ireland, 2007). The Commission recommended re-directing energies to the duties to promote equality of opportunity but failed to analyse the weakness and limitations of the concept of 'having due regard to promoting the equality of opportunity'.

Formally the Northern Ireland Equality provisions are unique in imposing a special requirement on public bodies to have regard to promoting equality of opportunity and to draw up an equality scheme for approval. However, strong enforcement and compliance laws refer only to employment measures. In practice the outcome of equality of opportunity policies in Northern Ireland is not wholly different from Scotland and Wales. The Scottish Parliament and Welsh Assembly and Executive have paid much attention to equality issues, taken a positive approach and have driven the agenda forward with new strategies and action plans and through the work of the Scottish Parliament and Welsh Assembly committees. (See also Chapter Seven).

In contrast, NIA has no specialist committee and while the OFMDFM committee covers equality it has not shown much interest in the topic. On the other hand, Northern Ireland has its own dedicated equality commission that takes on the major tasks in promoting equality of opportunity. It has more power and influence than the Equality and Human Rights Commission in Scotland and Wales, but is detached from the Executive and Assembly. The major innovative policy in Northern Ireland has remained the statutory monitoring of workforce composition by individual employers.

Elected health boards in Scotland

Another major proposed innovation in Scotland is the decision to move to direct elections to health boards in order to improve public engagement, involvement and accountability. This will allow the public to vote onto their local health board their own representatives and have a seat at the heart of the decision making process. This means a major democratisation on the NHS governance, with directly elected members and councillors nominated by the local authorities forming a majority of board members. The policy was questioned on the grounds of cost and several NHS bodies fear that party politics could destabilise services. However the legislation was approved and pilot projects for elections will be undertaken in 2010. The voting will be by STV and in another innovation the franchise will be extended to include 16- and 17-year olds.

Distinctive as universal provision

These policies and services may not be new but their provision on a universalist basis, free on the point of uptake, has been a major contribution of the devolved institutions. They are services which either have never been provided or have not been provided in recent years on a universalist basis.

Free personal and nursing care in Scotland

In 2002, free personal and nursing care (FPNC) on a universal basis was introduced in Scotland. This policy took on the status of a flagship social policy and was widely perceived as one of the major achievements of devolution and the Scottish Parliament and even as a defining moment in the development of the UK devolution (Dickenson et al, 2007). Perhaps of all the policies it is the one that has distinguished Scottish from UK social policy. The provision of personal and nursing care, which was free at the point of delivery and assessed according to need, was modelled on the UK Royal Commission report, *With respect to old age* (Sutherland, 1999). While the UK Government rejected this proposal, it was adopted by the Scottish Parliament's Health and Community Care Committee and after divisions in the Scottish Executive was eventually approved (Mitchell et al, 2001; Simeon, 2003). It was implemented through the 2002 Community Care and Health Act and covered people aged over 65, both at home and in care homes, and set out a list of personal care tasks to be covered. While local councils lead the implementation of FPNC and deliver some of the services directly, they are also able to commission personal and nursing care from private and voluntary providers. A key aim was to bring personal care into line with the medical and nursing care in the NHS, with the provision of free care based on need and funded through general taxation. The Scottish Executive provided additional financial allocations and from 2006/07 additional funding as part of councils' revenue. By 2007, 72,000 older people in Scotland received personal care services free of charge. The policy has had support in

Scotland from central and local government and from the voluntary and private sectors, and has proved very popular.

In 2006–07, the Scottish Executive commissioned an evaluation of the operation of FPNC and Audit Scotland produced a report on the funding. The evaluation study (Hexagon, 2007) found that the majority of people received FPNC services or payments without undue delay or complication, although some people had to wait for assessments or services. Delays were mainly due to staff vacancies, a shortage of care home places, user choice or service capacity. Some variation in interpretations by local authorities, for example of food preparation, was reported. The majority of service users were positive about their experience and the evaluation found strong support in Scotland for personal care being provided free without means testing. The Audit Scotland report focused on the costs, funding allocations, financial planning and the impact of FPNC (Audit Scotland, 2008a). Its key findings included a calculation of the total costs of FPNC for the first four years as £1.8 billion, but noted that councils would have spent around £1.2 billion of this even if the policy had not been introduced. It found initial cost estimates were difficult to make because of limited information. Monitoring the financial impact had been restricted, as had longer-term cost projections.

A number of ambiguities in both the legislation and guidance were noted, which has led to different interpretations by councils and variation across Scotland. Councils were using a variety of approaches to manage demand, and differences in the use of waiting lists and eligibility criteria meant that older people could therefore receive different levels of service. Most councils reported waiting lists because of: lack of staff to carry out assessments; limited capacity of care homes to meet demand; older people exercising a right to choose a care home; and councils managing services within available resources. Twenty-five councils had developed eligibility criteria or priority levels for their care services and all councils prioritised older people, based on their individual assessed needs and risks (Audit Scotland, 2008a, p 50). The Audit Scotland report recommended clarification on whether personal and nursing care should be a universal entitlement based on an assessment, or whether locally available budgets and resources should be taken into account. The report proposed a national eligibility framework (Audit Scotland, 2008a, p 5). It also recommended reviewing national allocation amounts for FPNC and methods for distributing this to councils as well as updating cost projections. There had been criticisms of the basis used to monitor costings, and assertions that cost increases over the first years of the policy were higher than expected (Cuthbert and Cuthbert, 2007).

Shortly after these reports, and with increasing demand for long-term care, the new Scottish government set up an independent review to take a closer look at funding, costs and sustainability. Lord Sutherland, author of the 1999 UK study, conducted the review, which identified problems with funding and variability of provision across the country (Sutherland, 2008). It confirmed that different interpretations by councils, for example, over food preparation and laundry services, had led to a variation in how FPNC was implemented. However, by far the most critical issue was the question of long-term costs and future affordability. The Sutherland review noted that in 2008 FPNC accounted for around 10% of the total resources used to support long-term provision for older people – free personal care is a relatively small component of the total costs of care. The review noted that, despite some practical difficulties in its formative years, the FPNC policy remained popular and has generally worked well, 'delivering better outcomes for Scotland's older people' (Sutherland, 2008, p 3). Benefits identified included reductions in the hospitalisation of frail older people and an increase in disposable income of some. The review endorsed a number of fundamental principles: that FPNC should be an entitlement for everyone, analogous with the NHS, and that access should be fair, equitable and transparent in terms of resources for the short term. It recommended: addressing the funding gap through the Scottish Government providing an additional £40 million for five years; that there should be clear national priorities; that local councils should consolidate the standardisation of assessment for services to common processes; and that there should be clearly stated target waiting times. Sutherland believed that the cost of the policy in the short term was affordable and action could be taken to stabilise it and to address variability in provision. It was recognised, however, that there were future uncertainties with demographic changes and health life expectancy. In the medium term it was recommended that demand should be reviewed and remodelled regularly to secure the policy. Also proposed was a holistic review of all the sources of public funding for long-term care of older people with more strategic planning (Sutherland, 2008, p 9). The Scottish Government has since stated its commitment to securing FPNC for the longer term.

The UK Government and WAG decided to implement free nursing care only on grounds of cost instead but WAG did introduce more heavily subsidised personal care services. The Welsh Assembly, while backing free personal care in 2002, took the view that UK Government action was necessary for implementation. Free home care for people with disabilities was considered but a commissioned report (Bell, 2006) concluded that the proposals would be costly. WAG has returned to the issue and is currently carrying out a consultation on the broader theme of creating a fairer and more sustainable system for paying for care in the future. The first Northern Ireland Assembly declared itself in favour of free personal care in 2007, but no further government action has been taken other than a commitment to a future review of options.

Universalising health benefits

There has been a cluster of health policies across the devolved administrations moving towards greater universalism, around removing charges for health services which are interpreted as a tax on ill health or a barrier to improvement of the health of people, particularly for those with long-term conditions. Thus the universality of the benefit is based on the principle that people should not be penalised financially because they fall ill and is seen as expanding or restoring the principle of healthcare free at the point of need. The abolition of prescription charges is the most significant example. This was seen as preferable to adding to the list of exempted conditions or groups. A phased reduction has been used in Scotland, Wales and Northern Ireland.

In Scotland prescriptions will be free for everyone from 2011. The existing costs will be lowered and phased out over a three-year period, as will the cost of prescription pre-payment certificates. The total annual recurring cost of this innovation by 2011 is estimated at £57 million.

In Wales action towards the abolition of prescription charges was taken earlier, with a freeze on the cost of prescriptions in 2001. This was followed in 2003 by a decision to reduce prices and to phase out charges over three years that meant that free prescriptions have existed in Wales from April 2007. This policy was again seen as benefiting those with chronic diseases and those on modest incomes and would encourage more people to see their GP and support people in making healthier choices. The argument was also made in Wales that the fear of losing access to free prescriptions may deter some people from taking up employment. The estimated cost in the first years of abolition is £29.5 million.

These developments have put pressure on the Northern Ireland Health Minister who set up a review group on the issue, but after media pressure announced in 2008 that all prescriptions would be free of charge by 2010, with an interim reduction of £3 from January 2009. The annual cost would be £13 million. The Health Minister's rationale did not differ from Scotland or Wales, stating that it was unacceptable that those who were ill should have to worry about finding the money to pay for their prescriptions, and that the system was unequal and unjust to rank people's suffering. The position in England is that the cost of a prescription was increased to £7.20 in 2008.

Scotland also introduced free eye tests and dental checks from 2006, an innovation that required primary legislation. Eye examinations are free and the testing process is also being broadened to provide a health assessment of each person's whole visual system – this can be seen as an innovation in public health and preventive care. Free access to dental checks in schools has been introduced, but the shortage of dentists has raised some concern about the national implementation of the scheme. Wales has moved more cautiously, although new ground has been broken in extending free eye health examinations to minority ethnic groups. A further distinctive move to universal health related provision in Wales was the decision in 2008 to abolish hospital car parking charges at almost all 130 NHS hospitals by 2011. Hospitals where parking is run by private companies will have to reduce costs until contracts expire. Charges were seen as a tax on the sick and on people who frequently attend NHS hospitals, whether as patients, staff or visitors. There have been concerns about monitoring access and also about the additional costs to the NHS – £5.4 million in Wales. Some hospitals have had to review or introduce car parking rules and checks to stop the misuse of free parking. Scotland has introduced a cap of £3 per day although only 6% of hospitals actually charge and some of these may move to free parking. In Northern Ireland only 20% of hospitals charge and a review of policy has led to certain categories of illness receiving exemption, but charges have not been totally abolished. Again, in contrast, almost all English hospitals impose parking fees – this Welsh innovation was criticised by the UK Health Minister as subsidising car parking.

Unique to Scotland or Wales or Northern Ireland

These policies are country specific and have developed as a unique feature of social policy. They are policies that do not exist in the other two devolved countries or in England. Some of the policies have been designed to meet particular needs of each country in terms of language or cultural factors.

Welsh voluntary sector scheme

The Welsh voluntary sector scheme is claimed as unique in the UK and 'probably the world' (WAG, 2007c). The scheme has a statutory basis in the Government of Wales Act and established principles and mechanisms to create a close working relationship between the voluntary sector and the Welsh Assembly and Executive. It also places the voluntary sector on equal footing with the local government and business sectors. A framework is set out in the Welsh voluntary sector scheme for all of the voluntary sectors' interaction with the devolved government, covering consultation, funding and support. Perhaps the main strength of the scheme is the regular meetings with the ministers with responsibility for services involving the voluntary sector. At these meetings current issues and mutual concerns are considered, and a record of decisions is published. The voluntary sector scheme is also supervised by a partnership council which originally contained Assembly members and ministers keep the scheme under review. It is not so clear that the outcomes for government–voluntary sector relationships for service provision are markedly different from the other three countries. A review of the scheme in 2008, while noting the key role of the structured dialogue and the international acclaim, suggested that the scheme could be more focused and effective in future to better enable an action-based dialogue between the voluntary sector and WAG (WAG, 2004a). Day (2009) does see the Welsh sector as developing strong upward connections to policy makers and suggests that engagement with ministers has promoted the capacity of the sector to influence policy making.

Distinct ethnic/national policies

All three countries with devolved administrations can be said to have a specific national feature that have an impact on social provision. A clear example is language, particularly the Welsh language. Twenty-one per cent of the population in Wales is Welsh speaking. The Welsh language has had official status since 1993 but its status was further strengthened with devolution, which has confirmed the language as an integral part of Welsh identity. Successive Welsh governments have been committed to supporting and promoting the Welsh language and to giving people the choice to live their lives through Welsh or English. A framework of organisations has been established to revitalise the language and to create a bilingual Wales. It was seen as essential that public services should be available in both Welsh and English and the linguistic preferences of individuals was respected. In 2003, a national action plan for a bilingual Wales had a particular reference to language choice in the delivery of health and social care. The Welsh language was also seen as important in fostering social inclusion. *The Welsh Language Scheme* is the statutory document that sets out how the Welsh and English languages are treated equally through policies and service delivery (WAG, 2008c). Education provision strongly reflects the language policy. Thirty-one per cent of primary schools (466) are Welsh medium and 15% of secondary schools teach Welsh as a first language and 84% as a second language. There has been a significant increase in the number of Welsh-medium teachers and support assistants trained to work in Welsh-medium early years work, and in Welsh language higher education developments. All NHS trusts are required to appoint Welsh language officers and the ability to communicate with service users is seen as contributing to the quality of care and as an integral part of the patient care pathway. A task group was set up in 2007 to strengthen Welsh language provision within health and social care, although language-sensitive practice has always been important, as has the use of Welsh-medium training and learning (Collins et al, 1997). Among the issues the task group is looking at is the Welsh language skills of the workforce, the Inspectorate's role in assessing Welsh language services and mainstreaming Welsh language considerations into childcare settings. The third sector is also identified as having an important role to play in supporting the language at community level and has led to a compact between the Welsh Language Board, WAG and the Third Sector.

The position of the Gaelic language in Scotland is very different in terms of the small proportion of speakers, but devolution has brought support for the language with a Gaelic Language Act in 2005 to help create a sustainable future. The number of primary school pupils in Gaelic-medium education in 2007 was 2,152, with a further 449 receiving Gaelic-medium education (Scottish Government, 2008d). In secondary schools there were only 449 receiving Gaelic-medium education. Devolved government has supported Gaelic education and there is a new Gaelic board, a national plan and guidance for public bodies on Gaelic language plans.

The position of the Irish language in Northern Ireland is different again, with much stronger political implications. Generally speaking Irish is embraced by the nationalist community but not by the unionist community. According to the 2001 Northern Ireland Census figures 10% of the population reported themselves as having an ability to speak Irish. In practice, language provision in schools raises issues not too different from Wales or Scotland. There are 31 Irish-medium primary schools with 2,630 pupils and 633 pupils attending Irish-medium post-primary provision, but Irish is also widely taught in Catholic secondary schools. The political context has resulted in major disputes at the Assembly and between ministers over a new Irish language Act. Despite commitments to such an act as part of the St Andrews Agreement, there is no consensus to promote and support the Irish language through legislation. There are no traditionally Irish-speaking localities in the six counties of Northern Ireland but the use of the language has grown and many public bodies now publish material in Irish.

The impact of other ethnic issues on social policy is also most clearly demonstrated by experience from Northern Ireland. The long-standing communal and sectarian divisions have continuing implications for aspects of social policy and the delivery and management of services. Major examples are the extent of residential segregation, especially in social housing estates, the mainly separate schools system, the cost of duplicating services and the need for anti-sectarian practice in social work. There is also a widely recognised need to deal with the legacy of the conflict in relation to victims, trauma and the regeneration of communities. Community relations policies have a special role and innovative strategies and action plans have been developed. The Good Friday Agreement led to the new devolved administration making commitments to improve community relations (NIE, 2002, p 30), exemplified in a key policy document produced under direct rule but influenced by the peace process and the restoration of devolution (Hughes et al, 2007). *A shared future* (OFMDFM, 2005) aimed at limiting sectarianism, reducing conflict at interface points and supporting the development of shared communities. The restored devolved government has been slow to progress this agenda because of fundamental party political disagreements over the whole issue. While this Northern Ireland issue is largely unique, a similar sectarianism has had some impact in Scotland and since 1999 there has been an increase in government activity tackling sectarianism in Scotland, focusing on education, sport, faith and parades (Flint, 2008).

While Northern Ireland is synonymous with religious division, a consensus of largely religious convictions has led to one other very distinct policy difference – the law on abortion. Abortion law has remained in Northern Ireland as it was in Great Britain before 1967. The prevailing 19th-century law means that a very small number of legal abortions are carried out, about 70-80, each year. Around 2,000 women travel each year to Britain to secure an abortion but they are not entitled to an abortion on the NHS. The UK Government has not acted to liberalise abortion law although it did legislate to bring the laws on homosexuality, civil partnerships and divorce into line. Views on abortion among the politicians of all the main parties are so hostile to change that Northern Ireland appears likely to continue with this major policy difference.

Self-identified flagship policies

The fourth category are policies which the administrations in Scotland, Wales and Northern Ireland have described and claimed as 'flagship policies.'

Student fees

The Scottish Government has accorded the status of a flagship policy to the abolition of graduate endowments. This had been a measure introduced in 2001 as part of a new set of student support arrangements which meant that Scottish graduates do not pay fees, set at £2, 289 for 2006-08 entrants, until 1 April after the graduation. The new Scottish Government took the view that the graduate endowment added to the student loan burden, and increasing debt remained a barrier to accessing higher education. The proportion of young Scots in higher education fell from 51.1% to 47.1% between 2001-02 and 2005-06 (Scottish Government 2007e). The abolition of tuition fees would not affect student support funding or university funding. In 2008, a flat fixed fee of £1,775 was introduced for students coming to Scottish universities from England, Wales and Northern Ireland (OPSI, 2008c). This policy has clearly put a major difference between Scotland, Northern Ireland and England, with a maximum tuition fee of £3,225 per year in England and in Northern Ireland. Most student support functions were devolved to the Welsh Assembly and ministers in 2006. WAG introduced deferred flexible fees from 2007/08. Fees were offset by the introduction of a non-means tested non-repayable grant of 60% of the fees payable directly to the place of study, but this grant is only available to students who normally live in Wales and who are studying on a course in Wales. The remaining deferred fee is repayable on a loan basis. The tuition fee grant is a Wales-only policy also designed to attract more Welsh domiciled students to study in Wales. The cost of this fee remission is estimated at £78 million for 2010/11 (Trench, 2008). An Assembly learning grant is also available, dependent on household income to all Welsh students wherever they are staying. The threshold for the maintenance grant is lower in Wales, which is another divergence with English policy. The Northern Ireland

Assembly has at times appeared to support abolishing tuition fees in debates in 2000 and 2008, but ministers baulked at the costs, resulting in Northern Ireland adopting a similar scheme to England, with a loan to cover the cost of fees but with a maintenance grant to students from low-income families. The difference in student fees between the four countries means greater financial support for Scottish and Welsh domiciled students. This 'convoluted patchwork of different fee regimes' (Trench, 2008, p 23) provides clear examples of distinctiveness in student support.

Approval of new medicines

The aspect of Scottish health policy under devolution that has attracted much public attention is the distinctive difference in Scotland in relation to the approval of new medicines. The National Institute of Health and Clinical Excellence (NICE) issues guidance for England and Wales, particularly on the cost-effectiveness of new treatments or medicines referred to it by UK ministers. Its advice also guides practice in Northern Ireland. Scotland has a separate body, the Scottish Medicines Consortium (SMC), set up in 2001, which advises NHS bodies across Scotland on the uses, costs and benefits of all newly licensed medicines (Dear et al, 2007). In some circumstances SMC advice may be superseded by a NICE multiple technology appraisal, taking into account the suitability for Scotland in relation to the principles and values of NHS Scotland, epidemiology and predicted uptake. The complexity of the application of NICE guidelines with devolution is set out in Table 3.3. SMC approved a range of drugs for NHS patients in Scotland that have been denied to patients in England and Wales, which has caused considerable media and political reaction and legal challenges. The Scottish body approved what are seen as life-saving drugs, such as Aricept® to treat Alzheimer's, Velcade® to treat bone cancer and Tarceva® for lung cancer, as well as other drugs for osteoporosis, muscular degeneration and head and neck cancer. SMC are able to make a recommendation of 'accepted for use', 'accepted for restricted use' or 'not recommended', and their advice is given up to 12 months more quickly than NICE (Dear et al, 2007, p 23). In practice, 80% of decisions are the same, but it appears that some devolution factors are at work in explaining differences, with strong support from the Scottish Parliament for making drugs available ahead of the rest of the UK. It is also the practice in Scotland that NHS boards can approve requests by clinicians to prescribe medicines not approved by the SMC (Scottish Parliament, 2008a).

Table 3.3: NICE guidance and devolution

England	Clinical guidelines Technology appraisals Interventional procedures Public health guidance
Wales	Clinical guidelines Technology appraisals Interventional procedures
Northern Ireland	Clinical guidelines (with advice on implementation from the DHSSPNI) Technology appraisals (with advice on implementation from the DHSSPNI) Interventional procedures
Scotland	Multiple technology appraisals (with advice on implementation from NHS Quality Improvement Scotland Interventional procedures

Source: NICE (2009)

Conclusion

Flagship policies have tended to be innovative and have sparked interest and debate throughout the UK. This has led at times to copying of a particular policy, or a considered decision not to pursue the innovation, which acts to emphasise the divergent status of the policy. Since devolution it seems that the trend to divergence in social policy has been led by health and social care and it is in this area that the main examples of distinct universalist policies are to be found. It is rather inherent in the nature of the operation and assessment of devolution that flagship policies are seen as coming from Scotland, Wales and Northern Ireland, but not really identified as coming from England. The identification of a flagship social policy is not a precise exercise and some policies for which the status has been claimed may fall rather short and more in a category of significant divergence.

FOUR

Divergence in social policy

Policy divergence is defined as a category of policies and strategies where significant differences can be identified between Scotland, Wales, Northern Ireland and England as a consequence of decisions by the devolved administrations. These policies fall short of major innovations or totally distinct policies, but diverge in significant ways. The main examples in this category fall into the health category plus other examples from social care, education and equal opportunities.

Health structures and governance

In the early years of devolution the organisation of the NHS was a key matter of debate for the devolved administrations – WAG's first request for Wales-only legislation related to a restructuring of the NHS, which was eventually passed as part of a general UK bill in 2003. This created a dual structure for the NHS in Wales, but a flatter structure than in England. There were 14 NHS trusts, 12 covering hospitals and two specialist trusts for cancer and ambulances. Twenty-two local health boards were responsible for primary healthcare and commissioning secondary health services and were coterminous with local authorities in Wales. There was no strategic health tier as in England. Three regional NHS business centres were set up but their role was supportive rather than directive for modernisation, continuous improvement and inter-agency cooperation. Within the NHS Wales structure were a number of specialist centralised bodies including: Health Commission Wales, which commissioned specialist services on an all-Wales basis; the Wales Centre for Health to improve health in Wales; the Health Care Inspectorate; and a National Leadership and Innovation Agency (WAG 2008b). The dominant thrust in this organisation of health services was described as reflecting localism and as a distinctive Welsh approach (Greer, 2004). The system was locally responsible, had local councillor representation on local health boards and local councils working in partnership with the NHS. The introduction of 22 local health boards coterminous with local authorities has been described as providing a very effective platform for developing strong community partnerships and had become a valued way of working (WAG, 2005a, p 38). However, the proliferation of local bodies, 60 in all, for the delivery of health and social care, did raise difficulties. Localism brought with it pressure on resources and the local health boards were small for commissioning purposes. Seven NHS trusts merged into three and groups of local health boards formed consortia for some services. A review of the NHS had judged the system of health and social care as unsustainable, including the configuration of health services (WAG, 2003c). A separate review of Health Commission Wales also judged it not fit for purpose, with unclear overlapping with the role of local health boards (Alyward, 2008). The outcome was proposals for the abolition of the commissioning role of local health boards. Following a consultation process a proposal emerged for seven health organisations in Wales to take on the functions of both NHS trusts and local health boards. The government's proposals reiterated that the principle of localism was of fundamental importance (WAG, 2008d). However, the change to a smaller number of larger bodies would seem to suggest a movement away from the distinctive Welsh localism. WAG will exercise influence through a national advisory board chaired by the Health Minister and a national delivery group chaired by the NHS Wales chief executive.

The first coalition executive in Scotland had moved quickly, with Scottish legislation to implement the new UK Labour Government's commitment to end the NHS internal market and GP fund holding. The division between trusts and health boards became a strategy/service division and action was taken in 2001 to unify boards with NHS trusts. Achieving integrated healthcare was a key policy aim (Scottish Executive, 2005a). Scotland moved to a flatter integrated structure than England or Wales, with a single tier of organisation comprising 14 area health boards, to assess need, plan provision, allocate resources and deliver services. A key feature of the reforms was the vision of a seamless healthcare service (Robson, 2007). The 2004 NHS Reform (Scotland) Act also provided for community health partnerships, of which there were 37. These functioned as sub-committees of NHS boards and became the key drivers for health improvement. Their main function was to bring together community-based services in a decentralised system, to provide a focus for the integration of primary care and acute services, to feed local needs into health board planning and to resource allocation and develop joint working with local authority social services. The underlying approach has been identified as a rejection of a command and control management approach in favour of public participation as the key feature (Stewart, 2004b). This unified structure of primary and secondary care was based on the use of networks and partnerships. The *Better health, better care* action plan (Scottish Government, 2007c) saw community health partnerships continuing, with a more flexible range of delegated resources and providing a wider variety of services at local level. Policy on NHS structures in Scotland has continued to demonstrate the principle of full integration of healthcare based on cooperation (Woods, 2004). There are some centralised aspects and NHS National Service Scotland is responsible for commissioning and performance managing, national screening programmes, specialist clinical services and national managed clinical networks.

Despite its traditional full participation in the NHS, since the 1970s Northern Ireland had a different form of organisation, with a largely integrated structure of health and social services. At the time of the introduction of devolution there was an existing two-tier structure of four health and social services boards and 18 health and social services trusts, 11 of which provided primary healthcare and social services and some also secondary healthcare, but there were still seven hospital trusts. The four boards were originally set up to deliver the full range of health and social services under the direction of the department. With the creation of the internal market in the 1990s the boards became commissioners of services and the main providers of services were the trusts. The new devolved administration committed itself in the paper *Developing better services* (DHSSPS, 2002a) to review the appropriateness of existing structures to the new environment of partnership and cooperation, signalled in the Executive's programme for government. The paper set out a number of options for structural reform specifically focused on creating a regional authority to replace the boards and combining the trusts. At this point the review of health structures was put on hold and absorbed into the wider review of the devolved system of public administration in Northern Ireland (Review of Public Administration, or RPA). The first RPA document (RPA, 2003, p 32) echoed the 2002 paper in noting that any new structural arrangements should facilitate coordination between primary, secondary and community care. The Direct Rule administration continued with the RPA in expectation of the return of devolution. *A further consultation* was published in 2005 (RPA, 2005) and contained major proposals for restructuring the health service. These were based on a number of principles: changes should be based on the integration of health and social services; the commissioning and delivery of services need not be separated organisationally; and the development of structures should be characterised not by the need to generate competition but by the creation of partnerships between commissioning and delivery (RPA, 2005, p 64). The document proposed that the existing four boards and 19 trusts would be replaced by a flat system of five or seven new integrated health and social services agencies. The consultation process showed general support for the proposals. However, when the Secretary of State and the Northern Ireland ministers announced the final proposals (NIO, 2005), they were significantly different. The new proposals were for the establishment of one statutory health authority that would commission services and be advised by local commissioning groups, although these would not be statutory bodies. Services would be provided by five trusts that meant a lack of coterminosity with the reformed local government structure. The main reason for this change was the response to an independent review of health and social care commissioned by the government (Appleby, 2005). Appleby recommended a separation between the providers of services and the funding/commissioners of services on the English model to sharpen incentives and drive performance, and suggested a single Northern Ireland commissioning body. It is doubtful if competition could work in Northern Ireland and there was support for structures based on the Scottish model of Health Boards, but the Health Minister, Mr Woodward, was to adopt the new proposal (Jervis, 2008). Legislation followed to reduce the trusts to five and came into effect in April 2007. When devolution was restored in 2007 the new health minister instigated his own review that led to further changes with a single regional health and social board, a separate regional support organisation and a new regional agency for public health (DHSSPS, 2008a). The new structures mean that Northern Ireland differs from Scotland and Wales in having a commissioner/provider structural division, a highly centralised commissioning system, and large delivery quangos with little recognition of localism.

One aspect of all three devolved health systems, which is different from England, is the administrative unification of primary and secondary healthcare.

Health commissioning/internal markets

The operation of an internal market was established in the early 1990s with a purchaser/provider split, but this had not been popular in Wales and Scotland. Wales had quite a low key health commissioning system, with the 22 local health boards as commissioning bodies responsible for commissioning both primary and secondary care and community healthcare services for all people resident in the area, except for specialist services that were the commissioning responsibility of Health Commission Wales. Commissioning implies a process encompassing the identification of health need, the specification of services and their procurement from provider organisations. In Wales the local health boards could commission services from NHS trusts but in practice commissioning was from the local trust, with little involvement of alternative providers and in reality no market choice existed for the majority of care (WAG, 2008c, paper 2). The local health boards could also be seen as too small for effective commissioning and the efficiency of the two-tier commissioner–provider system was questioned. This led in 2008 to the implementation of the commitment in the *One Wales* agenda to move to end the internal market and to replace it with an ethos of partnership. Local health boards would be abolished as commissioning bodies and there would be a change from a commissioned to a planned system, with a national advisory board, chaired by the Health Minister, allocating resources directly to trusts. The 2004 NHS Reform Bill, which introduced health boards, had finally ended the NHS internal market in Scotland and replaced commissioning. However, in Northern Ireland the Appleby Review in 2005 led to the endorsement of commissioning to improve performance and the new Northern Ireland Health Minister has continued with a form of commissioning. The organisation of the NHS now displays a number of significant differences in relation to key components, as set out in Table 4.1.

Table 4.1: Divergence in health structures

	Scotland	Wales	Northern Ireland	England
Health configuration	Integrated	To be integrated	Integrated	Not integrated
Integration of health and social care	Not integrated	Not integrated	Integrated	Not integrated
Commissioning/ provider divide	No	Change to no	Yes	Yes
Public involvement	Local schemes	Community councils	One council	Local government involvement networks
Public health		Central body Some localism	Central body	

Mental health

Mental health is an area of devolved responsibility and Scotland, Wales and Northern Ireland have brought forward their own mental health strategies and policies. Devolution in Scotland saw a change in the previous pattern of amending mental health policy and laws in Scotland after England and Wales, but with little policy difference (Atkinson, 2006). Mental health was one of three national clinical priorities, along with cancer and heart disease, and Scotland was to develop legislation that was not mirrored in England or Wales. An early initiative was the 2000 Adults with Incapacity (Scotland) Act, which provided for decisions to be made on behalf of adults who lacked legal capacity. This was the first major act of the Scottish Parliament and was seen as setting an example of the new Parliament's commitment to serving the interests of vulnerable people (Cheetham, 2001). The legislation also demonstrated the value of the parliament in avoiding delays at Westminster. When a major review of mental health legislation and community-based services commenced in England, Scotland was able to set up its own review. The Scottish Parliament produced a policy document, *Reviewing mental health law*, based on the Millan Report (Scottish Executive, 2001a), followed by the 2003 Mental Health (Care and Treatment) (Scotland(Act, which came into effect in 2005. The new Scottish Act set out 10 guiding principles. It defined mental disorder as mental illness, learning disability or personality disorder, and provided for three kinds of compulsory powers: emergency detention, short-term detention and a compulsory treatment order which has to be approved by a new mental health tribunal. It also established new rights for users and carers and access to independent advocacy services. The Scottish legislation differed from the proposals for England and Wales in an assumption against compulsion, less emphasis on public safety and a focus on high-level risk using the term 'significant risk', as well as confering a right to advocacy.

The proposed new legislation for England and Wales had a controversial focus on risk minimalisation and compulsory treatment which resulted in such opposition by stakeholder groups that it was withdrawn and not finally enacted until 2007, although the revised new version still had echoes of detention and treatment (Pilgrim, 2007). It was suggested that the Scottish outcome reflected a more collaborative style of policy making and genuine consultation rather than major differences in policy substance (Cairney, 2007). With the new legislation in Scotland the Executive published a delivery strategy, *Delivering for mental health* (Scottish Executive, 2006a), which concentrated on benefits, rights and care, improving patient experience, responding better to depression, early detection and better management of long-term conditions, enhanced forensic services and improved child and adolescent health services (CAMHS). The Scottish Executive had already published a framework to improve the mental health of children and young people through integrated inter-agency working (Scottish Executive, 2005b), including a named mental health link person available to every school. *Delivering for mental health* made 14 commitments with a timetable for mental health (Payne, 2007). A limited review of aspects of the 2003 Scottish Mental Health Act was launched in 2008, specifically concerned with named persons, second opinions, advance statements, mental health officers, availability, tribunals and the suspension of detention.

Wales was normally covered by Westminster legislation but had autonomy across some mental health measures. The first WAG made mental health one of its top three priorities and by 2007 had published two mental health strategies, one for adult mental health which largely followed Great Britain trusts in a move away from large institutional services to community services (WAG, 2001a). The second strategy was for improving Child and Adolescent Mental Health Services (CAMHS), and set out a four-tier concept for CAMHS covering: first, primary contact services; second, first-line professional services; third, CAMHS teams providing specialist services; and fourth, a tier of very specialist interventions (WAG, 2001b). The tier-based scheme required continual review and was later criticised as inadequate and poor (Williams, 2008).

A National Service Framework (NSF) for adult mental health services was developed in 2002 to drive up quality. This focused on health promotion, social inclusion, user and carer empowerment and normal daily life services. Following a review, the NSF was revisited in 2005 to set out standards for mental health services across the whole of Wales. *Raising the standard* (WAG, 2005g) set out eight standards and 44 key actions for service commissioners and providers. This document was based on the four principles of equality of access, empowerment of users and carers, effectiveness, and quality and efficient partnership working. The Welsh policies had also taken on board a mental health and social exclusion review published by the UK Office of the Deputy Prime Minister. The 2005 document also repeated the commitment to mental health as a top health and social care priority for Wales. In 2006, WAG published for consultation *Mental health promotion action plan for Wales* (WAG, 2006a), which included some new ideas, for example, mental health first aid to fill gaps in provision. The settings discussed in the document were roughly similar to those in the UK Social Exclusion Unit's 27-point UK government action plan and listed seven themes: parenting and early years, children and young people, workplace employment, older people, communities, health and social care services and mental health literacy. Targets have been set in new areas of adult mental health, in the areas of assertive outreach, liaison psychiatry, early intervention in psychosis and advice on CAMHS. An all-Wales mental health promotion network led by an advisory board is regarded as a flagship initiative using a collaborative approach to promote the mental health of the whole population of Wales. The controversial UK 2007 Mental Health Act applied to England and Wales, with a new definition of mental disorder, the introduction of supervised community treatment and a new mental health advocacy scheme. A Mental Capacity Act had similarly applied to Wales. WAG established an implementation project for the new 2007 Act and there was a new Mental Health Act code of practice for Wales. It has been suggested that while, as in the rest of the UK, there was a move towards community-based mental health services, there had been a continuing tendency to develop and deliver mental health services in a hospital setting. There are many parts of Wales where the shift to community care had not yet been fully funded or achieved (Williams, 2008, p 23). NHS Wales has taken steps to develop a national dementia plan in which this issue will be crucial. This followed a new strategy in England and Scotland, setting national targets for dementia diagnosis and care.

In Northern Ireland the main mental health strategy to emerge from the first period of devolved government was part of the Investing for Health Strategy, *Promoting mental health* (DHSSPS, 2003), based on a 2000 consultation. The rate of psychiatric illness was some 25% higher than in England. This strategy had more of a public health approach and was couched in more general terms of improving mental health through life circumstances and life skills support and raising awareness of the determinants of mental health. It did, however, set a target to reduce the proportion of people with a potential psychiatric disorder to 19.5% by 2008, with implementation based on an inter-agency approach. However, the scale of the budget spent on mental health remained at a low level, and this mental health strategy had little impact. The main piece of legislation was the 1986 Mental Health Order, similar to the 1983 Act for England and Wales and the 1984 Act for Scotland. It appeared that mental health law, policy and service provision were simply not adequate. In 2002, in response to increasing concern, the new minister in the devolved administration established the Bamford Review of Mental Health and Learning Disability. This comprehensive review highlighted gaps, difficulties, under-investment and the continuing domination of hospital services.

Encompassing 10 detailed reports the review did not conclude until 2007, and it was the new Executive minister who produced the response *Delivering the Bamford vision* (DHSSPS, 2008b). The Executive has formally adopted as a strategy the Bamford vision of person-centred, seamless community-based services, informed by the views of service users and their carers, and making mental health a key priority. It is anticipated that new legislation on mental capacity will come into effect in 2011, with an advocacy service and service frameworks. A Bamford monitoring board was established to exercise a challenge function throughout implementation and expressed concern at the commitment to progressing the Bamford recommendations and at the lower proportion of expenditure on mental health compared with England (McClelland, R. 2007). The plans for the major structural reform of health and social care did not accord any special attention to the impact on mental health services. Northern Ireland continues with less developed community care, and hospital care still takes up 43.3% of mental health resources.

Private sector involvement in health

PPPs introduced by the UK Labour Government were used in Scotland for capital projects but proved controversial. For example, the new Edinburgh Royal Infirmary, opened in 2003, was predicted to cost the taxpayer £990 million because of repayment charges, compared with £180 million through an outright payment from government (McCafferty, 2006). The SNP Government has decided to fund the new £842 million Southern Central Hospital in Glasgow entirely from public capital. Northern Ireland trusts, under pressure from the health department, have used PFI for major projects including a new hospital in Fermanagh. Escalating costs of a PFI-funded laboratory and pharmacy centre were criticised in an audit report (NIAO, 2008) and a study claimed PPPs in Northern Ireland had led to very high costs (Hallowell et al, 2008). PFI/PPPs had little impact on Wales, with hostility to the introduction of such measures – it has been suggested that there is little private sector capacity. Wales began to use private finance to fund capital development within the NHS, rather than PFI or PPPs, and WAG decided there would be no new PFI schemes introduced in the NHS in Wales (Roy, 2008).

In 2005 the Scottish Health Minister confirmed the use of private healthcare to help cut waiting lists and waiting time targets (Jervis, 2008, p 59), although it was recognised that the use of the independent sector should not detract from the duty of the NHS health boards to develop NHS services (Talbot-Smith and Pollock, 2006). However, the new government in 2007 identified private activity as only operating at the margins and 'that there was no significant private sector delivery and that is how the SNP government intends to stay' (Sturgeon, 2008, p 1). Action was also taken to close legal loopholes that might permit what was called the 'commercialisation of general practice'. The *One Wales* delivery plan in 2007 stated its intention to eliminate the use of private sector hospitals in the NHS by 2011, to end competitive tendering for NHS cleaning contracts with no renewal of existing contracts and to ensure any use of NHS facilities for private purposes would be appropriately remunerated.

The legislative provisions in the UK 2003 Health and Social Care Act to establish foundation hospitals did not apply to Scotland, Wales or Northern Ireland, and the Scottish Parliament and Welsh Assembly had rejected the principle. The Scottish Executive rejected foundation hospitals as going against Scotland's public sector ethos (Stewart, 2004b, p 112), and their policy of meeting demand in house and ensuring sufficient capacity. Northern Ireland has only a small private health sector and the NHS has used only a few short-term outsourced contracts to private providers from England to clear waiting lists.

England is divergent in making greater use of the private sector than any of the other countries, by purchasing capacity from the independent sector for the treatment of NHS patients and in adopting the policy of foundation status with greater freedom for provider trusts. With devolution there has been a probable strengthening of resistance to follow the new frameworks and policies in England for greater private sector involvement in the NHS.

NHS: public and patient involvement

There have been significant differences in how patient and public involvement have been treated in each country since devolution. In Wales, the involvement of people in decisions about health was central to the Assembly's new direction in health and social policy – Chapter 3 of the *Improving health in Wales* strategy (WAG, 2001c) was entitled 'The people's NHS'. The plans included a new charter, better information, public and patient involvement plans, an annual report on views of patients and representation of local councillors on health bodies. The 2003 Health (Wales) Act had retained community health councils (CHCs) and gave them new powers including the handling of complaints and the right to be consulted on major changes in their areas. The proposals in 2008 for a reduction in the number of health delivery bodies will mean a reduction in CHCs to seven, but with area associations to cover local authority areas. The *One Wales* programme contained a commitment to reinstate democratic enlargement at the heart of the Welsh health service. The new CHCs will have a strengthened role in scrutinising both the planning and delivery of health services and providing complaints and advocacy services. A further Welsh initiative envisaged local health board stakeholder reference groups to represent organisations with an interest in the health service.

Since devolution, successive Scottish governments have also been committed to improving public engagement and involvement in health. Scotland had produced a document on *Patient focus and public involvement* (Scottish Executive, 2001b) before the major restructuring, to encourage a proactive approach to public involvement that would move from a low priority to a day-to-day reality. This led in 2003 to a new public involvement scheme, with a Scottish health council to provide leadership in securing greater public involvement in NHS Scotland and with local advisory councils in each health board area. Community health partnerships were also charged with involving patients in the decision-making process and public partnership forums have made progress in involving local communities in the design and delivery of health. The Scottish Health Council supports community health partnerships and public partnership forums through providing advice and training. The *Better health, better care* strategy (Scottish Government, 2007c) proposed that people have real involvement, representation, a voice that is heard and are involved in the design and delivery of services. Specific strategies were to be produced for strengthening the public's role. *Better together: Scotland's new patient experience* programme aims to encourage and empower patients, carers and staff to work together in partnership to provide patient-centred care, and is described as making NHS Scotland a world leader in involving patients in the design of healthcare services. Also under consideration in Scotland have been direct elections to NHS boards (see also Chapter Three). The proposals would give the public the opportunity to vote their own representatives on to their local health board. Elected health boards were seen as giving power back to local people and the single biggest way possible to re-energise public engagement with the health service. This would represent a radical form of public involvement and democratisation and would be a highly distinctive Scottish policy.

Public involvement in the health system in Northern Ireland has never been a priority area to the same extent as in Great Britain. Four health and social services councils, coterminous with the four commissioning and planning boards, have, to date, been the only mechanism of public or patient involvement. The health strategy document produced in 2005 contained a commitment to 'involve people in the assessment of need, planning and designing services and the management of bodies delivering service' (DHSSPS, 2005a), and spoke of citizens rather than patients. However, nothing happened to implement these ideas and the view that the NHS in Northern Ireland is noteworthy for public participation (Campbell, 2007) is difficult to support. The proposed structural reforms will replace the four councils representing the public with a single patient and client body for the whole of Northern Ireland. Its role is largely limited to promoting the involvement of the public, although it has visiting rights. Northern Ireland is also different from Great Britain in giving local government councillors a limited role in health and social care. There is no representation on health and social care trusts although the new Minister of Health has agreed to improve local government representation on local commissioning groups, the patient and client council and the new regional public health agency. In all the health reform documents, public involvement appears tacked on to the end, very different from its position in Scotland, Wales and England. Policies on public involvement in health differ between each country and are significantly different from England, where a number of innovative policies have been attempted, and in 2008 patient forums were replaced by local involvement networks (LINks). These will operate in each local authority area to give local individuals and groups a stronger voice in how both health and social care are delivered, with a central NHS Centre for Involvement to give advice and support, and will operate along with the existing local authority Overview and Scrutiny Committees which scrutinise the operation of services.

Integration of health and social care

This has been a major issue throughout the UK, especially since the modernising social care and community care policies of the late 1990s. Following devolution, there was an overall commitment in all four countries to further promote collaboration, working together and integration between health and social care. There was an immediate initiative in Scotland to improve joint working. A post-devolution summit of senior NHS and local authority personnel led to a joint venture approach to community services with joint resources, joint management and single shared assessment. A special health and community care ministerial steering group and a Joint Future unit implemented this policy. The Joint Future policy was applied initially to older people's services from 2003 but was later extended to other care groups. Legislation allowed further flexibility in joint working, through pooled budgets, joint management and the delegation of funding, and made payments across organisational boundaries possible. The focus of the Joint Future initiative was mainly on older people's services and mental health and dealing with delayed discharge (Scottish Executive 2000a). However, community health partnerships were to become the main mechanisms for integrated working between social care and community-based healthcare, mostly renamed community health and social care partnerships. These brought together health services, including mental health, with local authority social services. These partnerships have been seen as an opportunity to mainstream partnership working in a fairly uniform way throughout Scotland, although they faced a number of barriers in terms of organisation, culture, staffing and the dominance of health (Cook et al, 2007). Scotland, however, has been seen as having a greater interest than the other countries in following a network governance model (Hudson, 2007). The flat structure of unified NHS boards in Scotland has made easier a uniform system of local partnerships with social services whereas England has a more fragmented and diffuse pattern of partnerships. However, research (Freeman and Moore, 2008) has also indicated tensions in Scotland, with problems caused by fears of a health takeover, separate NHS and local government budget processes and human resources challenges. Scotland also faced the lack of one-to-one coterminosity between local authority and health boundaries. Overall, Scotland has been seen as making more progress with integration than England (Evans and Forbes, 2009).

The pursuit of integration in Wales reflected the organisational structure. Here complete coterminosity between local authorities and health boards facilitated joint working, but the development of partnerships was largely left to local areas and local initiatives, as in England, using the flexibility of the 1999 Health Act. In 2005 the Welsh Assembly Health and Social Services Committee reported on the interface between health and social care. This report (NAW, 2005) recorded much close working, but identified the need for stronger action to promote unified assessment, to effect hospital discharge planning and to involve the independent sector. The report was noteworthy for identifying a list of barriers to more integrated working which included differences in structure, lines of accountability, lack of understanding of different professional roles and cultures, different performance systems, confusion over pooled budgets and problems in sharing information with different information and communication technologies (ICT) systems. In 2006, the Welsh Assembly agreed to review the adequacy of the capacity of the system to use services more efficiently to reduce delayed discharges from hospitals. Local multi-agency arrangements to ensure the greater protection of vulnerable adults developed in the period 2004-07, but partnership working in Wales continued to be largely determined by local arrangements. The 2007 social work strategy document, *Fulfilled lives, supportive communities* (WAG, 2007d), called for an increase in joint commissioning with health. Assessing that strong formal partnerships were under-used, it urged that formal health/social services collaborations should become the norm rather than the exception.

Northern Ireland is significantly different in having in operation since 1972 a structurally integrated system of health and social care, with a two-tier system of commissioning boards and delivery trusts. Up until 2007, of the 18 trusts, 11 were community health and social care trusts and 7 were hospital trusts. The community health and social services trusts provided a comprehensive range of primary and community health services and social work services and some were also responsible for all the hospitals in their area. When the new Health Minister turned her attention to restructuring health and social services, the minister's document stated it was essential that organisational structures supported a partnership approach (DHSSPS, 2002a, p 32). The RPA set up in the first period of devolution identified integration as one of the strengths of the health and social care system. This principle was never questioned and the new proposals, even as determined by NIO ministers in 2005, approved a more integrated structure now encompassing all the acute and teaching hospitals. With the restoration of devolution, while there was some concern at aspects of the ongoing restructuring, the principle of fully integrated trusts covering primary, secondary and community healthcare, and social care, was fully accepted. Integration in the delivery of health and social care is implemented through a programme of care approach, with integrated professional teams and integrated management structures. Achievements have been noted in hospital discharges and the closure of hospitals facilitated by a single employer body, but some problems have remained in terms of domination by the acute sector and lack of integrated professional education (Heenan and Birrell, 2006). In some respects the full potential of integrated structures has not been realised.

Education policy

Historically education systems have differed significantly between all four countries (Reynolds, 2002; Paterson, 2004). Nearly all aspects of education policy are devolved and the devolved administrations have all produced strategies embodying commitments to high-quality education to suit each country's needs. Wales produced *The learning country* (NAW, 2001), described as a blueprint with some distinctive aspects (Rawlings, 2003 p 150) subsequently revised up to 2010, based on proposed close links between schools and the community and with targets for policy delivery. Scotland had *Ambitious excellent schools* (Scottish Executive, 2004a), building on five national priorities in Scottish education set in 2000 (Clarke, 2006), and specifying 12 measures to improve schools. The first programme for government in Northern Ireland had an investing in education and skills section (NIE, 2001, p 37), which focused on improved standards of achievement, post-primary structures and a revised curriculum. Despite the apparent cross-national consensus on improving schools, the curriculum, improved outcomes and increased participation in higher education, it is still possible to identify some quite significant differences in education policy that have emerged.

Historically education provides a major example of policy divergence in Northern Ireland in its system of secondary education, based on academic selection through the 11 plus, with the traditional divide into grammar and secondary schools. The policy issue was opened up by the Direct Rule Labour Government before devolution in 1999, but the first programme for government had only referred to a review of post-primary education. The problem identified was that of low and under-achievement, not the issue of children from higher socio-economic groups accessing grammar schools in much larger numbers than those from lower socio-economic groups. In 2000, a committee was appointed by the Sinn Féin minister that proposed replacing the 11 plus with a system of formative assessment and schools organised into collaborative networks (Gallagher, 2006). Following a major postal consultation of all households in Northern Ireland, which produced a contradictory result of 54% wishing an end to the 11 plus but with 54% also wishing academic selection to continue, the Education Minister, Mr McGuinness announced the abolition of the 11 plus in order to create a more socially inclusive fair education system (Donnelly and Osborne, 2005). During the suspension of devolution the issue continued to be divisive between the parties as the Direct Rule minister worked on the introduction of informed parental choice. Sinn Féin strongly advocated the abolition of academic selection. This was less strongly supported by the Social Democratic and Labour Party (SDLP), but both unionist parties wished to protect the traditions of excellence of the grammar schools that annually produced the top A level and GCSE results in the UK. Another rather paradoxical comparative difference with England, Scotland and Wales is that there are no fee-paying independent secondary schools in Northern Ireland – basically it is a public sector system. The issue was so politically contentious that the St Andrews Agreement, which paved the way for the restoration of devolution in 2007, contained a negotiated provision that the decision to commence the pending legislative order to end academic selection would rest with the NIA, provided the Assembly could be restored (House of Commons, 2006). However, the new Sinn Féin Education Minister subsequently confirmed the ending of the 11 plus in 2008, but was much criticised for not having a clear process of transfer to secondary schools in place. Possible strategies involving transfer at 14 plus, local planning and a phased transition from academic selection have been discussed, while a large number of grammar schools set up their own shared transfer test. The political impasse has in part destabilised the new Executive, leaving uncertainty if Northern Ireland will continue this major divergence in policy.

The Northern Ireland secondary school system contrasts markedly with Scotland and Wales, where there is a strong commitment to comprehensive education, and also with the dominance of comprehensive education in England. The Scottish strategic paper *Ambitious excellent schools* (Scottish Executive, 2004a) gave strong support for a comprehensive system with common standards of provision. Wales has had a similar strongly articulated traditional commitment to non-selective secondary provision. England displays more divergence with retention of grammar schools in a small number of areas and initiatives to create different types of non-selective schools, especially through the creation of academies. The four countries have also adopted different concepts of specialist schools. This has evolved mainly in England with government grants plus private sector sponsorship supporting the development of an educational specialism in individual schools. Northern Ireland has introduced a rather similar principle, involving a partnership arrangement and evidence of an ongoing private sector sponsor. Scotland and Wales have no specialist schools and this has been interpreted as a drift away from the comprehensive ideal. However, Scotland does have perhaps a more ideologically acceptable status of *schools of ambition* that is aimed at schools with ideas for transformation and innovation. The focus is wider than specialist schools and aimed at enhancing the curriculum, developing pupils' confidence and strengthening community enterprise and creativity. The Scottish government provides all the additional funding.

Curriculum development has been a major priority in Scotland and Wales, with evidence of divergent approaches. The Scottish Government followed a national debate on education in 2002 and created a single coherent curriculum from 3-18. The *Curriculum for excellence* (Scottish Executive, 2004b) aimed to achieve a better balance between academic and vocational subjects and to broaden the range of learning experiences. There was also a declared intention to relate the curriculum to the values of Scottish society, expressed as children becoming successful learners, confident individuals, responsible citizens and effective contributors. The new Scottish Government has made it clear that it is committed to continue the development of a curriculum for excellence and to introduce flexibility to the traditional subject-based curriculum. Scotland is now moving ahead through its examination board to consider the next generation of national qualifications to ensure that the qualifications framework fully reflects curriculum excellence. In Wales, the abolition of testing for seven-year-olds and key stages 2 and 3 set out an approach to assessment described as diverging strongly from that pursued in England (Rees, 2007). Action was also taken to introduce 14-19 learning pathways as one of its early flagship policies to break down the barriers between academic and vocational education and a Welsh Baccalaureate has aimed to transform learning by providing a broader experience than traditional programmes. It combines personal development skills with existing qualifications like A levels, NVQs and GCSEs to make a wider award. The Welsh Government is also proposing a new approach to the 14-19 curriculum learning pathways that will offer a wider range of choices. Raffe (2006) sees the home countries' approach to secondary pathways and the relationship between vocational and academic learning as convergent in some respects. Northern Ireland maintains set A levels, NVQs and GCSEs with its own examination boards. This is similar to England and Wales and pupils can also sit English board examinations. Northern Ireland does not have such a tradition of major innovation in curriculum or examinations. Overall divergence in curriculum and assessment remains significant.

Divergence in education policy has also arisen from the devolved administrations simply not following initiatives introduced for England, for example, grant-maintained schools, city technology colleges, assisted places schemes, beacon schools and academies. Really distinctive aspects of education policy and provision are limited. It has been noted that Scotland has continued to balance innovations with traditional approaches (Humes and Bryce, 2003). However, Scotland, Wales and Northern Ireland were keen to launch some initiatives to suit their country and were reluctant to always follow the English agenda. Apart from the major differences in arrangements for fees and student support, (see Chapter Three) there are a number of differences with respect to higher education. These include the national structures for the funding and governance of higher education, greater collaboration between further and higher education in Scotland, differentials in fee income between universities in the four countries and the lack of foundation degrees in Scotland (Gallagher and Raffe, 2008).

Equal opportunities policies in Scotland and Wales

While Northern Ireland had innovative equal opportunities policies (as discussed in Chapter Three) following devolution the Scottish and Welsh administrations have made commitments to mainstreaming equality of opportunity as an integral part of all policy making and to move beyond anti-discrimination approaches. In Great Britain there are three major public sector equality duties in force for race, disability and gender, which require key public bodies to publish schemes setting out what they will do to promote equality. While equal opportunities is a reserved matter (see also Chapter Seven), the Scotland Act allows the Scottish Parliament to encourage equal opportunities and to impose duties on Scottish public bodies to meet equal opportunity requirements in carrying out their functions. The Scottish Government interpreted this broadly (Scottish Executive, 2003b), and has had an equality strategy in place since 2000 and an equality unit 'placing equality at the heart of policy-making' (Georghiou and Kidner, 2007). The strategy outlined how government would eliminate and prevent discrimination on the grounds of gender, marital status, race, disability, age, sexual orientation, religious or political beliefs, to an extent pre-empting what will be in the new proposed Single Equality Bill for England, Scotland and Wales (Government Equality Office, 2008). The Scottish Executive and Assembly have made a strong commitment to the systematic integration of equality perspectives into the everyday work of government. Legislation proposed by the government must be accompanied by a statement of its impact on equal opportunities. There is also a mandatory parliamentary equal opportunities committee that reports on the equal opportunities aspects of the Scottish budget and has investigated specific issues such as age and carers, female offenders and barriers facing people with disabilities. The Scottish Executive has also launched equality-based campaigns, for example, against racism, and has been able to introduce stronger legislation against hate crime. It has encouraged bodies to go beyond their legal obligations to be innovative and creative. However, there have been criticisms that action plans based on the equality strategy have not always been substantially followed through, for example in the case of gender (Breitenbach, 2006; McKay and Gillespie, 2007). The new government in 2007 stated that it was revising the structure and policy approach of the Scottish Government, endorsing a mainstream approach in integrating equality into the everyday work of government and planning to develop research, statistics and awareness. Two comprehensive equality schemes for 2008-11, for gender and disability (Scottish Government, 2008b, 2008c), have been produced, setting out policies and targets for all government directorates and public bodies.

Equality of opportunity is also a non-devolved matter in Wales but a clause in the Government of Wales Act states that the Assembly should make appropriate arrangements with a view to securing that its functions are exercised with due regard to the principle that there should be equality of opportunity for all. This principle is replicated in the 2006 Government of Wales Act. WAG, as in Scotland, began with a commitment to take equality of opportunity into account, as a priority, in every policy decision. Mainstreaming equality was seen as a fundamental driver of the government's agenda, defined in 2004 as treating people equally in status, rights and opportunities, through a set of policies and actions with the aim of securing equality of outcome for all (WAG, 2004c). The Welsh Assembly has a mandatory equality of opportunity committee and published an equality annual report. A significant number of pieces of secondary legislation have included references to equality. Despite this approach, Chaney and Fevre (2002) identified a failure to fully implement a mainstreamed approach to equalities with piecemeal measures and a lack of specific and measurable targets. Wales could claim to have the only cabinet in the world where the majority of the members were women. A new mainstream equality strategy was agreed in 2006 with the general aim of integrating equality of opportunity principles, strategy and practices into the everyday work of the Assembly and other public bodies. Chaney (2006) identified significant advances in the promotion of equality but also found progress checked by limited resources and institutional resistance to reform. Wales has also made progress to a distinctive equality agenda with a multi-strand equality impact assessment. Each government department has an equality champion, an equality audit of assessment, policy strategies and programmes and disability, gender and race equality schemes were launched in 2006-07

(WAG, 2007b). This was followed by a single equality scheme in 2008 which set new benchmarks covering age, gender, sexual orientation, religion or belief as well as disability, gender and race, thus moving beyond the statutory duties.

Conclusion

This group of significantly divergent policies are restricted to education and health and social care, which indicates that devolved powers in these areas have been used for more autonomous policy formulation. Significant differences in the organisation of health and social care in Scotland, Wales and Northern Ireland have a history before devolution. Similarly there is a long tradition of differences in aspects of education policy. It can also be noted that health and education are the two areas of highest expenditure in all three devolved administrations. It is now possible to examine if more limited policy differences between the countries are also to be found in the same social policy areas or range more widely.

FIVE

Incremental change and low-level differences

There is a substantial policy area where the basic principles of policies have largely remained the same throughout the UK. With devolution, however, some lower-level differences have emerged during the implementation of the policies. These more subtle differences are often identifiable in administrative structures, strategies and action plans, and reflect differences in local needs, priorities or well-established practices. Quite significant policy areas can be seen as falling into this category, including the voluntary sector, housing, aspects of health and children's services. Also in this category are components of policy areas and examples discussed are direct payments, anti-poverty, child poverty and social inclusion strategies, early years and childcare strategies, children's services, overall health strategies, the regulation of social care and housing policies and strategies.

Voluntary sector

Since devolution the upward growth of voluntary organisations has continued, with an expansion in roles, functions and the voluntary workforce. Estimates vary, but there may be around 45,000 voluntary and community groups in Scotland, 28,000 in Wales, 5,000 in Northern Ireland, probably a substantial underestimate (Acheson, 2009) compared with some 140,000 in England. In each country the voluntary sector provides between 2% and 4% of employment. The introduction of devolution coincided with the separate production in each country of a compact, which set out a new relationship between the state and the voluntary sector, and clarified the way they would work with each other. All were couched in similar language. Wales made a stronger statement in setting out to establish a unique working relationship between the Welsh administration and the voluntary sector (see also Chapter Three for description). However, the actual operation of voluntary organisations under devolution mainly demonstrates more minor differences of policy and approach, despite the diversity of the sector. In all four countries the key themes and issues relating to the voluntary sector are the same, largely producing differences of emphasis in government action. These issues can be listed as: financial resources, service delivery contracts, charity law, social enterprise/social economy, support for umbrella organisations, work with hard-to-reach groups, specialist and innovative practice and volunteering. Devolution has also seen a general movement away from grant-based dependency and EU funding to mainstream funding and more long-term funding to promote sustainability. The continuing growth of contracts with statutory bodies has led voluntary organisations to become more business-like and bureaucratic. Strategies introduced by the devolved administrations have also had a strong focus on capacity building and training.

If the broad approaches were similar, what kind of differences did devolution account for? The role of the voluntary sector in Scotland had been somewhat inhibited, given the dominant position of the public sector. The development of devolution did herald strong commitments by the Scottish Executive and Scottish Government to work in partnership with the voluntary sector, and to move to a relationship built on greater trust. However, there were still elements of a preference for the traditional 'social democratic service delivery model' (Maxwell, 2007), and a reluctance to engage with the voluntary sector or community group representatives. This distinctive approach was demonstrated in the debate on including a public benefit test when the Scottish Government passed regulations for Scottish charities. There was no specialist minister in Scotland for the voluntary sector as in England, or indeed a public champion. The relationship of the sector with the Scottish Government has also been fraught at times, with lack of trust (Fyfe et al, 2006). Concerns about lack of engagement, equality of treatment and esteem and local government concern about the capacity and infrastructure and the fitness for purpose of voluntary bodies have continued (COSLA, 2008). However, it has argued that devolution has contributed to a new dialogue (Burt and Taylor, 2009) and since 2007 Scottish Government has identified collaboration in service provision, community capacity building, policy development and social enterprise activity as priority areas for government support. The new economic strategy on tackling poverty states the third sector has a crucial role to play and should be a full partner in the process (Scottish Government, 2008f, para 63) The Voluntary Issues Unit in the Scottish administration had taken forward the Scottish compact, providing support for voluntary groups, community initiatives and volunteering and this has now been replaced by a Third Sector Division located more strategically within the Public Service Reform Directorate (Burt and Taylor, 2009, p 9). Despite the unique process for the relationship with the voluntary sector, the Welsh Government did identify some difficulties with the sector and produced a new strategic action plan for the voluntary sector scheme, *The third dimension* (WAG, 2008e). A number of spheres for improvement were identified: better services that were more sensitive to needs, building stronger communities and contributing to better policies – in fact, much the same three objectives as have been declared by the Scottish Voluntary Issues Unit in Scotland. The Welsh administration sees the voluntary sector as a major asset and as a force for improvement and a contribution to social, economic, and cultural well-being. *The third dimension* strategy sees the third sector as having a major role in helping to fulfil the *One Wales* programme for government. It has a strong emphasis on raising standards, increasing volunteering, promoting social enterprise and empowering communities. As well as defining social capital as valuable in moving communities from a position of dependency (WAG, 2008e, p 23), the strategy also identified specific added values such as confidence building, user ownership, employability skills and citizen voice and advocacy.

Since 1970 Northern Ireland had experienced a rapid growth in voluntary organisations but particularly in community groups, caused originally by social protest and a self-help ethos (McCready, 2000), and sustained by community conflict and by special EU and other funding. The 2001 programme for government referred to the advantages of this vibrant and large community sector making a significant and crucial contribution. A commitment was given to developing a strong partnership with the voluntary sector and implementing fully the Northern Ireland compact. A department voluntary activity section, later the Voluntary and Community Unit, took forward strategies on funding, support and volunteering. A Joint Government Voluntary Sector Forum has also been established, bringing together civil servants and representatives of the sector. This deals with resources, capacity building and collaboration, but it has little influence on policy, and it operates at a lower level than the Welsh scheme. Policies and strategies have developed in a way that generally reflects UK-wide strategies to the sector. Acheson et al (2008) report that research shows that the view that the voluntary and community sector has mediated communal divisions and helped peace building is exaggerated. Although voluntary services provision in such areas as social care is not as developed as in Great Britain, the sector has encouraged an expansion of community development, engagement with government, community and neighbourhood services, local partnerships and a strong equality agenda.

Development of direct payments

Direct payments were introduced in Great Britain before devolution by the 1996 Community Care (Direct Payments) Act. This meant that social services departments could make payments to people with disabilities (and later older people), parents of children with disabilities and, except in Scotland, carers. It meant that users could spend the money to purchase their own community care needs rather than receiving services from the statutory authority. The legislation was originally enabling, but was later to become mandatory in all parts of the UK for eligible groups. Direct payments fell into devolved services and its implementation and development across the UK was to demonstrate significant differences in priorities.

The early years of policy implementation in Scotland were characterised by a low take-up (Pearson, 2004). Research (Riddell et al, 2005) showed that Scotland made less use of direct payments than England although it had a higher proportion of users than Northern Ireland or Wales. Pearson (2006) notes that the Scottish Executive made a concentrated push to encourage local authorities to develop the implementation process. In a four-country study of the implementation of national direct payments policies, of the 59 authorities which reported more direct payments than the mean average, only five were outside England, three in Scotland, one in Wales and one in Northern Ireland (Riddell et al, 2006). The study also found that 65% of staff had designated full-time direct payments posts in England, with 23% of staff in Scotland and only one person in Wales and one in Northern Ireland. Variations were also found in support mechanisms. A specific project was set up in Scotland to deliver support, organisation and training, but in Wales funding for support was targeted at local authorities. In Northern Ireland support was through one body, the Centre for Independent Living, whereas in England support was channelled through a range of voluntary organisations (Pearson, 2006, p 26).

Government prioritising and commitment was much stronger in England, bolstered by targets and performance. In Scotland there were no set targets, no ministerial support and direct payments were seen as only one of a number of ways to deliver improved services. In Wales and Scotland there was also professional and trade union opposition to what was seen as 'back door privatisation' (Pearson, 2006, p 60). Riddell et al (2006) report that there have been markedly different opportunity structures for policy development and implementation in England, Scotland, Wales and Northern Ireland, reflecting the commitment of different devolved governments. In Scotland and Northern Ireland direct payments has remained a minority service.

Most recent trends indicate that direct payments are increasing in Scotland, Wales and Northern Ireland, but at a slow rate, again confirming mainly a difference in priorities.

Anti-poverty, child poverty and social inclusion strategies

One of the first matters to receive the attention of all the new devolved administrations was child poverty and social exclusion. This was accompanied by a commitment in all three countries to work towards the UK Government's target to eradicate child poverty by 2020 (see also Chapter 8 for discussion on cooperation). The range of options directly available to the devolved administrations were similar, but the strategies and options adopted demonstrated a degree of difference and an element of country-specific approaches. In Scotland, an initiative to tackle poverty and social exclusion was launched as early as November 1999. *Closing the opportunity gap* (Scottish Executive, 2002) became the Scottish Executive's strategy to tackle poverty and disadvantage and followed an initial social justice strategy to promote social inclusion. It focused more closely on action that the Executive could take under devolved responsibilities to tackle poverty in Scotland. The main aims were described as: preventing individuals and families from falling into poverty, providing routes out of poverty and sustaining freedom from poverty. Its six major objectives were to: increase chances of sustaining employment; improve the skills of disadvantaged young people; reduce vulnerability to indebtedness; regenerate neighbourhoods; improve the health status of people in deprived communities; and improve access to services within deprived rural communities. Within these six objectives 10 specific targets were set. An evaluation found that the programme had been integrated into departmental targets and sustained an Executive-wide approach to addressing social inclusion (Scottish Government, 2008e), but progress towards the 10 special targets was varied. The main achievements were in work, poverty, benefit dependency and health inequalities. The main targets not achieved were: in the proportion of young people not in education, training or employment, pupil achievement and achievements of young people leaving care. In Scotland the 2005 target for reducing child poverty was achieved ahead of the rest of the UK.

Since 2005 Scotland has also developed a financial inclusion action plan, covering debt advice, affordable credit and financial capability. In

2008, a discussion was initiated on the future direction of anti-poverty policy in Scotland as part of an overall government economic strategy. The discussion paper set out the basis for a revised strategy for action by the Scottish Government, identifying three main ways in which it could tackle poverty: preventing poverty and tackling the root causes, helping to lift people out of poverty and alleviating the impact of poverty on people's lives (Scottish Government, 2008f). These three ways were somewhat similar to the three main aims of *Closing the opportunity gap*, and the details were also similar to the Scottish Government's three 'golden rules' of it's economic strategy on solidarity, cohesion and sustainability. (Scottish Government 2007f). The cohesion golden rule involves greater priority to more balanced growth across Scotland. The sustainability golden rule relates to enhancing the environment. The solidarity golden rule focuses on reducing inequality in Scotland and was reflected prominently in the discussion paper in tackling poverty (Scottish Government 2008e, para 8). The solidarity target is expressed as 'to increase overall income and the proportion of income earned by the three lowest degrees as a group by 2017'.

Successive Welsh administrations in 1999 and 2005 have had a strong commitment to anti-poverty activities. Tackling social disadvantage was one of the major themes in 2007 in the *One Wales* document (WAG, 2007a). WAG is committed to developing Wales-specific solutions to child poverty, and in the third term of Welsh devolution child poverty remains at the top of the agenda. The second WAG published a specific strategy for tackling child poverty, with the declared aim of eradicating child poverty by means of mainstream services, through access to employment, financial inclusion measures, encouraging benefit take-up grants for further and higher education, the school curriculum and improving children's services. This strategy, *A fair future for our children* (WAG, 2005b), led to an implementation plan which developed ideas relating to child poverty proofing of Assembly initiatives. This included programme bending to ensure the needs of the poorest children were met first, setting targets and milestones and family income maximisation initiatives. The implementation plan also proposed a target that there should be equality for all children in Wales up to the age of five by 2030, which would go beyond the UK child poverty target (WAG, 2006b). The new Welsh Government did not produce another strategy document, preferring to build on it through new actions and measures (Gibbons, 2008). The main aims remained similar: improving life opportunities through early years provision, employment and health interventions, financial inclusion initiatives and encouraging greater uptake of tax and benefits support. A legislative competence order was introduced in 2008 to allow the Welsh Assembly to introduce legal measures to tackle child poverty, including top-up payments to child trust fund accounts, legislation on child poverty proofing, free childcare and local authority funding, more support for vulnerable children and young people leaving care and a proposal for a commitment by public agencies to help WAG with its child poverty objectives. Wales has also established Child Poverty Solutions Wales, a partnership of the Government, Local Government Association and Save the Children, to offer support and advice to local authorities in tackling child poverty, and it has undertaken a pilot project to maximise the leverage of local government in reducing child poverty. The 2009 Children and Families Wales measure will place a duty on Welsh ministers to prepare and publish an assessment report every three years, and also a duty on specific Welsh public bodies to produce strategies to eradicate child poverty by 2020.

In 2001, the programme for government of the new devolved administration in Northern Ireland contained a section on tackling poverty and social disadvantage and a declared aim to reduce levels of deprivation unemployment and benefit dependency (NIE, 2001, p 19). Northern Ireland had higher levels of benefit dependency and economic inactivity than any other regions of the UK. The actions described by this document were directed mainly through existing targeting social need (TSN) and promoting social inclusion initiatives. TSN was a strategy introduced before devolution to direct resources within government departments at those areas, groups and individuals in greatest need. It had been criticised for adopting variations in the definitions of social need and having little influence on departmental spending, and overall had no specific budget (Quirke and McLaughlin, 1996). TSN was relaunched as New TSN in 1998 and was promoted by the new NIE as its major policy for combating poverty. But the strategy attracted criticism, for example, for not using deprivation statistics (Tomlinson, 2000). It was also criticised for targeting groups and areas that did not accurately reflect individual or family needs. In 2006, the Direct Rule administration used New TSN to develop a Northern Ireland anti-poverty and social inclusion strategy. This strategy was declared to be the result of a commitment by the previous devolved Executive (OFMDFM, 2006). It identified the number of children and pensioners in poverty, and used multiple deprivation measures of high unemployment, crime and low educational achievement to focus on budgets for education, children and employment. The strategy was written largely in general terms but contained the UK-wide specific target to lift 65,000 children out of poverty by 2010 on the way to full eradication by 2020 (OFMDFM, 2006, p 31), that is, 50% by 2010. The legislation following the St Andrews Agreement in 2006 resulted in an amendment to the 1998 Northern Ireland Act, obliging the Executive to adopt a strategy setting out how it proposed to tackle poverty, social exclusion and patterns of deprivation (House of Commons, 2006). With the restoration of devolution, a new programme for government appeared for the period 2008-11, but this contained only a brief reference to tackling disadvantage (NIE, 2008a). The accompanying budget document repeated the target to work towards the elimination of child poverty in Northern Ireland by 2020, including lifting 67,000 children out of poverty by 2010 (NIE, 2008b). Otherwise the key government actions related to this target were associated with benefit uptake and promoting paid work and improving deprived areas (NIA, 2007a). The restored Assembly was to formally adopt the 2006 anti-poverty strategy in 2008. But the new Executive has been criticised for its inactivity in adopting a revised anti-poverty strategy. The public services agreement published along with the programme for government gave a more specific ambitious target, although qualified as 'working towards' the elimination of 44,000 in severe child poverty by 2012 (NIE, 2008b). This was added to the target of reducing child poverty by 50% by 2010. When the Assembly Committee of the OFMDFM carried out an inquiry into child poverty, it expressed concern at the lack of more government-specific measures and timetables (Committee of OFMDFM, 2007).

Within the UK strategy to eradicate child poverty there have been elements of different emphases and approaches in the details of action plans between Scotland, Wales and Northern Ireland. Social exclusion is also an area where devolved administrations have been keen to develop their own strategies using devolved powers, but in practice these strategies have not varied too much from each other's or from English strategies.

Communities First was developed as a flagship programme to improve the living conditions and prospects for people in the most disadvantaged communities across Wales; it originally launched in 2001 and was revised in 2007 (WAG, 2007e). It used the Welsh Index of Multiple Deprivation to target the most deprived areas in Wales, and covered 20% of the population. The strategy used the idea of 'programme bending', a process whereby the service delivery organisations ensure that mainstream programmes are targeted on Communities First areas. A further component was the involvement of local partnerships to develop community action plans and to focus on the root causes of poverty and disadvantage. With the financial recession Communities First has prioritised child poverty, economic activity and job creation.

The Northern Ireland programme for government in 2001 had relied on the existing New TSN strategy to target extra resources towards disadvantaged neighbourhoods and communities. The policy of targeting public expenditure towards areas in greatest need was a strategy that preceded the not dissimilar 'programme bending' of Communities First in Wales, but was less specifically targeted and did not have a separate budget. A neighbourhood regeneration strategy targeted 36 areas of concentrated multiple deprivation across Northern Ireland and, as in Wales, suggested a partnership approach.

Scotland has a long tradition of area-based approaches and the Scottish Executive has continued to pursue these since 2004. The Scottish Executive *Closing the opportunity gap* strategy had as one objective the regeneration of the most disadvantaged neighbourhoods. Again, partnerships have been a core component: first, social inclusion partnerships and subsequently community planning partnerships using mainstream funding. In 2006, the Scottish Executive complemented this with *People and place* (Scottish Executive, 2006f), setting out a strategy on area regeneration as part of building a strong communities portfolio.

Early years and childcare strategies

This was an area of priority for New Labour and a national childcare strategy was formulated (with a new childcare tax credit) just before the introduction of devolution and implemented with some differences in Scotland and Wales. Both countries were to see major developments of policy and provision during devolution. Wincott (2005) identified diversity within a common expansion and as differences of emphasis in adopting policy to local circumstances rather than a fundamental variation in the quality or level of services. It has been suggested that Wales undertook a more radical examination from first principles of policies, despite its lack of formal legislative powers, and took the most innovative approach (Wincott, 2006a). WAG identified children's development as paramount, rather than other social and economic objectives. Scotland's strategy documents were wide-ranging, from *For Scotland's children* (Scottish Executive, 2001c), which set out the strengths and weaknesses of existing services to a major consultation on an early years strategy in 2003, but the development of provision was less dependent on major strategic initiatives. It is only with the restoration of devolution in Northern Ireland that a specific early years strategy is being produced and provision has lagged behind Great Britain.

The strategies produced in the three countries provided differences of emphasis and implementation for childcare, pre-schooling, integrated school-based services and out-of-school provision. Wales moved to the integration of pre- and primary schooling embracing two phases. First, a foundation phase for children aged from 3-7, piloted in 2004. This foundation phase placed children's personal and social development and well-being at the heart of a curriculum of seven areas of learning and became a major pillar of WAG's early years programme (HMI for Education and Training in Wales, 2007). An evaluation of the foundation phase was somewhat critical about measures to assess children's progress and noted the need for appropriate funding (Estyn, 2008). This foundation phase was augmented by the Flying Start programme for the 0-3 age group in the most disadvantaged communities, which provided additional health visiting, free childcare and basic skills and parenting programmes. In 2006, the basis of allocation was changed from using eligibility for free school meals to permit local partnerships more discretion in choosing catchment areas. Concerns have been expressed about sustaining the programmes (Children in Wales, 2007), but WAG has been strongly committed to enhancing early years provision.

Following devolution, the Scottish Executive was also committed to putting early years provision on the map as part of making children's issues a key priority. The 2000 Standards in Scotland Schools Act had imposed a duty on local authorities to provide pre-school education, enforced since 2002. The main strategic review, *For Scotland's children report* in 2001 (Scottish Executive, 2001c), had made major recommendations on all aspects of children's services and put particular emphasis on joined-up working. There was an early education and childcare division within the Education Department and the Executive promoted social inclusion through early years intervention. The Scottish Executive had pledged to provide quality part-time pre-school education for all eligible three and four-year-olds. With this expansion of services came the introduction of more universal entitlement to free pre-school education for three and four-year-olds. By 2005, 81% of three-year-olds and 98% of four-year-olds were registered with pre-school education centres (Scottish Parliament Education Committee, 2006, para 61). The Scottish Executive has moved closer to the Welsh strategy, with a commitment to bring the 3-5 years and primary one curriculum closer. A joint statement between the Scottish Government and Scottish local authorities has set out an early years framework as the responsibility of both national and local government (Scottish

Government, 2008g). The aim is to provide integrated wide-ranging early years services (Kidner 2007).

The Welsh and Scottish administrations were broadly sympathetic to the use of school facilities for wider community purposes (Wincott, 2005). An early recommendation of WAG proposed setting up new children's integrated centres for a seamless service of daycare, early education, play, parenting support and health, bringing all early years services under one roof. Family centres have also developed but not as extensively in Scotland, with only around 80 provided by local authorities. In Scotland new community schools were fundamental to the strategy of raising educational attainment and promoting social justice. Over 400 schools were involved in a pilot study of the integrated provision of school education, which meant having social work, health, psychological family support and other children's services in selected schools. By 2007 this strategy was extended to all schools, and renamed 'integrated community schools'. Although akin to extended schools in England and integrated learning in Wales, this distinctive Scottish policy has not been evaluated as a total success in research findings (HMI, 2006).

All four governments have been interested in expanding childcare, particularly in disadvantaged communities. Wales produced a specific childcare action plan in 2002 based on a review of the UK Government's national childcare strategy. This was replaced in 2005 with the *Childcare is for children* strategy (WAG, 2005c), which was a response to both a WAG childcare working group and a UK government strategy announced in 2004, *Choice for parents: The best start for children*, which had a major focus on childcare (HM Treasury, 2004). The Welsh strategy acknowledged the patchy availability of childcare and aimed to make childcare more widely available and affordable and also addressed issues of regulation and the childcare workforce. WAG used the UK 2006 Childcare Act to bring Wales into line with England in introducing a statutory duty on local authorities to secure a sufficient supply of childcare within their areas by 2010. A new Children and Families Wales measure will place a duty on local authorities to secure free, high-quality and targeted childcare. The distinctive Welsh Flying Start strategy gave free high-quality childcare for two-year-olds in deprived areas while Genesis was an EU-supported project for a comprehensive package of advice, support and childcare for individuals seeking access to work. There was also extensive out-of-school childcare supported by Lottery funding and school breakfasts were piloted. Childcare places increased in Wales by 18,000 between 1999 and 2005 (Bryson et al,

2006) and all three-year-olds in Wales whose parents want it now have a free half-term school place.

Cymorth is a joined-up WAG approach to funding intervention projects in early years. It absorbed five previous funds: Sure Start, the Children and Youth Partnership Fund, the National Childcare Strategy, youth access initiatives and PlayBoard. Unified funding covered the enhancement of early years provision, parental support, prevention of school exclusion, play opportunities and health promotion. The childcare strategy has included the training of care workers, expansion of places, sustaining provision in sparsely populated areas and strengthening the framework of regulation. The benefits of the implementation of Cymorth were seen as targeting services, plugging gaps, encouraging greater and improved partnership working, supporting innovative projects and providing flexibility and security of funding (WAG, 2005d). The Children and Families Wales measure will put Cymorth on a new legal framework.

Scotland had a childcare strategy developed before devolution, but the Scottish Executive made an early commitment to develop it and deliver in each neighbourhood quality childcare services that were accessible and affordable. Childcare partnerships were created in each local authority area to develop provision. A specific innovation was the Working for Families Fund that provided childcare to enable people to access training or employment in a selection of local authorities. It started in 2004-05 as part of the wider *Closing the opportunity gap* strategy. Subsequently the Scottish Executive did not produce an overarching strategy and Scottish Parliament's Education Committee made a strong plea for the implementation of a new vision for the early years sector, and a requirement on local authorities to prepare plans for pre-school services (Scottish Parliament Education Committee, 2006, paras 40 and 56). This envisaged high-quality childcare to supplement the entitlement to pre-school education for three and four-year-olds. The Scottish Executive responded, stating that it shared many of the Committee's objectives. In 2003 the Scottish Executive had produced a consultation document, *Integrated strategy for early years*. However, no finalised strategy was ever published although the Executive decided to move ahead on integrated services and pre-school education. The 2007/08 Budget reiterated a commitment to increasing the availability of affordable childcare and the Scottish Government is preparing an early years and early intervention framework, and a 10-year strategy.

Northern Ireland has been developing early years and childcare provision from a position described as woefully inadequate (NIA, 2008b). Only one childcare strategy, Children First, has been produced, and that was at the start of devolution in 1999 (DHSSPS, 1999). The principles were similar to strategies in Great Britain, aiming to promote quality, affordability, accessibility and flexibility, and implementation was through new childcare partnerships. Although the main components were similar to the other three countries, a later review (DHSSPS, 2005b) reported limited development compared with Great Britain. The total number of childcare places had only increased by 5%, pre-school education was only available in the immediate pre-school year, out-of-school childcare places were small in number and only 25 Sure Start schemes had commenced. The review called for a reshaped childcare vision and mainstreaming, rather than short-term voluntary sector schemes dependent on EU funding. The Direct Rule administration in 2006 allocated funding to early years including Sure Start, daycare and extended schools, which provide study support, parenting and specialist services. Surprisingly the 2007 programme for government made no specific reference to early years, childcare and education, and the 2006 funding package was not mainstreamed or extended. The new administration has supported an expansion of Sure Start and published a review of pre-school education that envisages a pre-school expansion programme. Extended schools were only piloted in four areas in 2007 and there has been little attempt to integrate extended school policy with childcare and labour market participation (Gray and Carragher, 2008). In 2008, the Northern Ireland Department of Education considerably reduced the resources available for extended schools, which contrasts markedly with the proposals in Great Britain that will see all schools with a core set of extended activities. The continuing administrative division in Northern Ireland between education and children's care services has contributed a greater gap in early years provision between Northern Ireland and Scotland and Wales.

Delivery of children's services

All four governments in the UK have made similar commitments to action across a spectrum of services for vulnerable children, but differences in implementation have emerged. A Children First programme was among the first major initiatives by WAG in 1999 and it continued as a catalyst for improvement (Hill, D., 2008). The Laming Inquiry in England had an influence throughout Britain as the *Every Child Matters* agenda was developed and evolved into support for an integrated structure between local authority children's services and education services. Children First in Wales set key objectives for children's services encompassing integration, advocacy, children with disabilities, looked after children and children leaving care. The basic child protection procedures across the UK are similar, but the implementation structures can differ. A uniform structure for children's trusts was not implemented in Wales and local authorities were not required to create a single director for children's services. Partnership working was promoted through children and young people's partnerships but they were not responsible for direct service provision. In the third term WAG has been focusing on support for children with disabilities and reducing child poverty, but has taken action for the future with a Welsh legislative competence order. The 2009 Children and Families measure will create new integrated family support teams to help children and families with complex needs.

Getting it Right for Every Child became the overarching programme for Scotland, providing for more integrated services for children and families with schools, joint working, improved integrated assessment and workforce development. Revised in 2005, it led to linkages between child protection, health, education and youth justice (Scottish Executive, 2006b). This facilitated more integrated children's services planning and continued Scotland's welfare-orientated approach and early intervention approach, an approach that the Scottish Executive has wished to extend across the wider social policy landscape (Hill, M., 2008). The Scottish Government has not been specific about how local councils organise services and how various administrative combinations of children, education and social work services operate. Scotland has a less centralised approach to provision than Westminster (Cohen et al, 2004) – there has been a concord with local governments and an emphasis on partnership working through health partnerships, childcare partnerships and child protection committees.

The main decisions taken in Northern Ireland before the second period of devolution in 2007 did not formally adopt the *Every Child Matters* agenda policy strategy although it had some influence on developments. A 10-year strategy for children and young people pledged to take forward such themes as partnership and collaboration, what works, whole child approaches and a rights-based approach. The document was weak on specifying robust local processes to deliver the plan and changes produced under Direct Rule were minimal (Pinkerton, 2008). Northern Ireland continues to operate with strong integration between children's services and health services but weak integration with education. The delivery of education including pre-school education is organisationally separate from child protection and family services which has led to the underdevelopment of early years social care.

Overall health strategies

In Wales there have been several strategy documents that have driven the development of devolved health policy but within the overall aims and principles of the NHS (McClelland, S. 2007). The 2001 plan, *Improving health in Wales* (WAG, 2001c), marked the launch of a new vision for the NHS in Wales and had a focus on improving primary healthcare and securing the network of acute hospitals and public involvement. This strategy emphasised the Assembly's direct responsibility for health services in Wales and had a policy context dominated by principles of collaboration and localism. *Designed for life* was a subsequent major 10-year strategy for health policy (WAG, 2005a). This was not just shaped by the previous 2001 review but also the *Wanless review of health and social care in Wales* (WAG, 2003c), which had endorsed the existing strategic direction but called for improved performance, more capacity in non-acute settings and a focus on prevention in the context of high demand on acute services, emergency admissions and concerns about quality standards. *Designed for life* set out a vision of reducing health inequalities, ensuring quality-assured treatment and care, developing local and user engagement and bringing health closer to patients in the community. A twin-track approach was set, tackling the causes of poor health and focusing services at the same time to combat ill health (WAG, 2005a, para 2.2). Jervis (2008, p 72) comments that a distinctive Welsh approach was being adopted. However, McClelland, S. (2007, p 31) suggests that the *Designed for life* strategy of public health, community care and a concentration of clinical experience led to an unpopular move away from services provided in hospital. With *One Wales*, a series of strategic health commitments has been adopted including a local emphasis, for example a rural health plan and a moratorium on changes to local hospitals.

Policy strategies in Scotland also moved more towards localism. The 2003 White Paper *Partnership for care* (Scottish Executive, 2003b) promoted a partnership between patients, staff and government to deliver local services in a community setting and with more accountability to local interests through community health partnerships. A further policy emphasis emerged from a special investigation in 2005, the Kerr Report, *Building a health service fit for the future* (Scottish Executive, 2005a), which proposed that services should be as local as possible, with a shift of emphasis to the community and away from acute care. A major focus of the report was on a rebalancing of NHS care from hospitalisation and emergency admissions to a stronger emphasis on preventive and anticipatory care (Robson and Payne, 2005). It called for a new approach to get the NHS in Scotland to work as a single whole system (Jervis, 2008, p 47). A White Paper *Delivering for health* (Scottish Executive, 2005c) followed the Kerr Report, and proposed more healthcare provided locally and confirmed the continuing development of a unified NHS and a partnership approach. The new Scottish Government produced an action plan in 2007, *Better health, better care* (Scottish Government, 2007c), with the intention of: maintaining the integrated health structure, strengthening public involvement, encouraging a greater partnership of patients, carers and health staff and further developing the performance management system. There was also a strategic emphasis on tackling health inequalities, emphasising anticipatory and preventive care and shifting resources to local community settings. Jervis (2008, p 50) reported that the Scottish major strategies were working and delivering benefits, with the system bedding down and performance management improving.

Health strategy papers in Northern Ireland have been somewhat derivative and brief documents and the original document *Building the way forward in primary care* (DHSSPS, 2000) was broadly developed from the English and Welsh plans (Greer, 2004, p 184). Just after the collapse of the Assembly in 2002 the Department of Health, Social Services and Public Safety published a regional strategy for health and personal social services from 2002 to 2022 that made some general commitments to reduce the need for acute hospitals services and to tackle waiting lists and health inequalities (DHSSPS, 2002b). Strategic thinking has been dominated by structural reform, with the 2002 *Developing better services* initiative (DHSSPS, 2002a) focused on hospital rationalisation and reforming structures. In 2005, under Direct Rule, a major health strategy was produced, *A healthier future*, covering a 20-year vision 2005-25 (DHSSPS, 2005a). This placed existing strategies within a developmental framework and five cross-cutting themes were identified: investing for health, involving people, teams which deliver, responsive and integrated services and improving quality. Probably the most significant aspect was the commitment to flexible integrated care with multi-skilled teams and networks, which is facilitated by the integration of health and social services in Northern Ireland.

Public health

The importance of public health strategies, particularly to tackle health inequalities, has been emphasised by the UK Labour Government and this underpins many aspects of health policy. Structural and behavioural causes of inequalities in ill health were significant in Scotland, Wales and Northern Ireland and the devolved administrations have devoted considerable attention to develop strategies and plans, but in some different ways. The extent and causes of poor health in Wales and the value of public preventive action strategies was a major focus for planning and strategies. Greer (2004, p 284) suggested that Wales was the country most signed up for the new public health agenda. Smith and Babbington (2006) also saw that the health agenda in Wales had changed since devolution, with the public health agenda becoming prominent. WAG had adopted the recommendations of the Townsend Review *Targeting poor health* to reduce inequalities through an integrated approach. These were incorporated into the strategy document *Well-being in Wales* (WAG, 2002), which recommended action to tackle the underlying determinants of poor health across WAG's policy areas. It stressed partnership working with other organisations and that every organisation and every individual had a shared responsibility for health and well-being. It has been suggested that Welsh health strategies have been notable for a focus on health as opposed to health services, thus prioritising public health (Robson, 2007, p 14). WAG also moved to set up structures to support action by creating a National Public Health Service (NPHS) as a centralised body to provide a range of public health services, as well as resources and advice for all other health bodies and local government. The NPHS assists with public health locally and can provide a public health director and public health team in each local board. The focus on policy innovations in public health has also been seen in Health Challenge Wales, launched in Wales as a national focus to contribute towards the aim of preventing ill health in the first place. Despite the public health priorities and progress and claims of a distinctive Welsh approach (Wales Centre for Health, 2008), there have been calls for the new Welsh Assembly legislation to put in place a new approach to sustainable health (Owen, 2007). A unification of public health services for Wales is envisaged (WAG, 2009) that will be based on a public health Wales NHS trust with a national remit. This will focus on inequalities between different areas and social groups. However, there would still be a director of public health on each of the seven local health boards. The actual implementation of the structures may cause some difficulty, with a public health split between the centralised body and the local health boards.

At the time of devolution in Scotland public health issues and health inequalities became a major issue. Originally the Scottish Office had published a paper *Towards a healthy Scotland* in 1999. Subsequently, the key health paper *Partnership for care* (Scottish Executive, 2003b) had taken a broad view to address issues of poor health in Scotland

and the more specific strategy *Building a health service fit for the future* (Scottish Executive, 2005a) identified the main challenges to health and well-being. It was widely recognised that Scotland's health was poor within the UK and with significant differences within Scotland. A minister for public health was created with a public health and well-being portfolio, to include key determinants of health. A ministerial task force on health inequalities was also established to prioritise practical actions including support for families, a multi-agency approach and health inequalities proofing. The implementation structure was similar to Wales with a centralised board, NHS Scotland, to take the national lead for improving public health. Each NHS health board also contained a public health department and a director of public health. The 2007 *Better health, better care* action plan (Scottish Government, 2007c) proposed investing in resources to prevent disease and revived the role of directors of public health. It recommended that community health partnerships should be able to call on adequate professional public health support and advice with regional managed public health networks. The ministerial task force on health inequalities had urged the more widespread application of anticipatory approaches across Scotland. The 2008 Public Health (Scotland) Act redefined relationships between ministers, health boards and local authorities in protecting public health, strengthened the powers of health bodies and assisted Scotland to meet international obligations. Public health initiatives have continued to develop and the framework for action to address Scotland's alcohol problem, including minimum pricing and a promotions ban, has been particularly radical.

Northern Ireland, like Scotland and Wales, had major public health problems, accentuated by the conflict and disturbances. The programme for government in 2001 had as a priority 'working for a healthier people', but local public health services tended to copy initiatives from Britain, for example, health action zones. A ministerial group on public health published *Investing for health* (DHSSPS, 2002c). This contained a framework for action to improve health and to reduce inequalities and was based on partnership working in four board areas, with separate strategies for drugs and alcohol, teenage pregnancy, sexual health, tobacco and mental health. *Investing for health* led in particular to a strong emphasis on a community development approach. Following devolution in 2008 the Minister of Health announced a new separate regional agency for public health to develop the role of an existing health promotion agency. This public health agency would have responsibilities for health protection and improvement and addressing health inequalities, but concerns have been raised in relation to the centralisation of public health functions apart from delivery trusts. Despite organisational differences, public health policy has tended in all four countries to become more prominent, and has had a similar emphasis on changing people's lifestyles and behaviour (Harrington et al, 2009).

Regulation of social care

The introduction of devolution led to four different bodies to regulate the social work profession. As Table 5.1 indicates, since devolution four organisations have replaced the former Central Council for Education and Training in Social Work, a UK-wide body.

Table 5.1: Social care regulatory bodies

• Scottish Social Services Council
• Care Council for Wales
• Northern Ireland Social Care Council
• General Social Services Council (England)
o Skills for Care
o Children's Workforce Development Council

The three councils for Scotland, Wales and Northern Ireland have similar functions in regulating the social care workforce, establishing codes of practice and regulating education and accrediting education and training. Since 2005 in England responsibility for standards and the qualifying framework for social care workers rested with two bodies, Skills for Care for adult skills and a separate body for the children's workforce. These five bodies join together as a UK network body, Skills for Care and Development, which is licensed to be the sector skills council for the adult and children's social care workforce. Differences in standards and qualifications are limited and the social work degree is the recognised professional qualification for all four countries.

One consequence of the territorial bodies has been the facilitation of some differences to suit local conditions. The development of post-qualifying courses for social workers has seen England committed to three academic levels but Northern Ireland to only one. Scotland has introduced a new award for social workers undertaking mental health duties and its early childhood degree-level qualifications has put Scotland in the forefront of developments in integrated qualifications for early years and childcare. Wales has also introduced a post-qualifying course for children's social work, and there have been developments to promote good practice in social care. A Social Care Institute for Excellence (SCIE) was established in 2001 with a UK-wide remit, but Wales introduced separately the innovative Social Services Improvement Agency to support and improve practice in social care services.

The arrangements for the regulation and inspection of social care again reflect the existence of four different territorial jurisdictions. Thus Scotland has a Social Work Inspection Agency which carries out performance reviews of social work services provided by or on behalf of local authorities, while the Scottish Commission for the Regulation of Care reports on the quality of care in institutions and agencies and deals with complaints. Scottish ministers have devised and published national care standards.

Wales, following devolution, had a similar dual structure, but in 2007 WAG announced that two bodies would amalgamate into a new Care and Social Services Inspectorate Wales, within WAG, to cover local authority inspection review and other agency regulation and inspection, and to provide a more integrated view of social services, early years and care. This reflected a strategy already adopted in England that was to move to integrated childcare and education inspections.

Northern Ireland has a care inspection body, the Regulation and Quality Improvement Authority, which covers social care, but this body also covers health services reflecting the integrated structure in Northern Ireland as well as the Mental Health Commission.

This model has been used in England, bringing together the Commission for Social Care Inspection and the Health Care Commission plus the Mental Health Act Commission. The differential impact of the configuration of services is also demonstrated in Scotland where the Social Work Inspection Agency carries out performance inspections of criminal justice services. Overall the regulation and inspection regimes mainly reflect variations in the structure of services and local priorities rather than major differences in principle.

Housing policies and strategies

It is difficult to identify major policy divergence in housing policy and practice as similar policies and principles tend to dominate. Differences that can be identified, however, have tended to emerge more through divergence in the implementation of policies. Murie (2004) has warned that it is important not to overstate the nature of the distinctiveness of housing provision in the different parts of the UK, which have had the same economic environment, the same political and public preferences for home ownership and the same financial institutions and taxation system. Such drivers are more important than housing policy in determining what has happened in housing. The similarity of trends in housing is best demonstrated by an examination of tenure change during the period of devolution – housing tenure is very important as an indictor of both housing policy and the housing market.

There have been largely similar incremental increases in owner-occupation over the years, with Scotland catching up. The proportion of social housing has continued to decline and is at a similar figure in three countries, but Scotland continues with its tradition of the largest social housing sector, although this is also declining. The private rented sector has doubled in Northern Ireland but the differences between all four countries are not great. Table 5.2 shows that it is difficult to isolate devolution as having a major differential impact.

Table 5.2: Dwellings by tenure (%)

	Scotland	Wales	Northern Ireland	England
1999				
Owner-occupation	63.1	71.6	71.2	69.0
Social housing	31.9	20.1	24.5	20.7
Private renting	6.7	8.6	4.3	10.4
2006				
Owner-occupation	67.1	72.7	72.8	70.2
Social housing	25.6	16.9	17.9	17.9
Private renting	7.4	10.4	9.8	11.9

Source: Wilcox (2008)

Stock transfer

Stock transfer has the status of a national housing policy to transfer the ownership and management of council housing to an RSL, usually a housing association. Stock transfer was carried out on a large scale in England including some 97 councils by 2001 (Mullins and Murie, 2006). The option was particularly attractive for councils who had difficulty finding the capital investment for improving the physical stature of their stock. However, with devolution the use of stock transfer has been much more limited in Scotland and Wales than in England.

Three councils in Scotland were to transfer their stock but Glasgow City Council dominated the issue with its 85,000 properties. This transfer was described as the 'highest profile example of housing reform in the period of the Scottish Parliament' (Kintrea, 2006). The Glasgow stock was transferred in 2002 with 58% of tenants voting in favour (Gibb, 2003). While the UK Treasury was willing to write off £900 million in housing debt, the Scottish Government have taken the view that they would be prepared to consider full or partial transfers, particularly in cases that qualify for the Treasury write-off of the debt, but only with the support of tenants and tenant involvement. Stock transfer has been presented as community ownership, giving tenants more say in the management of their homes, as well as transfer to non-profit landlords and realising investment to improve the quality of housing (Scottish Executive, 2005d). It has been argued that the presentation of stock transfer as community ownership was markedly different from England (Daly et al, 2005). However, in England, stock transfers have all moved towards greater tenant involvement and there were stronger measures to protect the stock from the Right to Buy following stock transfer than in Scotland or Wales. The commitment to local control in Glasgow was to lead to a further planned delegation to 60 local housing organisations, who could present plans for further smaller stock transfer to existing or new RSLs. Second-stage transfer became a unique aspect of the Glasgow system (McKee, 2007). The community ownership concept emphasised the social dimension of stock transfer and localised housing organisations and was a key element in delivering on tenant empowerment (McKee, 2007, p 330). In other areas, for example Edinburgh stock, transfer was still rejected after referendums. The new Scottish Government has raised the possibility of alternatives to stock transfer with local councils retaining their stock but establishing arm's-length management organisations (ALMOs).

The Welsh Assembly also encouraged transfer as a way for local authorities to improve their stock – it could not take place without the support of tenants and the consent of the Welsh Assembly. They put forward a model, the community model, seen as consistent with other priorities of the Assembly such as tenant empowerment and community regeneration. This marked some convergence towards the Scottish model in terms of governmental accountability and tenant involvement, but appeared to have little appeal to councils (Mullins and Murie, 2006, p 206). Welsh councils have been the least willing to embrace stock transfer and have faced the threat that if they are not able to finance improvements to bring the stock up to the Welsh quality standard by 2012, then there is no alternative to transfer to the private sector. Although the Welsh Assembly may have given mixed messages, a major independent study (IWA, 2006) argued that most Welsh local authorities would have to transfer their housing in order to meet the

Welsh housing quality standard. It noted the significant regenerative impact of investing the £3 billion needed to reach the standard. More movement has taken place with Monmouth and Wrexham voting 'yes' despite a Newport 'no'. Between March 2007 and March 2008 RSL units have increased by 32% (Local Government Data Unit – Wales, 2009).

It has been noted that ALMOs, which operate in England, have not been an option in Scotland or Wales and PFI was not an option for local authorities in Scotland or Wales (Smith, 2006, p 132). ALMOs manage one fifth of all social housing in England. While England has the most progress with stock transfer, some councils have decided to retain their stock using their own extra resources and there is still some public scepticism in all countries. Experience in Northern Ireland is somewhat different in that there is only one public sector housing body, which owns some 92,000 properties. Stock transfer has not been an issue on the agenda of devolved government and although the Westminster Government passed a facilitating order for Northern Ireland in 2003, it was not used (Paris, 2008). The main reasons are the small size of housing associations, the Northern Ireland Housing Executive's ability to meet investment requirements and the potential problems of community ownership in the context of communal conflict. Wilcox (2008) examined the prospect for the continued existence of council-owned housing across England, Scotland and Wales. In England it appears that one million former council houses will be with stock transfer landlords and two million with councils, half-managed by ALMOs. Scotland may have a larger proportion in new ownership but in Wales most council housing stock will not change. In practice Wales will also have a large proportion with social landlords. Northern Ireland will remain distinctive in this respect with no transfers.

Right to Buy

The Right to Buy policy has been implemented throughout the UK with little variation, and the devolved administrations have debated restrictions on the Right to Buy to protect the social housing stock. Since 1980 over 480,000 households in Scotland have taken advantage of the opportunity to buy their own home. In its first two terms the Scottish Executive took action to modernise the scheme, balancing the need to offer the opportunity of home ownership to those who might not otherwise have that chance against the need to offer accommodation to new tenants (Scottish Executive, 2005d). This has been described as 'rebalancing' rather than 'removing' (Jones, 2004).

Modifications have been made, to succession rights, to grounds for repossession, introducing less favourable terms with less discount for Right to Buy, enabling ministers to designate pressurised market areas where Right to Buy might be suspended. The Scottish minister made a commitment in 2007 to end the Right to Buy for all new social housing (Sturgeon, 2007), and is considering ending it for new tenants entering the social rented sector. The continual depletion of the social housing stock and the amount of affordable housing was seen as unsustainable, especially in the context of pressure to increase the supply. However, the mechanism of suspension in pressurised areas has not been used extensively and by 2008 in only 10 local authorities.

Half the original social housing stock in Wales has been sold, causing government concern with problems of homelessness and affordability. The Welsh Assembly has used its powers to introduce secondary legislation restricting the Right to Buy and to develop a distinctive approach tailored to the particular circumstances of Wales. These reduced the maximum discount, allowing landlords a right of first refusal to repurchase properties offered for resale within 10 years of the original purchase, and excluded a number of rural areas, where restrictions may be placed on resale in order to preserve the stock of affordable housing. In 2008, a legislative competence order was introduced to enable the Assembly to legislate to temporarily suspend or vary the qualification provisions of the Right to Buy and Right to Acquire in areas of housing pressure, whether in very small areas or covering specific house types (NAW, 2008b). This led to some opposition in the Westminster Parliament over granting the Welsh Assembly power to end the Right to Buy. In Northern Ireland the devolved administration has made little input into amending the scheme, which was extended to housing association tenants by the Direct Rule government in 2003; the Northern Ireland house sales scheme was revised in line with similar revisions in England and Wales and the discounts reduced in 2004. It can be noted that actions have been taken in England as well, through the reduction in maximum discounts and the adoption of a regional maximum discount to reduce the impact of the Right to Buy.

Affordability

The issue of affordability and help for first-time buyers has produced a range of initiatives to help those priced out of the market across all four countries. In Scotland, the government has established a low-cost initiative for first-time buyers, including government grants to subsidise low-cost home ownership shared equity schemes, and is considering a first-time buyers grant. The shared equity scheme introduced in 2005 enables people to purchase a shared equity home in partnership with a recognised social landlord. The scheme covered new houses but since 2008 has been piloted in an open market version. Scotland also has a mortgage to rent scheme to help people who are in danger of having their homes repossessed to stay in their home as tenants of a social landlord. In 2008, the Scottish minister announced a new Homeowners Support Fund to build on the mortgage to rent scheme by giving homeowners the option of retaining ownership of their home on a shared equity basis. There have been other measures to help accelerate the supply of affordable housing and to provide an improved safety-net for owners facing serious mortgage difficulties. An affordable housing investment programme has assisted housing associations to identify opportunities for accelerated investment in new stock for rent and low-cost home ownership, assistance with purchasing land and new criteria for housing associations to purchase unsold stock from developers.

Wales has introduced a not dissimilar range of initiatives, increasing the supply of affordable housing for both rent and purchase as an area of priority. These included releasing publicly owned land below market value, securing affordable housing on development sites and requiring local authorities to identify a five-year supply of land for housing of all types. Wales has a 'Welsh affordable housing toolkit' that encourages agencies to use all the powers and tools at their disposal to maximise the supply of affordable housing (WAG, 2006c). Homebuy is an Assembly scheme, operated by RSLs to provide an equity loan for 30-50% of the purchase price with the balance met by a conventional mortgage. An independent review of affordable housing in Wales was commissioned by the new government and reported in September 2008 (Essex, 2008), in the context of the *One Wales* commitment to increase affordable housing in the current economic climate. The housing association sector had been smaller in scale than in Scotland and England (Mullins and Murie, 2006, p 205). A major component of the recommendations related to more involvement by housing associations to increase quality and a new regulatory framework was proposed to allow housing associations to look at more innovative ways of creating more affordable homes. Affordability will be a key issue in the formulation of a new Wales national housing strategy.

For a substantial period Northern Ireland had the lowest house prices in the UK, but a sharp increase just before the restoration of devolution in 2007 brought the issue of affordability to the fore. The last year of Direct Rule had seen a major report on affordability (DSD, 2007), which recommended an increase in social housing, investing land for building, using surplus land and more equity sharing. In fact inter-party agreement on housing was one of the early achievements, with affordable housing as one of the priorities, and the Executive agreed to establish an interdepartmental task force on affordable housing. In 2008, the minister responsible for social development launched the *New Housing Agenda*, presented as the most radical housing initiative in a generation, to increase social and affordable housing. The package contained extra funding for social housing targets, a form of developer contribution, an empty homes strategy, amending the co-ownership part-buy rent scheme, use of surplus public land and a mortgage rescue scheme. Compared with Scotland and Wales, this may not appear very radical. There were no restrictions in Northern Ireland on the Right to Buy, house building was not restored to the Housing Executive and the level of grant to housing associations was cut. One innovation for Northern Ireland was the first localised shared equity schemes with builders/developers and housing associations. Continuing difficulties with affordability and a shortfall in the supply of social housing are reflected in a 50% increase from 2002 in the number of people on the waiting list in 2008 (NIHE, 2009).

England, like the other three countries, has also developed new low-cost home ownership schemes such as key worker and starter home initiatives and Home Buy schemes similar to the Welsh schemes. All four countries have also used planning powers to achieve levels of affordable housing in new developments. It has been suggested, with reference to Scotland (Maclennan and O'Sullivan, 2008), but it is true of all three devolved administrations, that they have focused too much on housing policy as affordability and instability, and not developed distinctive housing policies as a national policy.

Homelessness

Following devolution, Scotland's policy on homelessness was seen as a flagship initiative (Smith, 2006), and as representing a radical divergence with England (Fitzpatrick, 2004). Legislation in 2001 and 2003 increased support for homeless people. The *Homes for Scotland's people* policy document referred to 'the most progressive homelessness legislation in Europe' (Scottish Executive, 2005d, p 5). The new homelessness policy was based on abolishing limitations on rights to assistance and extending eligibility for permanent housing to nearly all homeless people. It was proposed to give all homeless people in Scotland, regardless of priority need, at least temporary accommodation, but with the intention of offering a permanent home to everyone unintentionally homeless by 2012. Other innovations included suspending the local connection rules and modification of the impact of the intentionality rule to allow the intentionally homeless a short assured tenancy. These reforms of homelessness legislation have been described as far-reaching compared with those contemplated in England (Kintrea, 2006, p 198), and explained by Fitzpatrick (2004, p 193) as reflecting a strong and broad consensus to give priority to homelessness on the policy agenda. It has been suggested, however, that practice in England has been to put more emphasis on preventive measures, and the radical reforms in Scotland were made possible by weak demand for social housing at the time (Pawson and Davidson, 2008). The *Firm foundations* strategy (Scottish Government, 2007d) put forward a shift in emphasis by suggesting the greater use of the private rented sector to re-house homeless households, which would also help remove pressure from the social housing stock.

Wales is largely covered by legislation and provision for England but has still launched its own initiatives, as homelessness has been a major social justice issue. Secondary legislation, the 2001 Homeless Persons (Priority Need) Wales Order, broadened the category of people to be considered in priority need to include care leavers, 16- to 17-year-olds, former prisoners and those fleeing domestic violence. This was introduced ahead of the 2002 Homelessness Act that was common to England and Wales. WAG published its first homelessness strategy in 2003, which had a commitment to partnership working to reduce homelessness and this strategy was revised for 2006-08 with an action plan (WAG, 2006c). This plan had an emphasis on preventing homelessness wherever possible by housing more people before they became homeless. The Northern Ireland Assembly Social Development Committee turned its attention to homelessness in 2002, contributing to a revision of the Northern Ireland Housing Executive's (NIHE) homelessness strategy (NIHE, 2002). Their report contained recommendations stressing the importance of partnership working, adequate support packages and the possible need to change the definition of homelessness (NIA Social Development Committee, 2002). Also influential was a Northern Ireland Audit Office report that criticised the value and quality of private sector accommodation. It noted that the average length of stay in private sector accommodation was 115 days compared with 26 days in Scotland (NIAO, 2002). The report recommended new-look quality interim accommodation and an increase in preventive measures. A new Housing Bill was prepared in 2002 with a section on homelessness, but this largely brought Northern Ireland legislation into line with Westminster legislation in relation to the definition of homelessness and ineligibility for homelessness assistance. There were three key strands: primary prevention to stop homelessness; the provision of high-quality temporary accommodation, not unlike the Welsh strategy; but the third strand was a somewhat different emphasis on the provision of appropriate support to sustain tenancies and prevent the recurrence of homelessness. A homelessness steering group was established from October 2007 to implement a strategy to promote the social inclusion of the homeless, with proposed action relating to increasing land for social housing, more priority for prevention, a housing approach to anti-social behaviour with eviction as a last resort, and close working with health and social care bodies (OFMDFM, 2007).

Fit housing

All four countries have established and put into operation a definition of 'fit housing' for all social housing (see Table 5.3). The 2006 Housing Scotland Act introduced the Scottish Housing Quality Standard to tackle chronic disrepair in Scotland's housing stock, and is seen as the minimum acceptable level of quality for Scottish social housing; it is expected that all Scottish social housing will reach the standard by 2015. The Welsh Housing Quality Standard is the most ambitious, calling for housing to be located in a safe and attractive environment (Wilcox, 2008, p 13). The Decent Homes Standard was introduced in 2001 in Northern Ireland to meet modern standards of fitness covering structure, energy efficiency and facilities.

Each country set a target date but with funding pressures the 2010 targets are unlikely to be met.

Table 5.3: Improving quality of stock

Scotland	Scottish housing quality standard	2015
Wales	Welsh housing quality standard	2012
Northern Ireland	Decent homes standard	2010
England	Decent homes standard	2010

Conclusion

A large component of social policy would appear to fall into this category of incremental divergence. There is a caveat that for some area of provision one country may display rather more divergence then the others, because of either a few innovations or because of falling behind the other countries through inactivity. It is clear that some complete areas of social policy, mainly housing, children's services and the voluntary sector, fall into this category but also some aspects of health and social care. Some services may have initially demonstrated aspects of divergence but subsequently major differences did not develop, as with early years policies in Wales. There is no doubt other examples of more minor differences that have grown incrementally. This indicates that there may be less difference than some of the rhetoric and labels surrounding policy and strategic initiatives. The main reasons for incremental differences lie with degrees of innovative thinking, variation in needs, different priorities and administrative structures. In a number of major social policy areas there is little evidence for even incremental differences.

SIX

Convergence in social policy

The convergence of social policies throughout the UK has usually arisen for two main reasons: first, because the policy area falls within policies reserved to the UK Government, leading to parity in legislation, policy and provision or, second, through a decision by all four governments to adopt or endorse the same policies. Under the convergence heading the most important social policy area is social security, which rather dominates the issue. In practice there are a number of other dimensions to convergence and a range of factors that promote convergence in social policy.

Unified system of social security

Before devolution in 1999 social security was organised largely on a UK-wide basis. Following devolution in Scotland, responsibility for social security, child support and pensions policy and administration was designated a reserved function under the 1998 Scotland Act. The UK Government administers a single security system for England, Scotland and Wales, and the Department for Work and Pensions operates as a unified entity throughout England, Scotland and Wales. The position of social security in Northern Ireland is different constitutionally, however, and is something of an anomaly.

Formally, social security in Northern Ireland is a devolved matter but in practice it is part of the UK's uniform system. Historically, the division of functions in the 1920 Government of Ireland Act meant that social security would develop as a devolved matter, but by the time of the postwar welfare state the principle had been established of parity of services and taxation between Great Britain and Northern Ireland. The 1946 National Insurance Act permitted arrangements to coordinate the two systems of insurance so that they could operate as a single system and the 1949 Social Services (Agreement) Act maintained the rates of contributions and payments in parity for a range of benefits. However, the principle of parity did not prevent some differences in the 1950s and 1960s, for example, in residence qualifications, to deter population movement across the Irish border (Ditch, 1988; Fahey and McLaughlin, 1999) and the 1972 Payment of Debts Act, which allowed the transfer of benefits to counter a rent and rates strike which was a political protest at the time. The 1998 Northern Ireland Act, re-establishing devolution, specified that the Northern Ireland Minister for Social Security and the Secretary of State for Work and Pensions should consult one another with a view to securing a single system of social security, child support and pensions for the UK. A joint authority operated, consisting of the two ministers and the Chancellor of the Exchequer, under the name of the Social Security, Child Support and Pensions Authority (NIO, 1998, para 88). The 1998 Act contains a list of social security legislation where reciprocal consultation and coordination is required. The formal existence of two social security systems in the UK is demonstrated by the practice of having separate social security legislation for Northern Ireland, yet in practically all circumstances, this legislation makes corresponding provisions to that applying to Great Britain. A change occurred when HM Revenue & Customs became responsible not just for tax credits but also for child benefit, and its remit covered the whole UK. Consequently, child benefit is no longer a devolved matter and the 2005 Child Benefit Act applied to Northern Ireland as well as the rest of the UK (Evason, 2006).

Social security legislation has largely remained in parity, and such is the degree of convergence that the Northern Ireland Social Security Agency carried out work for some London districts and the Northern Ireland Child Support Agency provided services to an area of eastern England under a partnership contract with the Agency in Great Britain (NIA, 2007a, p 8). Some differences in the departmental organisations and the service delivery model have remained, however. Northern Ireland's devolved administration has a Department for Social Development, governing mainly social security and housing as a central department, but a centralised public body, NIHE, administers housing benefit. In 2002, a new concordat between the Department for Work and Pensions and the Northern Ireland Department for Social Development provided guidance for consultation and communication in order to ensure that legislation in Great Britain and Northern Ireland remains the same, or that any divergence could be accommodated. This means that if the NIA wished to pursue alternative policies, it would require a financial settlement, with costs met from the Northern Ireland budget. The NIA and NIE have shown little appetite for attempting to break the parity principle in the main area of social security benefits.

The 2008 Pensions Act (Northern Ireland) made the same provisions as the UK 2007 Pensions Act, as part of the ongoing process of pensions reform. However, when the 2007 Welfare Reform Act (Northern Ireland) was introduced at Stormont, as corresponding to provisions contained in the 2007 Welfare Reform Act in the UK, there were objections by the Assembly Committee to a change in housing benefit. This would have introduced the practice operating in Great Britain of paying housing benefit to claimants in the private rental sector instead of to landlords, as was the existing Northern Ireland practice. The Social Development Minister decided to retain the existing arrangement, an example not just of divergence but also of a more conservative approach. Unlike Great Britain local taxation (rates) relief is also devolved. The final decisions of a rating review carried out by the new devolved administration imposed much more restricted rates relief than in Great Britain (DFP, 2007). A 25% discount to single occupiers was restricted in Northern Ireland to people over 75. The Northern Ireland rating review did not discuss the issue in the context of social protection and welfare entitlement.

The impact of the reserved status of social security is also demonstrated in other aspects of the UK social security structures. The Social Security Advisory Committee (SSAC) was set up in 1980 to give advice to the UK Secretary of State on social security matters, and to consider and report on social security regulations. The SSAC similarly advises the Department for Social Development in Northern Ireland. If the Northern Ireland regulations are the same they are exempt from referral. The chair of SSAC meets with the Northern Ireland Minister for Social Development, the Department's Permanent Secretary and chair of the Assembly Committee (SSAC, 2000). It has also been the established practice to include Northern Ireland in visits to social security organisations that SSAC makes. In 2003, a quinquennial review of SSAC recommended that the procedures by which SSAC was consulted by the Northern Ireland Department for Social Development could be improved to reflect operational divergence and outcomes, that SSAC should develop a closer relationship with the Assembly Committee and that proposed changes in provision should be examined for their differential impact on Northern Ireland (DWP, 2003a). The review also examined the impact of devolution in Scotland and Wales on the Advisory Committee's work. It noted concern with growing differences in service delivery and the need for reliable information on the differential impact of social security regulations in Scotland and Wales. It also encouraged the Scottish Executive and Welsh Assembly to provide the fullest information to them (DWP, 2003a, p 42).

A second category of structures that reflects the reserved status of social security is the regulatory and appeals system. Social security and child support commissioners determine cases on points of law from appeals, from tribunals in social security benefits, child support and tax credit. Their jurisdiction extends over Scotland, England and Wales, with commissioners in Scotland based in Edinburgh.

Northern Ireland has its own social security and child support commissioners and Court of Appeal whose rulings are binding on Northern Irish adjudication officers. Thus British case law is not legally binding in Northern Ireland, but it has been argued that it has persuasive force (Dickson, 2005). The actual appointment of the Northern Ireland commissioners is, however, an excepted matter under London control. There is also a separate Office of the Social Fund Commissioners in Northern Ireland. While the same commissioners are also responsible for Social Fund reviews in Great Britain, they operate under the different name of the Independent Review Service for the Social Fund. In practice, the role of reviewing Social Fund decision making, providing information and conducting research operates uniformly throughout the UK. The pensions regulator, set up in 2005, is also a UK-wide regulator of work-based schemes.

Following the establishment of the Scottish Parliament and despite the reserved status of social security, a concordat was published in 1999 (DWP, 1999) with a similar one for Wales, setting out ground rules for managing the relationship between the Scottish Executive and WAG and the then Department of Social Security. This focused on working relationships and liaison arrangements for officials, including the exchange of information, good communications, the handling of correspondence, parliamentary debates, committees and questions, finance and resolution of disputes, but did not directly cover policy issues. The concordat did not, however, provide clear guidance in the dispute over savings in attendance allowance payments with the introduction of FPNC in Scotland (Parry, 2004). Decisions by the Scottish and Welsh administrations on student fees have also had a differential impact on the claimant position of students between England, Scotland and Wales. To date, there has not been any major campaign for greater powers for the devolved administrations over social security. The major area of discretion for Scotland, Wales and Northern Ireland lies in the area of initiatives to encourage benefit take-up, advice and quality of claimant services. In theory this should be easier to accomplish in Northern Ireland because the Department for Social Development and the Social Security Agency are integral parts of the devolved administration.

Other reserved social policy functions

Legislation on equal opportunities, meaning anti-discrimination measures, is reserved to the UK Parliament for England, Scotland and Wales. Thus legislation for discrimination relating to gender, race relations, disability, sexual orientation, age, religion and belief and equal pay is dealt with at Westminster and applies throughout Great Britain. There are 35 Acts and 116 different pieces of equality legislation currently in force.

Legislative authority is devolved to Northern Ireland and this has facilitated distinctive policy and legislation on fair employment and religious discrimination (for details see Chapter Three). Northern Ireland has its own legislation on other equality measures but almost all of this legislation, on sex discrimination, equal pay, disability and sexual orientation, is similar to legislation in Great Britain. The 1995 Disability Discrimination Act covered the whole of the UK but a separate Disability Discrimination (Northern Ireland) Order mirrored the amendments to the 2005 Disability Discrimination Act that applied to England, Scotland and Wales. The UK Government has published a Single Equality Bill in April 2009 which will replace and strengthen anti-discrimination measures and produce a single equality duty on the public sector to bring together the three existing duties for race, disability and gender, with an extension to the issues of age, sexual orientation, gender assignment and religion or belief (Government Equality Office, 2008). A new Single Equality Bill would cover England, Scotland and Wales, but Northern Ireland would have its own bill that would differ in relation to existing Section 75 equality duty and enforcement but large sections including those for age, gender and disability would be similar.

The area of clearly reserved functions outside social security and taxation is fairly limited. The most significant examples lie within the health field – the regulation of the health professions is a reserved matter and a policy area subject to recent review. Regulation covers registration, conduct, clinical quality and education and operates through a number of bodies, including the General Medical Council, the General Dental Council and the Nursing and Midwifery Council. In 2003, a Council for Healthcare Regulatory Excellence was set up to ensure consistency and good practice in regulation throughout the UK. The UK-wide convergence was intended to achieve public confidence through national standards and to facilitate staff movement around the UK. In 2007, a UK Government White Paper (DH, 2007) confirmed the need to ensure the integrity of health professionals within the UK, but advocated a system with sufficient flexibility to work effectively for the different health needs and healthcare approaches in the NHS in England, Scotland, Wales and Northern Ireland. It recognised that a different approach in implementation may have to be taken by the devolved administrations in terms of operational practicalities, for example, there was different devolved delivery frameworks for handling revalidation and recording concerns/complaints.

The licensing of medicines in the UK is a reserved matter. This is in contrast to guidance on the use of medicines by the NHS that is in part a devolved matter (for details see Chapter Four). Pharmaceutical companies normally seek licensing approval through an application to the Medicines and Healthcare Products Regulatory Agency, which is responsible for the efficacy, quality and safety of medicines and medical devices, as well as bloods and blood products. It also investigates incidents and has the authority to withdraw products and suspend production. The Medicines and Healthcare Products Regulatory Agency operates as a UK-wide body, as does the Human Fertilisation and Embryology Authority, which acts as an independent regulator for this reserved function. It licenses and monitors clinics for IVF procedures, produces a code of practice, provides information for the public, patients, professionals and also advises the government. It has promoted its UK-wide remit in holding open authority meetings around the UK and its membership has representatives from Scotland, Wales and Northern Ireland.

Human genetics is also a reserved subject and since 1999 a Human Genetics Commission has provided advice and information on new developments, particularly on social, ethical and legal issues. While genetics policy is reserved, the delivery of genetic services is the responsibility of each devolved administration. The Commission also works within the context of devolution as it advises the devolved administrations, as appropriate, as well as the UK Government.

The operation of reserved functions only explains part of the convergence in social policy. There is a substantial area of policy convergence that is the result of the four governments deciding to introduce similar policies, and there are a number of dimensions to this trend.

Copying and policy transfer

Copying or policy transfer was one of the anticipated outcomes of devolution and the expression 'policy laboratory' became closely linked to devolution. The expectation was that each country would learn from each other and from new innovations in particular. A development in social policy in one country could transfer to one or more of the other countries. Stewart (2004a) suggested that it seemed likely that copying would become more pronounced as devolution unfolded.

The introduction of children's commissioners is an example of policy copying and transfer. A children's commissioner was originally introduced in Wales and the Scottish Executive and Parliament and NIE and NIA followed, as eventually did the UK Government and Parliament for England (see also Chapter Three). It has been acknowledged that the commissioners helped each other in establishing the new offices, drawing from previous experience, which meant they did not have to reinvent the wheel (Joint Committee on Human Rights, 2006). The commissioners and staff in all four countries had joint meetings to share best practice and common concerns and this represents a policy and practice transfer process.

The introduction by Wales of a commissioner for older people (see also Chapter Three) provides a more fragmented case of 'copying'. After the Welsh bill was introduced it appeared that Scotland was going to follow suit, when a member's bill was proposed by Alex Neill MSP to establish a commissioner for older people in Scotland. This would have had a similar function to the Welsh commissioner, to promote and safeguard the rights and interests of older people. The election of a new government resulted in an end to this policy copying process as the bill lapsed and the new government was not convinced of the need for the office given the proliferation of commissioners and ombudsmen. Northern Ireland, however, seems to have decided to copy the Welsh model, after commissioning a review of existing provisions and proposals in Great Britain (Deloitte, 2007). An interim older people's advocate has been appointed, pending final decisions on the role, remit and powers of an older people's commissioner, and whether it would exactly copy the Welsh model. In England, the *Opportunity age* strategy referred to the establishment of a Welsh commissioner as an interesting development and stated '… we will wait to see how it works' (DWP, 2005, para 5.8) – in 2008 it was announced that an independent and informal advocate for older people would be set up.

It is possible to see Scotland as leading in the UK with a complete smoking ban in public places, which may have also compelled England to largely follow the same path. Another example of mutual learning relates to the introduction in Scotland of employer-led regulation of healthcare support workers, based on safe recruitment, induction and continuing development. The UK Department of Health's (DH) White Paper on regulation for health professions recommended that on the evidence this approach might be copied and extended to the other countries of the UK (DH, 2007, para 7.20).

The new provision in Wales for legislative competence orders allows individual members as well as the Executive to introduce legislative proposals, and these may be inspired by copying and policy transfer. In 2008, a member proposed a legislative competence order to facilitate a mental health measure which would provide people with a right to assessment, a right to independent mental health advocacy and impose duties on the health service to provide treatment. This was acknowledged as based on Scottish experience. Scotland had used its devolved legislative powers to introduce rights for people with a mental disorder to an assessment of need and to independent advocacy. The 2003 Mental Health (Care and Treatment) (Scotland) Act had conferred rights on people with a mental disorder in Scotland not enjoyed by those in England and Wales. It was claimed that the Scottish model was much admired for adopting a humane and inclusive approach.

Since 2006, all four countries of the UK have decided to carry out separate fundamental reviews of the role and task of social workers, which suggests a degree of process transfer. In 2006 in Scotland, a review group report *Changing lives* was published (Scottish Executive, 2006c). In Wales, two key reviews were undertaken – *Fulfilled lives, supportive communities* set out a vision of social services and an implementation strategy (WAG, 2007d). A previous Welsh report *Social work in Wales: A profession to value* (Social Services Improvement Agency, 2005) had also reviewed tasks and workforce issues. At the same time the General Social Care Council in England was involved in an extensive exercise to produce a report, *Social work at its best* (2008). This followed a review on raising the status of social care (Platt, 2007). A similar Northern Ireland review was initiated, but not until 2007. This was undertaken by the Northern Ireland Social Care Council and could therefore be seen as copying the process in England. Policy transfer was underlined by the production of a briefing paper on lessons from the reviews in Scotland, England and Wales (Brand, 2008). The chief social services officer has given some indication that there will be similar issues in the Northern Ireland report (Martin, 2007).

The *Changing lives* review found social work in Scotland lacking in confidence in its own skills and distinctive contribution and not delivering to its potential. The *Social work in Wales* report also noted that social workers felt undervalued. In *Changing lives* the challenge was seen as protection and support for the vulnerable and socially excluded. In *Fulfilled lives, supporting communities* there was a similar commitment for social services to be acute champions of the needs of the vulnerable. Both papers *Changing lives* and *Fulfilled lives* recognised the significance of similar demographic and socio-economic factors: an ageing population, complex high care needs, fragmented relationships, social polarisation, ethnic diversity and people living alone. In both Scotland and Wales the response used the same four-tier pyramid of intervention to describe the task of social work categorised in Wales as universal/vulnerable/complex and acute tiers. Each tier was based on a different role for social workers and the nature of social work intervention. In looking at the way ahead there were three common themes.

First, engaging users and carers as participants to influence the design, planning, review and assessment of services. The Scottish document recommended building greater capacity to allow social workers to work with users and their carers to manage risk and resources and also to involve users in training, recruitment and inspection. The Welsh document described a vision that would be delivered in partnership with the service user.

Second, was the theme 'personalisation of services', seen in Scotland as unavoidable and desirable. In the Welsh document there was also a focus on person-centred care services.

Third, was the importance of collaboration with other agencies, integration in delivering community care and integrated work with health and education. In *Challenging lives* there was an expressed will to exploit more fully the potential of partnership working in Scotland. In *Fulfilled lives, supportive communities* there was a commitment to address the barriers to better collaboration. This was seen as best delivered by social services as a core service in local government working closer with other services. The Scottish report only briefly addressed the distinctive impact of devolution, noting that Scotland had been able to pursue its own evolution of services and underlined the social justice aspects of social work. The Scottish paper recommended that social work should remain a single generic profession and identified a range of functions only social workers could do, seen as a strong re-statement of core values (Brodie et al, 2008). In England a somewhat more ambitious discussion on the role of social work was included, based on remodelling the social work role with increased support from non-professional staff. The review of *The status of social care* (Platt, 2007) had raised for consideration a new type of worker straddling health and social care. *Social work at its best* also commented on the loosening boundaries between professional disciplines and the increasing variety of multi-disciplinary tasks. Social workers in all four countries are facing similar pressures with structural reorganisation, social workers working more in multi-professional teams, the demands of individual budgets and personalisation, and with social work located more in the voluntary and private independent sectors.

Copying and policy transfer often goes relatively unrecognised and a major source of copying remains the policies of the UK Government adopted for England. This can be demonstrated in the details of action plans, strategies and policies in such areas as tackling social exclusion or urban and rural regeneration. However, Scotland and Wales have increasingly tended to look to each other rather than England for policy transfer; for example, in 2005 members of the Scottish Parliament's Health Committee paid a visit to the National Assembly for Wales (NAW) to fact find on the phasing out of prescription charges. With SNP assuming power the Scottish Government has declared its intention to look in future to other European countries rather than England for policy transfer.

Use of legislative consent

This is the facility that allows the Scottish Government to use Westminster legislation although covering devolved matters (see also Chapter Two) – with the introduction of legislative devolution it was anticipated that there could be occasions when it could be more convenient for Scotland to be included in Westminster bills (Winetrobe, 2005) rather than introduce Scottish bills in Edinburgh. It is a convention that Westminster would not legislate on devolved matters for Scotland and Northern Ireland without the consent of the Scottish Parliament or the NIA. A memorandum explaining the bill is usually considered by the relevant Scottish Parliamentary Committee before what is now called a legislative consent motion is agreed by Parliament. Sewel motions became much more common than anticipated and 86 have been approved since 1999, with over half falling into the social policy or criminal justice categories, although some others are technical rather than policy related (Scottish Affairs Committee, 2006). In practice the Scottish Government and Parliament, in accepting legislative consent motions, are making a decision to adopt parity in policy with England and often with Wales as well. Thus the 2006 UK Health and Social Care Act contains provisions relating to community pharmacies and medicines that cover Scotland. The 2007 Further Education and Training Act introduced provisions relating to the Learning and Skills Council, career development loans and industrial training, while the 2008 Health and Social Care Act introduced provisions relating to the regulation of health professionals.

There are a number of different influences on the Scottish Executive and Parliament that led to such convergence legislation. These include convenience, in that parliamentary time in Scotland can be saved or the matter introduced more quickly, for example, to strengthen protection against sex offenders. Other reasons include the avoidance of potential problems of overlapping competencies or blurred responsibilities – the complex interrelationship between reserved and devolved powers can best be solved on occasions by a single Westminster bill, for example, in relation to the regulation of cross-border bodies, such as the Health Protection Agency, or in relation to closing loopholes between the two jurisdictions in criminal legislation, which could be exploited. It has been suggested that there may also be political or special reasons for the Scottish Executive wishing to use Westminster legislation and these have arisen in relation to legislation on tobacco advertising, gender recognition and the Sexual Offences Bill (Keating et al, 2003) and also with civil partnerships. By agreeing to Westminster legislation the Scottish Parliament can avoid what might be major controversies (Page and Batey, 2002). It can be suggested that to some degree Scottish Parliament has been marginalised by the use of the process – it has not been used to impose policies demanded by Westminster or to pass power back to Westminster. It was anticipated that the SNP Government would make less use of Sewel motions, yet their first year in office saw 10 such motions. The convention also applied formally to Northern Ireland and Westminster Parliament will not legislate on devolved matters except with the agreement of the devolved legislature. During the operation of the NIA only a few minor examples can be identified (Anthony and Morison, 2005, p 179), and the process was more informal than in Scotland.

Similar responses

A major factor in producing convergence in social policy has been a uniform response to the same problems in each country or the continuation after devolution of well-established policy responses. Key housing policies adopted by the devolved administrations demonstrate this trend. Many housing problems across the UK are similar, for example, housing supply deficiency, lack of affordable housing, compliance of the housing stock with quality standards, regeneration of difficult-to-let estates, homelessness, tenant participation and sheltered housing (for discussion see Chapter Five). Convergent policies can be identified in support of the growth of owner-occupation, the promotion of housing associations and RSLs, decent homes standards and the Supporting People initiatives. The operation of housing benefit on a largely common basis across the UK is a further example. It is also possible to quote the role of housing policy in contributing to wider uniform objectives of regeneration, energy efficiency and sustainability (Smith, 2006, p 136). Mullins and Murie (2006, p 10) suggest that, 'It seems unlikely that devolution will exert a sufficiently strong influence to overwhelm nationalising, unifying and converging forces' that lead to largely similar policy responses.

Similar policy solutions to similar problems can also be detected in aspects of educational policy. Despite the tradition of separate education systems, particularly in Scotland and Wales, there is a view that close scrutiny reveals a broad UK similarity in many respects (Raffe and Croxford, 2000). Rees (2007, p 8) suggests there are important continuities between pre- and post-devolution education policies in Wales and that this pattern has largely continued under devolution, while Poole and Mooney (2006) suggested that Scotland's schools were moving in a similar direction to England. Some of the main legislation has related to additional support needs, curriculum development, early years and targeting under-achievement. The 2006 Joint Inspection of Children's Services and Inspection of Social Work Services (Scotland) Act had similar outcomes to England and Wales, and enables joint inspections. A proposal in 2003 to extend ministerial powers to intervene in failing schools was also similar to England.

EU influence

The requirements of EU laws are a major factor contributing to convergence. The devolved bodies are under a statutory obligation not to legislate or act in a manner that is contrary to EU law, and two main types of EU legislation have a direct application to all four countries. EU Commission regulations have a direct effect in all member states but EU directives have a more territorial impact, as they have to be transposed into national law. They set out the objectives to be achieved but give some freedom to decide how they should be implemented. Normally the lead Whitehall department notifies the devolved administration of new EU measures that require action. For directives on devolved matters it is for the devolved administrations, in consultation with Whitehall, to decide whether the obligations arising from the new directives should be implemented or enforced in separate legislation in Scotland and Northern Ireland, in all three countries the parliament and assemblies can also pass regulations as secondary legislation to enforce directives.

Many of the devolved policy areas contain substantial components of EU matters and it was even suggested that three quarters of the work of the Scottish Government is, to a greater or lesser extent, influenced by decisions made in Brussels. At the transposition stage it is almost too late to influence change (Scottish Parliament, 2008b). In practice the majority of EU directives fall into the areas of the environment, agriculture, pollution, food and health and safety rather than social policy. However, European directives have played a key role in equal opportunities, equal pay, equal treatment and access to employment. Examples include the Equal Pay Directive, the 2000 Race Discrimination Directive and the 2002 Equal Treatment Amendment Directive on the principle of equal treatment for men and women. The EU 2000 Employment Framework Directive governs protection in employment in respect of age, disability, religion and belief and sexual orientation. A further employment directive established a framework for the elimination of discrimination and provided for reasonable adjustments for people with disabilities and there was also a 2007 EU Gender, Goods and Services Directive. These normally required only British and Northern Irish law, but the implementation implications regarding support for complainants required action by all the devolved administrations.

As European directives were mandatory they did not often produce conflict. The European Working Time Directive was an exception, however. This was a component of health and safety legislation but affected the working hours of doctors in NHS hospitals, causing particular problems for hospitals in the Scottish Highlands. There has also been concern over the possible convergence impact of other EU health measures and decisions influencing patient mobility and European support for an internal health market (Greer, 2005). The whole range of European funding programmes and initiatives also serves to impose similar policy approaches on the recipient regions, and these have included education, training, youth, social inclusion and equality and employment programmes.

International conventions

The UK is a signature to a number of UK conventions which impose obligations on the devolved administrations and have had an influence on decision making in devolved social policy areas. While the conventions may not be incorporated into UK or devolved legislation they are indications of international standards. The UK government has signed the UN Convention on the Rights of the Child and agreed to do everything it can to implement it (UK Government, 2007). The Convention has 42 articles covering social, economic and cultural rights. Both the Scottish and Welsh governments are strongly committed to it and have been very proactive in its implementation. Wales has adopted it as the framework of their seven core aims for their work with and for children and young people. The Northern Ireland Executive has more simply stated that it is committed to the Convention. The UK Government makes a periodic report on progress regarding implementation of the Convention and draws attention to where devolved administrations have made significant contributions in the main report. In addition, individual reports from the devolved administrations are appended (UK Government, 2007, appendices).

Other core international conventions that have influenced policy makers are the UN Convention on the Elimination of All Forms of Discrimination Against Women and the UN Principles for Older Persons, which has influenced strategies in Scotland and Wales. In 2009, the UK Government agreed to sign the UN Convention on the Rights of Persons with Disabilities.

Intergovernmental organisations

A number of intergovernmental organisations can be seen as forums for cooperative activity and the sharing of policy ideas, even if their influence is limited. It was originally intended that a joint ministerial council, set up following the introduction of devolution, would have this function as well as solving intergovernmental disputes, but between 2002 and 2007 no use was made of this mechanism, except for European matters (Trench, 2007). Somewhat oddly, an inter-governmental organisation, which was greeted with some scepticism, has operated with some success in bringing the political leadership or their representatives together. The British-Irish Council (BIC) was introduced after the Good Friday Agreement to provide a forum for the UK and Irish governments, the devolved governments in Northern Ireland, Scotland and Wales, together with the governments of the Isle of Man, Guernsey and Jersey. Known also as the Council of the Isles, it had the original purpose of giving assurance to Ulster Unionists about the importance of east–west relations in a British Isles context. BIC's role was defined at its inaugural meeting as a forum for members to exchange information, to discuss, consult and endeavour to reach agreement on cooperation over matters of mutual interest (BIC, 1999). It developed a multi-tiered level of functioning, meeting at senior ministerial level, at sectoral level with ministers and civil servants and, at the level of work sessions, visits and seminars. A programme of work was agreed with each country taking a lead role. BIC was not designed as a forum for internal cooperation between the devolved administrations and it could have collapsed after the suspension of the NIE and NIA in 2002. However, it continued to function and the Scottish, Welsh and Irish administrations developed some enthusiasm for the work; its activities have expanded (see Table 6.1).

Table 6.1: Areas of work of the British-Irish Council; lead country

From 1999		Additions post 2001	
United Kingdom	Environment	Jersey	Knowledge economy
Republic of Ireland	Tackling drugs	Guernsey	Tourism
Northern Ireland	Transport	Isle of Man	Telemedicine
Wales/Scotland	Social exclusion	Wales	Minority languages
Isle of Man/ Channel Islands	Knowledge economy	Scotland	Demography
		New work streams	Post 2008
		Wales	Early Years
		Scotland/UK	Energy
		Isle of Man	Digital inclusion
		Northern Ireland	Housing
		Northern Ireland	Spatial planning

Source: BIC Communiques (1999–2009)

BIC summits met in different locations, received responses from the sectoral groups and endorsed action plans. It was clear that the participants found the joint activities useful and BIC took on roles which were not contemplated when it started (Trench, 2004). It encouraged the sharing of best practice and information through reports, visits and seminars and promoted the adoption of some policy ideas and practices, for example, the social inclusion sector examined child poverty, the long-term care of older people and migrant workers. A report on disability and access to employment and training made recommendations on using IT to improve service delivery. To some extent ideas on credit unions, smoking bans and criminal assets recovery were transferred. In 2007, Northern Ireland representatives returned to

BIC. The sharing of practice and joint studies continued on such topics as the misuse of drugs, health services in rural areas, the impact of the recession and the voluntary sector. This contribution led to a further expansion in BIC's work into new work streams including early years, housing, planning and energy.

A similar body, the British-Irish Inter-Parliamentary Body, had existed since 1990 but following devolution its composition was revised to include elected representatives from Scotland, Wales, Northern Ireland, the Isle of Man and the Channel Islands, as well as Dáil Éireann (House of Representatives of Ireland), and the House of Commons. Representatives could also be appointed from the House of Lords and the Irish Senate. This was again a forum for sharing ideas but it was able to exert some influence on policy makers mainly because it operated through four investigative committees that reported to the governments and received formal responses. Four committees cover constitutional, social, economic, European and also environmental and social issues. Topics covered have included rural development, higher education, pensions and young people in deprived areas (British-Irish Inter-Parliamentary Body, 2009). A number of other networks of statutory bodies have been set up, usually also involving the Irish Republic as well as the four home countries. Examples are the Joint Equality and Human Rights Forum, the British-Irish Ombudsman Association and the British-Irish Network of Children's Commissioners. This could result in learning from each other's experiences and engaging in joint activities, all of which serve to promote common approaches and convergence.

UK policy pressures for convergence

A number of UK-related factors can be seen as creating pressure towards convergence in policy, but five in particular, are worth a comment. First is the influence of the UK civil service and the networks of advisory bodies as a common source of policy ideas, with a long established policy-making capacity and expertise in key areas. In practice Whitehall-based bodies have often given the lead on policy innovations. This can be compared with a much less developed policy making and policy innovation capacity in Scotland, Wales and Northern Ireland. Second is the role of Great Britain's national political parties. Through devolution the Labour Party has been able to have a significant influence on politics adopted by the Scottish and Welsh Labour Parties, who have been in government positions for most of the time of devolution in Scotland and Wales. Third, and to date more of a potential convergence influence, is the continuing post of Secretary of State in each country. Their role and position in the UK Cabinet can contribute to convergence. The Welsh Secretary has engaged in discussions in the Welsh Assembly and the Scottish Secretary has been seen as hostile to SNP policy, but the Northern Ireland Secretary has largely avoided impinging on devolution matters. Fourth is the influence of UK-wide pressure groups and policy institutions. Campaigning organisations such as the Child Poverty Action Group, Save the Children, Action for Children, Shelter, Barnardo's, Gingerbread and the 4 Nations Child Policy Network tend to promote the same policy demands throughout the UK. The same is true of policy institutes such as the Institute for Public Policy Research, the Policy Studies Institute, the Pensions Policy Institute and the New Policy Institute and research institutes such as the Joseph Rowntree Foundation. In contrast Scotland, Wales and Northern Ireland lack policy think tanks, especially in the social policy areas. Fifth is the dominant role of England, stemming from its population, dominance at Westminster and Whitehall, and its size relative to the devolved administrations. The UK Government and Parliament, while in one respect now providing policies and services for England in devolved matters, are still the sovereign authorities that control ultimate financial, constitutional and legislative power. This results in an influence in setting agendas in key areas of social policy, for example, child poverty, benefits, welfare to work and higher education; however, as devolution has developed, the policy-making scenario has been changing, with pressure groups forming territorial sub-national organisations for each country and with the civil service in each country improving their country-based expertise in policy development.

Conclusion

UK membership as well as formal reserved powers create a strong focus for convergence in social policy. The impact and scope of EU directives also has some influence, although this is greater in non-social policy areas whilst UK conventions impose obligations in some discrete social policy areas on the devolved administrations. Policy transfer and copying has had a clear influence on legislation and policy initiatives in the four countries, encouraged at times by popular opinion. However, it is in social security, benefits and tax credits that the most important example of convergence for social policy is to be found. The UK government's role in reserved areas of social policy has significant implications for the activities of the devolved administrations and a number of areas present a formal mix of devolved and non-devolved functions.

SEVEN

Interfaces and overlaps

In theory, there should be no actual overlaps or shared functions between the devolved administrations and the UK government. In practice, however, it is not always easy to draw a neat distinction between reserved and devolved functions. Even if there is a clear distinction in constitutional responsibilities, interfaces exist between services that closely relate to each other, but are the responsibility of the different administrations, and this generates a need for coordination and collaboration. As devolution has progressed, interfaces and overlaps in social policy areas have become more of a feature of its operation and have had to be addressed. A number of different dimensions to overlapping function and interface engagement can be identified. These can be categorised as: interfaces and overlaps which require a need for coordination and cooperation; overlaps which produce entanglements; conflict over powers; cross-border activities; and structures for cooperation.

Interfaces and overlaps: the need for coordination and cooperation

The main social policy areas which require close coordination and cooperation particularly in the delivery of services are benefits and anti-poverty measures, welfare to work, social inclusion and aspects of health.

Benefits and tackling poverty

Social security is largely a uniform UK service but often interfaces directly with what are devolved services, particularly in the area of poverty, child poverty, social inclusion, New Deal, welfare to work and employment, area regeneration and fuel poverty (see Table 7.1).

Anti-poverty strategies are basically an overlap area of responsibility between devolved governments and the UK Government. The Scottish Affairs Committee at Westminster has a particular interest in reserved powers operating in Scotland, and has been active in emphasising the need for the UK Government to cooperate with the Scottish Government to ensure that national policies in tackling poverty are

Table 7.1: Social security-related interfaces

Devolved governments	UK government
Help into work	Benefits
Advice on benefits uptake	Delivery of benefits
Local council tax	Council tax rebates
Early years provision	Tax credit element
Energy efficiency	Energy policy, fuel tax
Social housing rents	Housing Benefit

delivered effectively and are joined up with devolved programmes. The Scottish Affairs Committee has argued that the Scottish Government needs to ensure that its own programmes dovetail with national provision, and that key responsibilities should operate within the Scottish context of tackling poverty (Scottish Affairs Committee, 2008a). The Scotland Office has stated the task of ensuring that the reserved policies that help tackle poverty reflect the Scottish context during both their formulation and implementation. The Department for Work and Pensions (DWP) and the Scottish Executive alert each other as soon as practical to new proposals, where there is a direct or indirect impact on the other's areas of responsibility – there is a concordat in place between the DWP and the Scottish Executive for consultation and clarification of relationships. The Scottish Government currently has a tackling poverty team as the central liaison point with the DWP, to work alongside the UK Government to maximise the impact of the welfare system for Scotland.

The Scottish Government stated that it was committed to sharing the UK Government's objectives to halve child poverty by 2010-11, on the way to eradicating it by 2020, and would continue to do all it could to ensure that Scottish policies and programmes made the maximum contribution (see also Chapter Five). Special policies on child poverty identified by the Scottish Government include: Workforce Plus; more choices for young people not in education, employment or training; free school meals pilots; skills strategies; early years policies; and a task force on health inequalities (Wakefield, 2008). The overarching approach of the first two terms of the Scottish Executive was to identify opportunities to sharpen the attack on poverty in strategies that complemented the approach of the UK Government. Six high-level objectives were set: increasing the chances of employment; improving skills; tackling over-indebtedness; regenerating neighbourhoods; improving health services in deprived areas; and providing quality health services in deprived rural communities. Successive Scottish administrations have continued to take a lead role in tackling poverty in Scotland.

In 2008, the Scottish Government's discussion paper on tackling poverty, inequality and deprivation, and child poverty in particular, addressed the issues of interface and overlapping responsibilities more specifically (Scottish Government, 2008f). It sought to clarify where the Scottish Government could maximise its impact on poverty, and identified three main levers available to the Scottish Government under the current devolution settlement to tackle poverty: first, the prevention of poverty and tackling the root causes, which included measures to address educational underachievement and disadvantage, poor health, disenchantment of young people, early years provision, area deprivation, worklessness and discriminatory attitudes; second, helping to lift people out of poverty which included improving employability, well-being, the quality of advice, the take-up of benefits, tackling substance misuse and homelessness and reducing reoffending; and third, alleviating the impact of poverty on people's lives which included free personal care for older people, the take-up of free school meals, tackling fuel poverty and the abolition of prescription charges. These activities were identified as being where devolved levers could have the greatest long-term impact. The paper acknowledged that UK-wide policies on aspects of tax and benefit arrangements, particularly tax credits and the National Minimum Wage, have had the greatest impact on poverty in Scotland, but that devolved policies have played an important supporting role, and that devolved and reserved policies need to work together more effectively to complement each other (Scottish Government, 2008f, para 49).

The responsible Welsh minister has also recognised that a 'substantial number of the key levers to meet child poverty targets are reserved to Westminster but I am determined that the Assembly government must continue to do whatever it can to help achieve our shared child poverty objectives' (Gibbons, 2008, p 1). When the strategy for tackling child poverty was published in 2005, WAG declared its determination to work closely with its UK partners. It was accepted that policies in all areas of devolved government needed to address the poverty issue, and ending child poverty would involve different Assembly departments. An integrated government effort was needed to encompass: family income benefit, maximisation initiatives, benefit and debt advice. In particular, it was accepted that a strong focus on children's early years was a way to make a greater positive impact (WAG, 2005b). However, it was also recognised that close collaboration with UK bodies was needed, in particular with HM Revenue & Customs (HMRC), to raise awareness of working tax credits. The desirability of a collaborative approach between WAG and the DWP has been widely supported, for example, in identifying four key approaches to tackling poverty: income maximisation, routes to employment, improving learning and skills and reducing indebtedness (Save the Children, 2008). WAG cited child poverty as a reason for facilitating Welsh-specific solutions such as top-up payments to child trust fund accounts, and it was agreed with the UK Department for Children, Schools and Families that WAG would administer the UK top-up for looked-after children, in addition to the Welsh Trust Fund Reimbursement Grant.

The Northern Ireland anti-poverty and social inclusion strategy was launched under Direct Rule, although based on the 2001 devolved programme for government (see also Chapter Five). The emphasis of the strategy was on cross-department working, but led by the local Department for Social Development, responsible for social security. It was not seen as likely that social security schemes different from Great Britain would be introduced (NIA, 2008c, p 4), and more attention was paid to benefit up-take campaigns. With social security administration devolved, the programme for government of the new administration in 2007 did not specifically raise interface issues and did not raise the need for a consultation on the policy implications for Northern Ireland of decisions by the DWP in London. A central anti-poverty unit exists within the OFMDFM but the degree of direct liaison with the DWP or HMRC is variable.

The Scottish Affairs Committee inquiries on poverty and child poverty in Scotland prompted separate responses by the UK Government and the Scottish Executive, although they were published together (Scottish Affairs Committee, 2008b), itself a recognition that liaison with the Scottish Executive was necessary. The DWP responded to almost all the recommendations, referring to where it worked with the Scottish Government. However, in response to certain recommendations, for example, resources for disabled families, looking after a member with a disability, the DWP stated that this was a devolved matter for the Scottish Executive. The Scottish Government was keen to build more effective links with the DWP around issues such as benefits take-up campaigns and reforms to housing benefit, and also to engage with the DWP early in the policy development phase, when changes were being considered that would impact on devolved policies and services. It was emphasised 'that positive benefits would accrue when the DWP did not attempt to adopt policies which rigidly adhere to a one size fits all approach across the UK' (Scottish Affairs Committee, 2008b, p 33). Basically, the most powerful levers in relation to child poverty are reserved benefits and tax powers, but with an important complementary and collaborative role for a wide range of devolved services.

Welfare to work

The overlap in the administration of employment policies is also demonstrated through the implementation of New Deal and welfare to work policies, stemming from UK Government policy that the best route out of poverty for most parents and their children is moving into employment (DWP, 2007a). Employment policy including the New Deal and National Minimum Wage are UK policies. The UK Government has the lead role in helping unemployed people with job search, but providing greater access to the labour market has involved both devolved and central government. In place since 2002, Jobcentre Plus is a major service provided to the public in Scotland from London. But the Scottish Executive has also played an important role in the delivery of the New Deal policy. The *Closing the opportunity gap* anti-poverty strategy endorsed helping people into work and was introduced in seven key local authority areas working through local partnerships with organisations that deliver employability. Scotland took the opportunity to harness the work of the key education, regeneration and health agendas. There was a particular focus on early engagement, post-employment aftercare and inter-agency cooperation. Workforce Plus involved close working with the DWP and Jobcentre Plus Scotland to develop jointly owned targets to get people, especially disadvantaged groups, into sustained employment. It was presented as a joint enterprise to share a UK long-term aim of 80% employment (Scottish Executive, 2006d). While the UK Government was responsible for employment and benefits, the Scottish administration identified many aspects of its responsibilities as having a critical impact on employability covering health, skills, disabilities, children, regeneration and enterprise. Thus Jobcentre Plus had to interact with the Scottish devolved administration in the areas of community regeneration, health, children's services and lifelong learning. In 2006, New Deal Plus for lone parents was extended to Scotland and Wales (Jenkins, 2008).

The Scottish Executive saw itself as working with the UK Government in implementing the proposals in 'a new deal for welfare empowering people to work' (DWP, 2006) through New Deal client groups, Pathways to Work, strategies for incapacity recipients, and New Deal strategies related to health, cities and lone parents. The devolved government could contribute support through childcare, advice, financial support and education for lone parents. The Scottish

Executive, DWP and COSLA signed a partnership accord for collaborative work to help the 'hardest to reach' into work and to help achieve the objectives of *Closing the opportunity gap*. Workforce Plus, the Scottish Executive's employability framework, was published (Scottish Executive, 2006d), with an emphasis on more effective local partnership working to help more people into work and cooperation with the UK Government. The DWP paper setting out the revised system, *Ready for work*, acknowledged that policy for skills, childcare, health, local government and regeneration were all closely linked to the proposals in the paper, but were the responsibility of devolved administrations (DWP, 2007b). DWP worked closely with Scotland and Wales to establish how to implement the reforms in a way that would meet their particular circumstances and needs.

The UK Government also developed a 'city strategy' that would make a concerted effort to tackle worklessness in the most disadvantaged communities in major cities. The pathfinder areas were identified to test the merits of localised, more flexible back-to-work support and the pilot cities included Glasgow, Dundee and Edinburgh. The city strategy also operated alongside the Scottish Workforce Plus strategy. Continuing barriers to increasing employment in Scotland have been identified as childcare, disability and employer attitudes, largely devolved matters.

Wales also had opportunities within the UK-wide framework to focus on Wales-specific solutions, with initiatives covering welfare to work and childcare and skills to boost employment. A joint report between DWP and WAG (DWP, 2007c) stressed the importance of working closely together to deliver employment support. The Pathways to Work programme was running in two of the four Jobcentre Plus districts in Wales. The city strategy covered Wales as well as Scotland, with two Pathfinders areas in Wales based on concentrating local resources on worklessness. Among specific Welsh-tailored initiatives was an EU-supported 'Want 2 Work' pilot to assist welfare recipients in removing barriers to entering employment, combining personal advice in the transition to work, health 'guidance' and financial incentives. WAG worked with Jobcentre Plus in the delivery of four 'Want 2 Work' pilots across Wales to test a range of measures to help claimants into work (DWP, 2007c, p 19). The introduction of new measures in the 2007 Welfare Reform Act to move people away from dependency on benefits into work led to some disagreement with the Welsh Executive concerning the rhetoric used in London (Wyn Jones and Scully, 2009).

Welfare to work policies in Northern Ireland operated somewhat differently. Employment and benefits were formally both devolved, so in one sense a close working relationship with the DWP or UK Government was not always necessary. As the benefit system was maintained in uniformity with Great Britain, in practice the same welfare to work agenda has also been adopted in Northern Ireland, with similar schemes and New Deal and Pathways to Work programmes developed. The Northern Ireland administration would also liaise with the DWP and decide on the most appropriate policies. There was a complication within the devolved administration in that responsibility for employment and benefits was divided between two government departments – Employment and Learning and Social Development – and this caused a delay in rolling out unified jobs and benefits offices. What was missing in Northern Ireland was detailed collaboration with the UK Government to discuss or formulate Northern Ireland-specific policies. Working within the same benefits parameters, Northern Irish departments did produce some local modifications. The devolution of employment services meant that the Northern Ireland administration had more discretion to amend the actual New Deal schemes than in Scotland and Wales (see also Chapter Five). Subsidies were available to employers for up to six months for employing participants on the New Deal for Lone Parents. A new Pathways to Work for Lone Parents initiative was piloted which included an enhanced personal adviser service, a work preparation programme and return to work financial support. Integrated support was also demonstrated by the Possibilities programme, involving personal development training, childcare and advice (PDP, 2007). This initiative involved the voluntary sector and had EU funding.

The significance of interfaces was acknowledged in 2007 when the Secretary of State for Work and Pensions brought his ministerial team on a visit to Scotland and Wales to discuss cooperation, the role of welfare to work and welfare reform. Mr Hutton, Secretary of State, referred to the success of welfare to work in Scotland as a direct result of a partnership between national programmes, the work of the devolved administration and local initiatives (Hutton, 2007). Yet *Reducing dependency, increasing opportunity* (DWP, 2007d), which recommended the use of the private and voluntary sectors in reforming welfare to work, made no reference to devolution. The UK Government moved on to introduce a new Employment Support Assistance benefit for the whole of the UK and issued the details of a new contract structure (DWP, 2008a). This made specific references to Scotland and Wales as contracts for outsourcing would cover large areas but not the whole of Scotland or Wales. Top-tier providers would operate in local partnership arrangements that in Scotland might include community planning partnerships and local employability partnerships and in Wales, Community First partnerships and local service boards. In a gesture to the importance of devolved interfaces, in Scotland providers would be expected to demonstrate knowledge of Workforce Plus and the employability framework and, in Wales, the Skills that Work for Wales strategy. The DWP would work with the new Skills Development Board in Scotland and the Employment and Skills Board in Wales.

There has been concern that not enough account has been taken of differences in Scotland and Wales, for example, in relation to provider capabilities. The DWP commissioning strategy paper made no reference to Northern Ireland at all, implying that as employment was devolved it was a matter of local choice. In practice the equivalent Steps to Work Programme in Northern Ireland will largely be contracted out following the same top-tier/prime contractor/sub-contractor model.

Social exclusion

Social exclusion policy is also split between devolved (see also Chapter Five) and non-devolved powers. A priority in tackling social exclusion is maximising and increasing income through tax credits and social transfers/benefits, but some measures and actions lie within the remit of devolved governments. Policies on social exclusion had been identified as a key issue in Scotland before devolution and were one of the priority agenda items for the new Scottish Executive. Shortly after the introduction of devolution the new Scottish Executive published *Social justice: A Scotland where everyone matters* (Scottish Executive, 1999b), and at the same time a Scottish social inclusion network, changing the emphasis from social exclusion, was set up to coordinate policy. The UK Government also had social exclusion as a major policy item and social exclusion policies again reflected the mixture of devolved and reserved matters. Close links were maintained between the Scottish Executive and the Cabinet Office's Social Exclusion Unit, and the Scottish social justice publication included references to targets for reserved matters. Scotland also set up a ministerial poverty and inclusion taskforce (Scottish Executive, 2000b), and there were still distinctive approaches in Scotland such as social inclusion partnerships. Following EU requirements for national action plans against poverty and social exclusion, the UK Government declared its responsibility to set up a strategy which covered the whole of the UK, but included roles for the devolved administrations of Scotland, Wales and Northern Ireland

(DWP, 2003b). Particular mention and use was made of the Scottish social justice annual report, the Scottish executive programme, *A partnership for a better Scotland*, WAG's commitment to improving public services within principles of social inclusion and also the strategy for children and young people in Northern Ireland. Consequently, the UK's national action plan on social inclusion (DWP, 2008b) integrated the contributions of the devolved administrations with a discussion of central government action. However, it was suggested that the national action plan was not actively pursued by WAG because it was a UK DWP policy that might not adequately reflect Welsh interests (Thompson et al, 2006). On the other hand, it has been suggested that in Scotland a combination of overarching UK-wide policies, along with initiatives at the level at which the Scottish Executive operates, contributes to combating poverty and the UK's Jobcentre Plus has combined well with Working for Families and other Scottish Executive programmes (Scottish Affairs Committee, 2008a, para 49). While childcare provision is mainly a devolved matter, it is not entirely so. Thus, for example, tax credits and maternity leave are reserved issues. The UK 10-year strategy document in 2004 on childcare did state that responsibility for the delivery of the strategy is shared, and that the UK government would involve all four countries in discussing its implementation (HM Treasury, 2004).

Division of functions in health

Health is almost totally devolved, but a list of non-devolved matters indicates the need for a degree of cooperation:

- international and EU business
- licensing and safety of medicines and medical devices
- coordination and planning for pandemic influenza
- ethical issues: abortion, organ transplants, embryology, surrogacy and human genetics
- oversight of the medical professions (Welsh Affairs Committee, 2008b)

There is an apparent clear divide between health professions whose regulation is a reserved matter and those new professions, for example, counselling and psychotherapy, where regulation is devolved. However, the UK Government has recognised that the regulation of health professions will have to be developed in close consultation with the devolved administrations to ensure they are appropriate for the whole of the UK. It also envisages that aspects of the appraisal and revalidation process for doctors and for non-medical healthcare professionals working in Scotland, Wales and Northern Ireland will be devolved (DH, 2007, para 8.4).

Mental health demonstrates an area that is devolved but is not entirely free of some interfaces. Mental health provision can interface with non-devolved areas, for example, in relation to the criminal justice system in Wales and Northern Ireland. When *Mental health promotion action plan for Wales* (WAG, 2006a) was published and used a policy pyramid it had to acknowledge the importance of the reserved areas of work and employment as well as criminal justice.

Overlaps and entanglements

A number of overlaps have resulted in some confusion about responsibilities or have produced some entanglements where it has been difficult to clearly differentiate responsibilities.

Children's commissioners

The children's commissioners for Wales, Northern Ireland and Scotland were set up with responsibilities over devolved matters (see also Chapter Three). Thus in Wales and Northern Ireland functions not devolved included the justice system, police, immigration, asylum, and in Wales and Scotland, social security. The issue of overlap and interface became significant when the children's commissioner for England was set up with formal responsibilities over non-devolved matters in Wales, Scotland and Northern Ireland. This gave rise to possible conflict and confusion with overlapping responsibilities. This could prevent the commissioners in Wales, Scotland and Northern Ireland formulating a strategic comprehensive view of the rights of children in their countries. As the children's commissioner for England operates under reserved powers this could in effect mean two children's commissioners operating in Wales, Northern Ireland and Scotland. It would also cause confusion by creating two routes of access. The commissioner in Wales also had to face constraints because criminal justice, youth justice and policing were not devolved. The children's commissioners were able to point out that children could not be divided into devolved and non-devolved (Joint Committee on Human Rights, 2007, p 61). The four commissioners have been involved in close cooperation and communication to mitigate against possible conflict and confusion. The commissioner in Scotland has interpreted the legislation as excluding the Scotland Office from investigating reserved matters but not from commenting on all issues. As it was put, 'there may be devolved matters but there cannot be devolved children' (Joint Committee on Human Rights, 2007, memorandum cc3). The four children's commissioners have issued joint statements: expressing concern at the effect of the asylum process on children, on issues of unaccompanied children and on the removal and detention and the physical punishment of children.

Fuel poverty

All the devolved administrations have developed strategies within their devolved powers to tackle fuel poverty and to contribute to its elimination for vulnerable households by 2010. Fuel price increases since 2007 means that increasing numbers of households are in fuel poverty, 34% in Northern Ireland, 22% in Wales and 25% in Scotland and targets originally set for eliminating fuel poverty now appear unrealistic. The division of powers means that the UK Government is responsible for energy market issues, prices, social tariffs and regulation of companies, benefits, tax credits, winter and cold weather payments, impact on incomes and some aspects of energy efficiency agendas. It is not within the current powers of the devolved government to solve fuel poverty on their own and the factors pertinent to fuel poverty are a 'complex mix of reserved and devolved issues' (Scottish Fuel Poverty Forum, 2008). Energy efficiency is largely the responsibility of the devolved administration, but funding streams come from both devolved and UK governments. The Scottish Government has acted to introduce a new energy assistance package for insulation and new central heating targeted at low-income families (Local Government and Communities Committee, 2008). The main programme in Northern Ireland was a warm homes scheme but in 2009 a household fuel payment scheme was introduced. £150 for those entitled to pensions credit or income support with housing benefit. This payment is made through the benefit system in cooperation with the UK DWP, although the scheme is not available in England, Scotland and Wales. Energy efficiency schemes alone are likely to have a limited impact on fuel poverty, which is determined more by fuel prices and household income. It has become recognised that UK and devolved governments need to work together to tackle fuel poverty (Scottish Affairs Committee, 2007).

Equal opportunities and the Equality and Human Rights Commission (EHRC)

In some areas the division of powers has led to a somewhat unclear demarcation line and almost an entanglement of powers. This is particularly exemplified by the subject of equal opportunities.

The 1998 Scotland Act made the subject matters of equal opportunities and discrimination a reserved matter. However, the legislation also gave the Scottish Government power to encourage equal opportunities, to observe equal opportunity requirements and to place duties on public bodies to have due regard to existing equal opportunity duties (see also Chapter Three). The 2006 Government of Wales Act requires Welsh ministers to have arrangements to ensure their functions are exercised with due regard to the principle that there should be equality of opportunity for all people. This effectively means that the main equal opportunities legislation is passed at Westminster, but most of the strategic action plans and initiatives are produced and implemented by the devolved administration. Thus the new proposed single Equality Act will cover Scotland and Wales (but not Northern Ireland), and has required regular meetings between the UK Government Equality Office, the Scotland and Wales Offices, Scottish Government and WAG. The policy framework for equal opportunities has been described as a complex one in which both UK and devolved governments interact (Breitenbach, 2006, p 11). This mix or even entanglement of reserved and devolved powers is demonstrated most clearly by the Equality and Human Rights Commission (EHRC). This was set up in 2007 as a UK-wide body bringing together the six equality strands of gender, race, disability, sexual orientation, age and religion and belief, and amalgamating the Equal Opportunities Commission, the Commission for Racial Equality and the Disability Rights Commission. The EHRC has duties to promote equality of opportunity, to challenge discrimination and to promote human rights. This raised a question of how they would interact with the general equality duties devolved to Scotland and Wales. It had no jurisdiction over Northern Ireland, which retained separate commissions for equality and for human rights. After a period of some confusion, the EHRC decided that it would have an office in Scotland, a commissioner for Scotland and a Scotland committee called the Equality and Human Rights Commission Scotland. These bodies would set priorities and oversee the work of the EHRC in Scotland, as it related to equality. Somewhat confusingly, however, there is a separate Scottish Human Rights Commission which has formally both devolved and reserved dimensions. The EHRC has duties to advise the Scottish Executive and Parliament on equality issues in relation to devolved legislation and to monitor Scottish legislation to ensure that it is in keeping with equality requirements. It can also advise the Scottish Parliament and Executive on promoting equality of opportunity. In practice, a process of close cooperation has been instigated, for example, in 2006 the Scotland Committee and the Disability Committee of the EHRC met representatives from the Scottish Government to discuss an Independent Living Scotland project. Measures are frequently supported by both bodies despite a division in responsibilities, for example, the Scottish Parliament strengthening hate crime legislation and the EHRC funding voluntary organisations (EHRC, 2008a). To date EHRC Scotland and the Scottish administration appear to work well together despite the potential for turf wars.

In Wales, the EHRC also has a Wales committee and a commissioner for Wales to reflect the needs and priorities of Wales, which works with the Welsh administration. The aim of cooperation is to ensure that the needs of Wales are taken into account in the Great Britain business plan and to implement a programme of work appropriate to Wales, described as 'finding the synergy between the EHRC and the Welsh Government activities' (EHRC, 2008b). WAG can influence strategies to deliver EHRC objectives in Wales, publicises EHRC aims and activities and may provide an evidence base. The EHRC can seek to influence WAG's equality strategies and its spending plans on issues such as domestic violence, equal pay and hate crime and the dual responsibilities can be seen as adding value to equal opportunities strategies. The new UK Single Equality Bill will replace the existing three statutory duties on race, gender and disability with a wider single duty. The Bill applies to Scotland and Wales but because of overlaps in responsibilities includes specific customisation measures for Scotland and Wales. The Bill also makes provision for Scottish ministers to impose specific duties on relevant Scottish authorities and confers additional powers on Scottish ministers to make secondary legislation. Welsh ministers are also empowered to impose duties on relevant Welsh authorities.

Conflict over powers

The area of overlapping policies and interfaces has thrown up a few conflicts and disputes. One contentious issue was caused by the introduction of free personal and nursing care in Scotland (see also Chapter Three). The existing funding systems which support the care of older members of the population are split between matters devolved to the Scottish Parliament, that is, health, social and personal care and housing, and those which are matters for Westminster, that is, attendance allowance and disability living allowance. As a result of the introduction of FPNC older people living in care homes in Scotland, who became entitled to free personal care, were no longer entitled to claim attendance allowance. This meant approximately £30 million per annum of attendance allowance payments were no longer paid to older people in Scotland's care homes (Audit Scotland, 2008a, p 13). The payment of social care from Executive funds implied less social security money from Westminster. Thus it was argued that the money saved in attendance allowance should be paid into the Scottish purse (Sutherland, 2008, ch 9). However, the UK Treasury ruled that the Scottish Executive could not have a call on money spent or saved by the UK departments as a result of changes on devolved policy. Simeon (2003, p 225) has suggested London's refusal was mainly political, to make divergence more difficult. A similar issue has emerged with the possible change to a local income tax in Scotland. The Scottish Government suggested that the UK Government hand over £400 million in council tax benefits to assist in the implementation of a local income tax, but the UK Government's position was that it would not hand over council tax benefits if there was no council tax.

Immigration and asylum are reserved to the UK government, but the exercise of this power in Scotland has also generated some intergovernmental conflict. In 2004, the Scottish Executive introduced a migration policy to attract fresh talent to help reverse population decline and to boost enterprise skills. The Home Office would not make special concessions to suit Scotland and this resulted in tension between ministers over a conflict of powers and interests. A similar conflict occurred in 2005 over the forced detention of children (a devolved matter) as part of the enforcement of UK policy on asylum seekers (a resolved matter) (Mooney and Williams, 2006, p 620). A further clash seemed possible at the time of the smoking ban proposed for Scotland, as basing the ban in Scotland on health and safety law and working conditions would run into reserved law meaning that legislation at Westminster would be required (Cairney, 2006). There was doubt about Westminster support for a total ban, but a solution was found by incorporating the ban into Scottish devolved public health legislation.

A further area of some tension has been in higher education where some of the responsibilities of the UK Department of Innovation, Universities and Skills are UK-wide, whereas others relate only to England. The UK Department is responsible for science policy and research funding, although WAG has funded university research. The Welsh Affairs Committee (2009) has called for better communication mechanisms to establish the territorial extent of any policies so that Wales is not overlooked, and there is a better understanding of devolution within Whitehall.

The potential for lack of clarity is also illustrated by domestic abuse policies. A separate strategy for tackling domestic abuse was pursued by WAG, but while adopting a Wales approach it recognised that there were non-devolution areas (WAG, 2005e). When the UK Government introduced the Together We Can End Violence Against Women and Girls strategy, there was confusion about how it applied to Wales, and discussion with the UK Government was required to determine which parts of the strategy Wales could adopt. The Welsh strategy had seen domestic abuse not just as a criminal justice issue but also as a social policy issue. Devolved responsibility in Scotland has assisted the development of a particular focus on children affected by domestic abuse. A Tackling Violence at Home strategy was promoted in Northern Ireland under Direct Rule and was largely based on England's experience.

Cross-border activities

The development of devolution and divergence in policies and structures created a relatively new dimension to overlapping provision – the question of cross-border activities, that is, England–Wales and England–Scotland, in particular Welsh and English populations crossing the border to access services (mainly health services). Patients are free to register with a GP on either side of the Welsh-English border, and an investigation by the Welsh Affairs Committee (2008b) reported that more than 19,000 patients resident in England registered with a GP in Wales, while nearly 14,000 patients resident in Wales were registered with a GP in England. The cross-border flow of patients for secondary care takes place more from Wales into England, in immediate border areas, because of the non-availability of certain specialist services – some English hospitals report a 20% occupancy rate of Welsh people. Some, but not all of this access is commissioned and WAG and the DH have drawn up a procedure for cross-border healthcare commissioning. However, the increasing divergence in health policy can cause difficulty. Patient choice has been a feature of health service reform in England since 2006, whereby patients have a right to choose between at least four hospitals in England for their non-emergency executive treatment; Wales does not have this system. The

Welsh Affairs Committee (2008b, paras 30-6) also noted the impact of longer waiting time targets in Wales, 26 weeks compared with 18 weeks in England, from GP referral to the start of treatment. In practice this has led to the development of two administrative channels within English hospitals, with English and Welsh waiting lists. Furthermore, the divergence in funding regimes has led to tensions between some providers in England and Welsh commissioners but the DH and WAG have worked at resolving the financial conflicts. Some issues such as patient–public involvement measures remain unresolved. The Welsh Affairs Committee (2008b, para 51) saw cross-border access to health services as inevitable and recommended a permanent protocol on the commissioning and funding of cross-border health services. They suggested that transparent and accountable links between jurisdictions should be established to ensure that the interests of cross-border patients were served. A number of controversial issues have arisen, for example that patients in North Wales may be required to travel to South Wales if specialist centres develop there, and English residents may register with a Welsh GP to access free prescriptions.

A number of issues have also arisen in relation to social care services. Four Welsh local authorities have a physical border with an English authority. Difficulties can arise if a Welsh local authority places a local resident in a nursing home in England. The Welsh council must pay the residential element of the cost but the English primary trust pays the nursing element. There are also different payment rates for nursing care and care home beds. Other issues have arisen in relation to patients from Wales who have received treatment in an English hospital but whose discharge is dependent on having social care in Wales. In addition, the delayed discharge fines scheme operating in England does not apply to Wales. An agreement between the four countries was made in 2006 (DH, 2006a) to cover out-of-area patients given emergency treatment that occurs outside of contracts between providers and commissioners of the four countries. This related to arrangements such as the body providing treatment invoicing the patient's responsible commissioner and refunds for prescription costs at English hospitals.

Cross-border activity in respect of education takes place under a number of headings. The highest profile relates to student flows in higher education that are quite significant between the four countries, particularly from Wales to England and from Northern Ireland to England and Scotland (Table 7.2). It is also the case that nearly 50% of full-time undergraduates at Welsh universities are from outside Wales.

Following devolution significant differences in higher education student finance have occurred, with implications for students attending

Table 7.2: Full-time undergraduates 2006-07

	Domiciled in			
	Scotland (%)	Wales (%)	Northern Ireland (%)	England (%)
Studying in				
Scotland	94.1	0.6	6.9	1.3
Wales	0.4	74.4	0.7	2.4
Northern Ireland	0.1	–	78.8	0.1
England	5.4	24.9	13.6	96.2
	100	100	100	100

Source: ONS Regional trends (2008)

institutions across jurisdictions (see also Chapter Three). This has led to coordination in respect of student finance, and 'quadrilateral' meetings are held between the countries as well as the student awards agency for Scotland. The Student Loans Company also attends the meetings and there is a UK project board chaired by the Student Loan Company for implementing student finance delivery each year. Issues remain about the application of differential fees, with students from outside Scotland and Wales paying higher fees to study in Scotland and Wales. The UK Department for Innovation, Universities and Skills and the devolved administrations meet regularly, as do the separate funding councils, and consider cross-border implications of policies (HM Treasury, 2006). Further education students also cross borders for geographical convenience or to attend specialist courses. The Welsh Affairs Committee (2009, para 23) has recommended that the Department for Innovation, Universities and Skills and WAG improve communication and work closely together to consider the potential impact of new policies relating to further education on both sides of the border and jointly keep employers informed.

The Leitch review of skills (HM Treasury, 2006) required extensive cross-border working on policy and administrative matters as skills are a devolved matter. The four devolved administrations agreed to the joint establishment of the UK Commission for Employment and Skills in 2008. Agreement was reached to appoint country commissioners and to align the work of the UK Commission with organisational arrangements appropriate to each country.

The 2008 order enhancing the legislative competence of the Assembly in relation to children and families has raised the potential for cross-border issues as there is considerable use of English services for vulnerable children ordinarily resident in Wales, for example, two thirds of Welsh-resident children are placed in specialist residential units in England (Welsh Affairs Committee, 2008b). A further issue has also arisen in relation to Welsh arrangements to safeguard and promote the well-being of children in circumstances that involve the UK Border Agency.

Although there are a few similar issues in Scotland, for example in relation to health treatment, the main cross-border issue that has arisen relates to the operation of cross-border public bodies. There are a considerable number of quangos with UK-wide responsibilities that include devolved functions. The 1998 Scotland Act designates no fewer than 65 public bodies as cross-border authorities, and examples are the Health Protection Agency, the Advisory Council on the Misuse of Drugs and the Community Development Foundation. For devolved matters the Scottish Parliament has been given the power to receive reports from cross-border bodies, is able to investigate any change in their terms of reference and has a right to be consulted on appointments. There are also UK-wide quangos who are responsible for non-devolved functions in Scotland, Wales and Northern Ireland, and various liaison arrangements often exist, for example the Scottish Parliament can still invite the submission of reports from the UK quangos.

Structures for cooperation

Originally a structure for intergovernmental consultation was set up through a joint ministerial committee (JMC) system which would consider non-devolved matters impinging on devolved responsibilities and vice versa, and also consider any disputes. By agreement it could also discuss the respective treatment of devolved matters in the different parts of the UK. Functional committees were set up for health and poverty but after 2002 only the Europe JMC met. There was instead a preference for departmental bilateral and informal meetings as necessary (Trench, 2004, p 178). A study of intergovernmental relations in health found ministers seldom involved and few problem health issues (Greer and Trench, 2008). In 2008, the JMC recommenced in plenary session for the first time since 2002, a move strongly encouraged by the Scottish First Minister. This development was justified as helping devolution work better and significantly aimed at addressing challenges that had to be tackled together and developing mechanisms to help overcome differences (Wales Office, 2008). The reinvigoration of the JMC, at least in part, is evidence of the growing importance of interfaces and joint working.

Conclusion

Interfaces and overlaps are inevitable given the split in responsibilities, and it is clear that this can give rise to a number of problems in social policy areas. First, there can be a complex mix of devolved and non-devolved responsibility in dealing with, for example, employability, energy and university research funding. Second, there is potential for confusion even among the politicians and administrations, for example on equality issues and domestic abuse in Wales. Third, clear anomalies can be identified, for example with professional regulation and funding university research. Fourth, there is a potential for conflict, as has occurred over housing powers in Wales and asylum children in Scotland. It can be argued that joint action and coordination has overcome some of the potential difficulties with interfaces, for example in relation to employment and training, child poverty, social exclusion and equality. Adjustments have been relatively easy to make between devolved and UK departments and there has been little resort to the formal resolution of disputes or to judicial review. The area of overlapping social policies has perhaps been greater than anticipated and has shown the need for collaborative models of working at a multiplicity of levels and bodies.

EIGHT

Underpinning values and principles

The operation of devolution, the formulation and implementation of policies and the production of policy strategies and rationales has highlighted the commitment of devolved governments, particularly in Scotland and Wales, to a set of values and principles closely related to social policy. Writing of Wales, Chaney and Drakeford (2004, p 121) referred to an explicit set of articulated ideological principles underlying social policy. For the purposes of this analysis, values and principles are categorised under four headings: social and political values, principles for service delivery, nation-building values and principles of social policy.

Social and political values

A number of social and political values have had a central role in the development and justification of social policy in the devolved administrations: formal narratives in policy and strategy documents; in the discourses conducted by governments, the assemblies, parliament and public bodies; and also in the political rhetoric. The main values that underpin social policy narratives can be listed as social justice, equality and collectivism.

Social justice

In one sense social justice was an overarching value justifying the demand for devolution and the setting up of the systems of devolved governance that would be a better guarantor of social justice for Scotland, Wales and Northern Ireland and for disadvantaged individuals, groups and areas. The strong Welsh commitment to social justice has been clearly articulated since 1999, demonstrated originally by the creation of a minister for social justice and social justice annual reports during the first two periods of devolution. It is central to Welsh Assembly policies and initiatives in tackling disadvantage, and was described by the Minister for Social Justice and Regeneration as 'a thread that has been woven through all the Assembly government's strategic plans'

(WAG, 2005f). A key principle of the Communities First strategy was 'to promote social justice', defined by Rhodri Morgan, the First Minister, as 'to ensure that all communities can share in the increased wealth and prosperity of Wales and the less well-off communities should be at the front of the quest to share in this prosperity' (WAG, 2007e, para 2). Tackling child poverty was a fundamental component of WAG's strategic plans.

Bransbury (2004) and Egan (2008) have also noted the tradition of using education to further social justice, a theme repeated in the *One Wales* document (WAG, 2007a), which refers to a learning culture as helping achieve social justice. It has been used to refer to the idea of a society encompassing all its individuals and in which no one is socially excluded, and the formation of the Labour/Plaid Cymru Government in 2007 meant no major change to the significance of social justice. As one of the five pillars to the inter-party cooperative agreement, Plaid Cymru put forward major commitments on social justice in relation to childcare, affordable housing, council tax and student debt. The agreed *One Wales* agenda presented 'a fair and just society', as one leading part of the vision with a joint inter-party commitment to the principles of social justice, sustainability and inclusivity (WAG, 2007a).

The Scottish Executive's commitment to the value of social justice was equally obvious from 1999 – *Social justice: A Scotland where everyone matters* stated that a commitment to social justice lay at the heart of political and civic life in Scotland (Scottish Executive, 1999b), and a social justice minister was also established. Analysis of the early rhetoric around social justice identified the values of fairness, equality and opportunity but without strong reference to wealth distribution (Stewart, 2004). In its narratives for social justice the Scottish Executive was also seen as having a preference for including everyone in Scotland rather than using exclusionary language (Fawcett, 2004). From 2000-03 social justice annual reports monitoring social justice milestones were published. The strategy for tackling disadvantage, *Closing the opportunity gap*, was essentially based on policies to drive the value of social justice, although social policies reflecting an 'opportunity for all' approach or 'targeting areas or groups' can fall short of the meaning of distributive social justice (see Ellison and Ellison, 2006). The SNP Government has maintained the social justice commitment but Scott and Mooney (2009) suggest within a neoliberalism approach.

Northern Ireland Government narratives, in contrast, have been lacking in references to social justice as a specific value, and the 2008 programme for government uses the much weaker term 'a fairer society' and 'fairness'. In part this may be a response to disagreements over the dominant position of equality and human rights agendas as well as reflecting a more conservative ethos among governing elites.

Equality

A commitment to equality can be more prescriptive than the value of social justice, especially if defined as equality of outcomes rather than equality of opportunity. The Welsh First Minister emphasised the difference in seeking greater equality of outcome as an ambition, overtaking the more conventional pursuit of equality of opportunity (Drakeford, 2007a). This can also be seen as moving beyond creating a more socially inclusive society (Chaney and Drakeford, 2004, p 128). The commitment to equality has also been linked with the principles of cohesion, participation and mutual aid. The programme for government, *Wales: A better country*, referred to delivering health, jobs and social justice based on the values of equality and sustainability (WAG, 2003a). A social justice annual report (WAG, 2005f), in asking *What is social justice?*, linked it closely to equality of opportunity, stating that social justice is about everyone having the chances and opportunities to make the most of their lives and to use their talents to the full. The principle of equality of opportunity has been more widely adopted and promoted through all four countries. The Welsh Assembly's work as a whole has been committed to embracing equality of opportunity and building this into all its social policies through the mainstreaming equality strategy (WAG, 2006d).

Scottish governments have also been committed to the principle of equality of opportunity, and to an ideal where everyone is encouraged and enabled to take part in society to their full potential.

A commitment to equality of opportunity was embedded in the Northern Ireland constitutional agreements, the legislation establishing devolution and the programmes for government. All the political parties accept the principle of equality of opportunity and its enforcement, if not equality of outcomes.

The value of equality is also strongly implicit in many strategies to tackle disadvantage and to combat social exclusion and reduce or remove barriers that create inequality. In 2003, the social justice agenda adopted in Wales to tackle poverty, poor health and disadvantaged communities was produced under the wider social justice agenda. The original Scottish Executive's commitment to social justice also had a major focus on the fight against poverty and set out milestones tackling the social, educational and economic barriers that created inequality. Scottish governments have committed to tackling inequality in all its forms, with an 'attack on disadvantage' signalled in *Closing the opportunity gap* (Scottish Executive, 2002). Many of the narratives, strategies and action plans relate closely to anti-discrimination measures and to tackling group inequalities as well as income inequalities. A wider view is often taken to cover housing, health and education inequalities. The 2008-09 programme for government and the government's economic strategy both highlight tackling inequality. They invoke both a 'solidarity golden rule' to increase low incomes and also a 'cohesion golden rule' to regenerate communities suffering from multiple deprivation' (Scottish Government, 2008f).

The *Closing the opportunity gap* strategy in Scotland for 2003-06 had adopted an equality ethos, of everyone contributing to and sharing in increasing prosperity. However, the narrative accompanying the strategy was close to the values of reducing inequalities and providing equality of opportunity. Thus Lister (2007) refers to the discussion in Scotland in terms of closing the opportunity gap in meritocratic rather than equalitarian terms. The 2007 *Progressive Agenda for Wales* also directed its attention to the principle improving the quality of life especially for the most vulnerable and disadvantaged.

The programmes for government in Northern Ireland have not demonstrated similar underpinning egalitarian values. Even the first document, produced under devolution, did not move beyond the implementation of statutory requirements for equality of opportunity, although there was a general commitment to combating poverty and disadvantage. The details of the narrative demonstrated a much more conservative underpinning: 'We recognise our responsibility to ensure a reasonable standard of living for those who cannot support themselves and are committed to providing a fair system of financial help to those in need, while encouraging personal responsibility and improving incentives to work and save' (NIE, 2001, p 19). Northern Ireland's equality agenda is underpinned by the liberal value of quality of opportunity rather than any commitment or concentration on equality of outcomes or an intention to create a more equalitarian society. In political reality the definition of equality has become part of sectarian political positioning (Wilson, 2007). The St Andrews Agreement legislation in 2006 did place a duty on the new power-sharing Executive to adopt a strategy for tackling poverty and social exclusion and patterns of deprivation, but to date there has been no new anti-poverty strategy. The draft programme for government 2008-11 was brief and tended to use the concept of fairness rather than social justice or equality. Although containing references to the promotion of social inclusion, it gave priority to economic growth and increased prosperity to help reduce poverty and disadvantage (NIE, 2008a, p 5). A report on an inquiry by an Assembly committee into child poverty has been one of the few indicators of unanimous support by a cross-section of local politicians for a properly resourced, robust anti-poverty implementation plan (NIA 2008d). This report took an instrumental approach rather than articulating underlying values. There has not yet been a comprehensive government response to the recommendations.

Collectivism

What can be viewed as a more social democratic value has been identified in Scotland and Wales as 'collectivism'. Scottish and Welsh Governments see the relationship between government and citizens as based on social solidarity and collectivism rather than individualism. Poole and Mooney (2005) identified a commitment to collectivism, long since abandoned in England. It has been suggested that in the prevailing culture in Scotland collectivity is regarded as more important than the individual, and there is a strong expression of social solidarity (Tannahill, 2005). Paterson (2002) characterised the dominant Scottish social philosophy as 'social democratic communitarianism', leading to a belief in collective provision in social policy. Kerr and Feeley (2007) discussed how the development of the NHS in Scotland revealed the related underpinning values of collectivism, collaboration, involvement and community.

Drakeford (2007a, p 176) noted the strength of support in Wales for the collective ownership of public services and assets. The Welsh First Minister gave a more practical definition, as 'no matter what organisation in the public service they work for people see themselves as part of a bigger network of organisations' (Morgan, 2005, p 31). The Welsh communitarian tradition has been seen as inspiring the universalism at the core of Aneurin Bevan's NHS (Michael and Tanner, 2007), which continues to the present day. Sullivan (2005) described Welsh health policy as a distinctive package driven by a 21st-century collectivism, stemming from a reworking of 'old Labour' values and a sort of quasi-syndicalism. A collectivist ethos then tends to permit the policies of the main political parties and has influenced policy makers, professionals and public sector managers in Scotland and Wales. Stewart (2004b, p 115) refers to a popular, professional and political ethos, broadly supportive of the public sector, while Keating (2007a, p 248) refers to fragmentary but consistent evidence that the public service ethos in Scotland may be in a healthier condition than in England.

This collectivist ethos has underpinned support by the Scottish and Welsh Governments for the welfare state and comprehensive welfare provision. However, there has been some questioning of whether Scottish opinion in general is so strongly supportive of collectivism. Keating (2005) makes a more cautious assessment that there is a small but consistent bias towards more collectivist solutions. It can be argued that commitments to a particular set of values in strategies and narratives are not always reflected in policy outcomes because of constraints such as electoral concerns or finance.

Principles for service delivery

The determination of principles governing the delivery of social and public services has been a key issue in Wales, has been addressed in relation to specific services in Scotland and has been a major issue in the Review of Public Administration in Northern Ireland. The salience of the principles of citizenship of public involvement, mutualism and co-production, partnership working and localism can be analysed.

Citizenship and public involvement

Devolution itself is, of course, an expression of citizenship and participation and brings decision making closer to the public in all three countries. The commitment to the value of participant democracy is particularly strong in Wales (Chaney and Drakeford, 2004, p 129) – the idea of putting citizens at the centre has been a feature of WAG commitments, which has emphasised the individual as an active citizen rather than as a passive consumer. *Making the connections* laid the foundation during the second Assembly term for public service delivery and transformation (WAG, 2004b), and most notably adopted a 'citizens at the centre' approach. This envisaged delivering citizen-centred services that would be responsive and open to all who needed them, encouraging participation in design, planning and delivery as well as feedback. This 'citizen model' was to be endorsed by a commissioned review of local public service delivery in Wales (Beecham, 2006). The model relies on 'voice' to drive improvement together with the design, management, regulation and delivery of services, all operating in the interests of the citizen, with the potential to build up trust and a long-term relationship between the citizen and public services. It also emphasises the citizen's rights and responsibilities, and implies delivery organisations should be focused on outcomes for citizens. The citizen model does not see choice on customer dissatisfaction as the driver of improvement, as in the consumer model. Beecham (2006) has gone on to argue that all parts of the delivery system have to be congruent. Thus *Making the connections* and *Beyond boundaries* sought to reform public services in Wales based on the citizen model, also seen 'as a constant reminder of why public services exist and that the citizen comes first' (Beecham, 2006, p 7). Devolution in Wales has continued with the same value of citizen-centred service delivery, and Beecham has proved enormously influential, having a major impact on all aspects of delivery and citizen encouragement. WAG's response to Beecham (WAG, 2006e) endorsed the values of putting citizens first and working together, and the new Welsh Government has continued the citizenship model, with proposals for citizen-centred governance principles. All Welsh policy makers have supported a model of delivery rooted in collaboration and citizen engagement and seen as fundamentally different from England (Martin and Webb, 2009). One of the major outcomes of the model for engaging with citizens was the creation of local service boards to operate in every area by 2010. These were officially described as a new model for engaging the whole of the Welsh public service in a new way of working with citizens. The voluntary sector scheme in Wales has also promoted voluntary activity as a part of active citizenship.

The devolved administration in Scotland is also committed to making public involvement a core driver of decision making, but it has not enunciated the citizenship model so clearly as in Wales. However, it has been argued that the value of citizenship based on social rights rather than consumerism has also been favoured in Scotland (Pawson and Davidson, 2008, p 42). The idea of active citizenship has become a frequent element in narratives and discourses about the advantages of devolution, while public participation has become a central plank of public policy making. The major Scottish document, *Transforming public services* (Scottish Executive, 2006e), expressed five elements in their approach, the first and foremost of which was user-focused and personalised, the others relating to quality, efficiency, accountability and joined-up services. The description of 'user-focused' spelt it out as ensuring that services were organised around the needs and aspirations of service users and citizens rather than the convenience of the service provider. The value of the user focus was strongly exemplified in health delivery structures involving patients and carers, while the report on the future of social work (Scottish Executive, 2006c) had involved the concept of citizen leadership. In Scotland there has also been support for strengthening 'voice' and advocacy, which has influenced legislation for mental health service users and parental involvement in schools – the SNP Government has confirmed 'user focus' along with effectiveness and value for money as three principles to govern the delivery of services.

The new Scottish Government has continued the strong emphasis in the devolved NHS on the patient and user at the centre. However, in outlining public service reform linked to these proposals, the Scottish Government is proposing a reduction in national public sector organisations, based on values of increasing efficiency and productivity (Salmond, 2008). This raises the question of whether such a streamlining of the public sector landscape may reduce the opportunity for citizen and user involvement.

The Scottish provision for public involvement may not be markedly different from participation and patient empowerment in England, and the major changes in the institutionalism of public participation in health and social care in the 2007 Local Government and Public Involvement in Health Act. In England the review of patient and public involvement saw the focus on choice as not making 'voice' a less important value (DH, 2006b).

Public involvement has not been a major value promoted by government in Northern Ireland outside formal consultations and special initiatives such as tenant participation. The view was expressed in a recent study on NHS values across the UK that in Northern Ireland there was a commitment to the values of democratic participation and 'having a say' (Campbell, 2007). However decisions on the establishment of only one patient and client council for the whole country and with very limited functions does not provide evidence that any strong commitment has been given to public and user involvement in health and social care in Northern Ireland. The restructuring of public administration has resulted in fewer opportunities for public and user participation.

Mutualism and co-production

In Scotland, *Better health, better care* (Scottish Government, 2007c) took the concepts of citizen, user and public involvement in the NHS towards a more radical value of mutualism. This defined the Scottish people and staff of the NHS as partners or co-owners in the NHS, and spelt out a new ethos of a more mutual NHS, where ownership and accountability have shifted to the people of Scotland. The principle of mutualism emphasised sharing a common purpose and a mutual organisation serving its members: 'the concept of a mutual NHS organisation sits extremely comfortably with the Scottish government's commitments to stronger public involvement, improving the patient experience, clearer patient rights and enhanced local democracy. We intend to ensure that NHS Scotland is based on a mutual ethos' (Scottish Government, 2007c, para 1.1). Associated with mutualism was a modernising version of co-production, whereby the user/recipient should be viewed as a co-producer of the services, and whose involvement is essential. Co-production as an idea also recommends the use of the user's talents. The Scottish Governments proposal to introduce public elections to health boards also gives practical effect to the mutual/co-ownership concept of the NHS in Scotland. The concept of co-production between the consumer and producers of services has gained increasing attention (Needham, 2007). In fact, the Beecham review (2006, p 9) in Wales made a passing reference to the tradition of mutual and common purpose. *The third dimension* (WAG, 2008e, p 34) also noted that the voluntary sector's often closer relationships with users helped the co-production of outcomes.

Collaboration and partnership

Making the connections, produced in the second Welsh Assembly, endorsed the principles of collaboration and working together for service providers. The values of cooperation and collaboration were also taken forward by *Beyond boundaries*, which was described by Rhodri Morgan (WAG, 2004b) as in contrast to the model of public service that puts substantial weight on competition between public services providers. Cooperation and collaboration were seen as a benefit to the needs and circumstances of Wales.

Partnership structure was also identified as a critical success factor in realising the values of collaboration, and in this case did not really conflict with the UK Government's modernisation agenda. The Beecham review (2006, p 63) had strongly recommended greater working across boundaries and greater partnership ambition. The value of collaboration was also compatible with an effective working relationship with the voluntary sector, and the expansion of the voluntary sector had a major influence on the expansion of partnership working. The preference for collaboration over rival competitive mechanisms also had some direct implications for social policy developments, for example the abolition of school league tables and star ratings for local government or health boards. The first devolved government for Scotland actually entitled the programme for government *Making it work together*, with commitments to civic participation and partnership working (Scottish Executive, 1999a).

More recent Scottish Government strategies and narratives on collaborative working have had more of a service improvement orientation (Scottish Executive, 2006e) rather than referenced to a more fundamental interpretation of collaboration. Thus the community planning initiative in Scotland has drawn much criticism for not achieving full public participation or effective collaborative outcomes (Audit Scotland, 2006). In 2008, the Scottish Government confirmed part of its vision was to achieve collaboration and joint working (Salmond, 2008). Local community planning presents an interesting value-based development in the devolved administrations as it is based on ideas of citizen/user engagement, collaboration and localism. It is possible to identify some variation in the weighting of values in the systems operating or envisaged. In Wales, local service boards are intended to engage the leadership of delivery bodies fully in dialogue with all citizens and to develop more cooperative responses. In Scotland, community planning has been developed at the local level, with more equal weighting between: the objectives of joint working, better coordination, central–local policy linkages, and the engagement of local people and communities in decision making. The restructuring and reform of local government in Northern Ireland makes provision for what will be a new function of community planning. Statutory agencies have to work with councils to produce a community plan. However, there is an obvious difficulty in councils taking an effective leadership role as they are not responsible for delivering any major social or welfare services. The original Direct Rule government statement did refer briefly to councils consulting all its constituents (RPA, 2006, p 7), but subsequent government statements have tended to omit references to this. In England, local strategic partnerships developed as part of the local government modernisation agenda, and brought together local public services providers in health, social care, housing, education and the voluntary sector, but these partnerships are largely underpinned by the community leadership role of local authorities (Downe and Martin, 2006).

Localism

Localism expresses the value of devolving power and resources away from central control to local decision-making structures and local communities (Stoker, 2004). The 'new localism' has been applied mainly to the specific context of local government in England, but has also been used in relation to other bodies, for example the governance of foundation hospitals (Pratchett, 2004). Among the devolved administrations localism is most clearly identified with Wales, followed by Scotland, and has three dimensions. First, the idea of empowering local communities, demonstrated by the delegation of health delivery in Wales and Scotland down to local community level. Greer (2004, p 147) described the dominant thrust in post-devolution Welsh health service organisation as localism, a locally based and responsive health service. Second, localism can be closely identified with the operation of local government. Devolution in Scotland and Wales has recognised and accepted the status and values of local government with little dilution of local government's role in planning and delivering services and facilitating close local links with health services. The third dimension is to connect localism with smallness. Wales is seen as a small country with a small population and mostly small communities, and therefore it is seen as appropriate to have small public bodies, referred to in the Beecham review as small country governance. Ponton (2008) describes the three key dimensions to localism in Wales as community leadership, governance and action.

Attitudes to localism by devolved government in Northern Ireland have been confused and contradictory. The devolved Executive in 2002 drew up the terms of reference for a major RPA and listed a set of values/characteristics that the system of public administration should reflect. This included the issue of the responsiveness of services to local needs (RPA, 2003, p 39), and subsidiarity as the principle that powers should be delegated to the most local level consistent with efficiency. The Direct Rule ministers in 2005-06 continued to present subsidiarity as one of the key principles underlining the reforms. The actual proposals were almost the opposite of subsidiarity, with centralised large quangos replacing more localised bodies and a large reduction in the number of local councils. These proposals were reviewed by the restored devolved ministers and there was some acceptance of a more localised structure, with an increase in the number of proposed new local councils from seven to eleven. The main reasons for this change, however, were political and pragmatic, and streamlining and giving structures has become a more dominant value than localism.

Nation-building values

Nation building can be seen as a value closely linked to the role of distinctive social policies in each country, which has contributed to a deepening of national identity. McEwen (2002) discussed how sub-state governments with responsibility for social policy could draw on the symbolic resources of the welfare state to provide national solidarity.

Osmond (2004) saw distinctive governance, law, policy and public engagement as generating a Welsh civic consciousness, while Mooney and Williams (2006, p 610) discerned in Scotland and Wales a new form of welfare nationalism that conveyed understanding and assumptions about people and their needs. Welsh and Scottish social policy are seen as critical to a national vision of a better Wales or a better Scotland, even as a prerequisite for progressive social change. McEwen (2002, p 87) pointed out that the national parliaments could be a guarantor of social services and social protection replacing the UK Government in this role. A parliament for each country with responsibility for a range of social policies could clearly express national interests and identity. Thus Scotland, Wales and Northern Ireland have become the frame of reference (Williams and Mooney, 2008, p 496) for the construction and delivery of social policies and solutions to each country's social problems. In Northern Ireland, the devolution of social policy has not so much of a relationship to national identity, since that has remained divided and contested, but has consensual appeal and support as local politicians replaced control over social policy exercised by ministers from London.

Social policy has therefore been linked to dimensions of nation building through devolution. Welfare policies have traditionally been seen as contributing to social solidarity and the social dimension of citizenship that has contributed to the formation of nation states (Wincott, 2006b). Comprehensive universalist policies can be seen as building up civic solidarity, and the idea of a national community sharing risks. Therefore a comprehensive system of social welfare can serve to reinforce identification with and belonging to a national state (McEwen, 2008). The argument has also been made that national systems of education have had a role in shaping national identity (Paterson, 2002). The identification of distinctive Scottish or Welsh social policies is problematic. Rhodri Morgan's assessment about policies made in Wales (Morgan, 2005) or doing things the Welsh way is a somewhat different issue. Williams and Mooney (2008, p 496) note that in Scotland policies on free personal care or student fees are couched in terms of their 'Scottishness', or Scottish and Welsh solutions to Scottish and Welsh problems. A specific nationalist content of social policies would be unusual, and social policies inevitably reflect ideological values and principles. As with welfare, policies can reflect certain ways of life, behaviour, needs, priority or the social make-up of its people (Clarke, 2005). Loyalty to a national identity and the existence of territorial government and decision making need have nothing to do with different views on the role of the state in social policy (Jeffery, 2006b).

A nation-building approach is also exemplified in the Scottish Government insisting that it does not necessarily have to look to England for either policy inspiration or as a reference point for welfare comparisons. The election of the SNP Government has also meant an increased emphasis on nation building, towards an independent Scotland. In such a scenario, a Scottish government and parliament would have full executive and legislative powers over all current devolved and reserved matters. Growing divergence and practices in the main areas of social policy can be seen as contributing to the case for Scotland as a fully independent nation.

Principles of social policy: universalism

Choices between the principles of universalism and selectivity are important in explaining the nature of developments in social policy. The devolved governments in Scotland and Wales have shown strong support for the principle of universalism, the provision of comprehensive services free for all at the point of delivery, irrespective of income. This has been clear in their support for existing universalist services and opposition to any proposed dilution or any dilution by the UK Government, for example, in relation to the NHS. It is also evident in extensions to a universalist provision of services. The most significant example was free personal and nursing care in Scotland for everyone over the age of 65. The fundamental principle was extending universalism analogous with the NHS to social care. Universalism stands in contrast to the selective provision of services and the forms of selectivity connected to means testing and targeting. The support for universalism has also been supported by government acceptance of criticisms of means testing, that it can lead to poorer quality services, or two tiers of services, stigma and inequality of treatment and in particular, low take-up of entitlements. Drakeford (2007a) identifies the relationship between selectivity and poor services as a potent argument in Wales.

A significant application of the principle of universalism in all three countries is free prescriptions. Other examples are free bus travel for pensioners in Scotland and Wales, and in Northern Ireland free bus and rail travel from the age of 60 plus, free school milk and free breakfasts in schools. Some universalist innovations have elements of targeting but are based on a move away from means testing, as with free school dinners, or from charging, for example through free access to museums and leisure centres. Universalism also implies a principle about the treatment of the state of all its individual citizens. Politically, it is related to traditional principles for the delivery of the welfare state, described by Keating (2007a, p 242) as Scotland retaining the univeralist assumptions of the old British welfare state. Devolved administrations have been seen as moving towards greater universalism without implementing total universalism, and policies and provision in childcare fall into this category (Wincott, 2006a).

In Northern Ireland, initiatives and approaches have an assumption in favour of selectivity rather than an exploration of universalism. This is expressed in the dominance of the targeting social need principle, and is exemplified in the outcome of the 2007 Rating Review when the NIE rejected more universalist reliefs, criticising them in ideological terms as 'blanket assistance' and a 'blunt instrument' (DFP, 2007, p 19).

'Progressive universalism' is a term that has been ascribed to the development of the universalist principle in Wales. Drakeford (2007b) regards WAG as a believer in progressive universalism. The progressive element is a top-up or an addition to a universally provided service. This can be demonstrated in extra provision for deprived sectors of the population and disadvantaged areas as with the case of trends in early childhood care provision in Wales or in a top-up to the child trust fund. The principle can be open to interpretation in relation to the nature of the original basis of entitlement from which additional resources and services can be delivered to the worst off. The UK Government defined progressive universalism as 'some support for all and most support for those who need it most' (HM Treasury, 2004, para 1.15). It can be seen as combining the benefits of universalism with some of the benefits of targeting. The essential feature is that it is additional to a universal service – as Drakeford described it, universalism with a progressive twist (2007a, p 174). Since devolution, how significant has the shift been to an extension of the principle of universalism, based on the concept of the traditional comprehensive welfare state? McEwen and Parry (2005, p 58) refer to 'the occasional promotion of universalist policies'. The use and scope of the principle have continued to develop in Wales, perhaps less so in Scotland and to a small extent in Northern Ireland. A more radical expansion of universalism would also be difficult under the current funding arrangements and the Barnett formula which means the main allocation of expenditure is not devolved.

Rejection of market values

The discourse on Scottish and Welsh policy and narratives in strategy documents not only demonstrates a commitment to the values discussed but also a specific rejection of conflicting or alternative values, many of which are associated with the UK Government. Paterson (2002, p 116) refers to the traditional perception in Scotland that, on the one hand, there was a Scottish social philosophy, and on the other, laissez-faire conservatism, a position later replaced by New Labour policies. An expression of this was given by the Scottish Minister of Health in 2008 when she stated that there was 'a real battle of ideas between different parts of the UK about the future direction of health care. It is a battle between the values of the market, internal competition and contestability on the one hand and the values of public ownership, cooperation and collaboration on the other' (Sturgeon, 2008, p 1). WAG has also firmly rejected the privatisation of NHS services (WAG, 2007a, p 8). There has also been a rejection of private sector involvement in other key social policy areas, as when the Minister for Education in Scotland ruled out using private companies to rescue failing schools (Stewart, 2004b, p 109), and Wales and Scotland have rejected the idea of academies. Other examples were a rejection of competition when school league tables were abolished in Scotland, Wales and Northern Ireland, the abolition of SATS in Wales and the abolition of the purchaser/ provider competitive mechanism in health provision in Scotland and Wales. Rhodri Morgan, in the introduction to *Making the connections*, presented the argument for rejecting the English model of competition in service delivery in Wales and opting for cooperation (WAG, 2004b). The Beecham report (2006) also rejected the value of consumerism as not facilitating empowerment, and noted that consumerism does not find favour in Wales on grounds of both principle and practicality.

Since devolution, analysis by academics, if not politicians, has clearly identified a rejection of neoliberalism, as exemplified in many New Labour policies. Martin and Webb (2009, p 125) assert that 'the Welsh rejection of competition and user choice is more than just rhetoric' and 'is reflected in significant and increasing divergence' with England. Wincott (2006a, p 292), while Poole and Mooney (2005) describe how the Scottish and Welsh Labour Parties largely rejected New Labour values. Thus New Labour has been seen in Scotland and Wales as attempting to build a renewed sense of national purpose around neoliberal agendas (Mooney and Williams, 2006, p 625). In relation to Northern Ireland, it was suggested that the restoration in 2007 of the Executive and Assembly would offer some hope of local politicians halting neoliberal policies introduced under Direct Rule, such as PFI (Horgan, 2006). There has been little subsequent evidence to identify the Executive and Assembly opposing such policies or values, however, with PFI being fully embraced. Northern Ireland is different from Scotland and Wales in its promotion and acceptance of more welfare state values or universalist principles to underpin social policy. However, in some areas of social policy this is debated in Northern Ireland political forums in terms of rejecting progressive 'English' or 'Direct Rule' ideas.

Conclusion

The devolved governments in Scotland and Wales have demonstrated strong support for welfare state values, and an extension of universalism rather than selectivity and have adopted a strong participatory, localist and citizenship view of public sector delivery and modernisation. All administrations in Scotland and Wales have been enthusiastic in articulating commitments to the values of social justice, equality and collectivist action and in relating these values to national identity and devolved governance. Northern Ireland remains somewhat different in that government narratives display much less discussion of principles, less clear commitment to welfare values and less commitment to participation and localism. This reflects a more dominant conservative ethos among political parties and also attempts by civil servants to adopt what are perceived as non ideological positions. All three devolved administrations have been accused of adopting 'populist' positions in social policy areas. Populist responses tend to be identified as governments giving way to popular demands or winning popular support at the expense of more strategic, long-term considerations, pressing financial or their normal ideological positions. Devolution may make government more susceptible to populist responses by moving decision making closer to local people, the local media and local pressure groups. Devolved decisions on such matters as hospital closures, free prescriptions, free travel and council tax and rates freezes have produced accusations of populism. However in Scotland and Wales, if not Northern Ireland, such decisions are generally not incompatible with the underpinning values and principles of the respective devolved governments.

NINE

Comparison of outcomes by country

To what extent has devolution delivered better services, increased provision, greater expenditure, improved well-being and care? Is there statistical data and evidence to back up the rhetoric and claims, and have targets been achieved? Are there any significant differences in performance between the devolved administrations and between the four countries? It is possible to examine available statistical evidence relevant to the achievements of devolution and compare statistics between the different countries. A number of different types of evidence are available based mainly on national statistics analysed on a regional basis, public expenditure data, specific analysis by the devolved administrations and official but independent evaluations by the respective national audit offices. Some research and implementation reports of this data also facilitate an examination of trends over time, including the period since the introduction of devolution. There may be some difficulty with the accuracy of data or differences in quality or definitions in making comparisons, however. For example, Alvarez-Rosete et al (2005) referred to the difficulty and in some cases the impossibility of obtaining valid comparable basic statistics on the NHS in the four countries. With variations in the quality of the data, different definitions and data taken at different times, the view has also been expressed that the serious shortage of good quality comparable data undermines our ability to learn from different policy approaches (Halpern, 2009). The continuing problem with the lack of comparable data on health over time was reiterated by Dixon (2009). Studies by the New Policy Institute and Joseph Rowntree Foundation (2008) of UK differences of poverty also refer to the statistics not being directly comparable and to statistical gaps. It is a complex question of how far this data on differences in outcomes between the four countries can be interpreted as determined in whole or in part to be the direct consequence of devolution. Statistical comparisons can also be valuable in giving some indication of differences in need between the four countries, as well as indicating possible differences in service provision.

Five different types of comparative evidence are examined in this chapter:

- socio-economic and health indicators
- input of public expenditure per head on services
- data on aspects of provision
- assessments by the devolved administrations
- national audit office evaluations of performance

Use is also made of a number of research reports and evaluations that are relevant to comparing provision and performance.

Socio-economic and health indicators

Analysis can be made between the four countries for selected key statistics that provide a comparative socio-economic profile and a profile of health indicators. The statistics presented in Table 9.1 relate to aspects of age, economic activity, income and benefits, health and housing, and mainly relate to the last available data which was for 2006.

Comparing these selected statistics gives a broad snapshot of socio-economic conditions across all four countries, as well as giving some indication of what can be interpreted as differences in social need.

The data compares key population characteristics; unemployment and economic activity; child poverty; and earnings, income and benefits. The data also covers health indicators including life expectancy; infant mortality; percentage of adults with disabilities; and the incidence of smoking and major diseases. Some information on children and young people is also covered.

In broad overall terms as indicating need, Northern Ireland has the highest needs in terms of income poverty. Northern Ireland may also have the greater need for children's services but Wales has the greatest need for older people's services and employment. Scotland would appear to have the highest needs in terms of ill health. The profile for England is not always very different statistically from the other countries.

Table 9.1: Selected key socio-economics statistics on need 2006 (% except where indicated)

		Scotland	Wales	Northern Ireland	England
Percentage under 16		18.0	18.9	21.8	19.0
Percentage over 65		16.4	17.7	13.7	15.9
Dependency rate		37.2	39.6	38.1	37.6
Unemployment rate (2007)		4.6	5.8	3.8	5.7
Employment rate (2007)		77.1	72.2	70.6	74.4
Economically active (2007)		80.9	76.7	73.4	78.5
Percentage claiming who are over 12 months unemployed		15.1	13.1	21.0	16.6
Average gross weekly income per person		£235	£209	£188	£257
Median weekly earnings (2007)	male	£482	£450	£425	£498
	female	£381	£362	£372	£398
Income distribution – bottom quintile		20	24	23	20
Income for households with children – bottom two quintiles		46	54	52	52
In receipt of incapacity benefit		34	38	43	29
In receipt of child benefit		26	29	34	28
In receipt of income support		14	14	17	13
In receipt of tax credits		18	17	21	17
Prescription exemption		92.7	92.6	94.3	90.0
Birth rate		16.9	11.3	13.4	12.5
Infant mortality rate		4.5	4.1	6.1	5.0
Neonatal mortality rate		3.1	2.8	3.8	3.5
Disabled people 16-64 %		15.8	20.0	17.6	14.8
Life expectancy	male	74.6	76.6	76.1	77.2
	female	79.6	80.9	81.0	81.5
Smoking %	male	27	22	25	25
	female	24	21	26	22
Cerebrovascular disease (per 100,000)	male	67	58	56	53
	female	62	52	52	49
Respiratory diseases (per 100,000)	male	102	90	98	90
	female	78	65	72	65
Looked after children (per 10,000 population)		115	70	56	55
Children on Child Protection Register (per 10,000 population)		23	36	48	27
Young People not in Education, Employment or Training		13	12	9	11

Sources: ONS (2008a, 2008b), WAG (2008f)

Comparison of public expenditure per head on services

HM Treasury statistical analysis of UK public expenditure has, for some years, detailed expenditure per head on major services. Consequently the trends in expenditure per head are identifiable between the four countries of the UK and over the years of devolution. This is significant for assessing the working of devolution as the actual allocation of expenditure on services has been determined by the devolved administrations since 1999 (see Table 9.2).

Table 9.2: Expenditure on health per head (£)

	Scotland (£)	Wales (£)	Northern Ireland (£)	England (£)
1998–99	913	862	862	784
1999–00	968	918	940	816
2000–01	1,042	983	1,030	893
2001–02	1,106	1,027	1,111	991
2002–03	1,324	1,188	1,224	1,082
2003–04	1,455	1,438	1,345	1,220
2004–05	1,517	1,444	1,452	1,350
2005–06	1,681	1,548	1,545	1,436
2006–07	1,771	1,664	1,671	1,514
2007–08	1,919	1,758	1,770	1,676

Source: HM Treasury (2005, 2008)

In practice there has largely been an incremental increase in each country each year, but Scotland has maintained its position of spending more on health per head during each year of devolution and the gap with the other countries has increased with recent years. Expenditure on health per head in Northern Ireland has remained just ahead of Wales.

A more detailed compilation has calculated the combined expenditure on health and personal social services, and provides a different order of expenditure per head (see Table 9.3).

Scotland still has the highest expenditure per head, but Wales remains consistently in

Table 9.3: Expenditure on health and personal social services per head

	1999	2006-07
Scotland	1,197	2,313
Wales	1,116	2,109
Northern Ireland	1,098	2,096
England	963	1,915

Source: ONS (2008b)

second place. This also clearly demonstrates the comparatively lower expenditure in Northern Ireland on social care and may bring in a factor about local government involvement.

Table 9.4: Expenditure on education per head

	Scotland	Wales	Northern Ireland	England
1998–99	792	708	958	663
1999–00	855	756	1,004	694
2000–01	910	820	1,080	753
2001–02	1,005	890	1,119	838
2002–03	1,062	1,005	1,202	894
2003–04	1,123	1,067	1,259	1,007
2004–05	1,198	1,132	1,297	1,070
2005–06	1,278	1,187	1,310	1,149
2006–07	1,388	1,255	1,372	1,192
2007–08	1,455	1,322	1,475	1,278

Source: Hm Treasury (2005, 2008)

An examination of expenditure per head on education shows Northern Ireland as the highest, ahead of Scotland until 2006-07 when Scotland became the country with the highest expenditure but in 2007-08 Northern Ireland had the highest per capita expenditure again (see Table 9.4). Wales has continually been in third position, just higher than England. The high expenditure in Northern Ireland reflects the high number of schools as a result of religious division and different types of schools, rather than a response to other needs or innovations.

Table 9.5 Expenditure on housing and community services per head

	Scotland	Wales	Northern Ireland	England
1998–99	93	97	79	67
1999–00	75	74	164	57
2000–01	108	76	158	72
2001–02	165	84	160	96
2002–03	250	98	350	70
2003–04	247	79	417	89
2004–05	186	90	459	117
2005–06	275	160	507	155
2006–07	311	184	502	168
2007–08	387	193	439	184

Source: HM Treasury (2005, 2008)

The noticeably high level of expenditure in housing and community services in Northern Ireland was a response to the salience of these services in reducing community conflict and in promoting post-conflict regeneration rather than clearly evidenced differences in housing need or unfitness (see Table 9.5). In 2006-08 expenditure began to increase significantly in Scotland and reduced the gap with Northern Ireland. Since 2005 Wales has increased its expenditure per head compared with England, but has remained behind Scotland and Northern Ireland by a significant margin.

Expenditure on social security benefits is directly related to need, as defined by eligibility for uniform UK benefits, and therefore does not reflect devolved administration policies other than perhaps benefit take-up strategies. Thus Table 9.6 tends to reflect poverty, incapacity and unemployment levels and England has the lowest expenditure per head. There have been little differences between the other three countries, and during 1999-2002 Wales had the highest expenditure per head.

Table 9.6: Expenditure on social protection per head

	Scotland	Wales	Northern Ireland	England
1998–99	2,059	2,334	2,234	1,885
1999–00	2,191	2499	2,316	2,008
2000–01	2,257	2,637	2,433	2,090
2001–02	2,514	2,743	2,643	2,211
2002–03	2,660	2,753	2,779	2,357
2003–04	2,804	2,914	2,995	2,512
2004–05	2,940	3,054	3,185	2,640
2005–06	3,028	3,166	3,227	2,737
2006–07	3,123	3,241	3,363	2,814
2007–08	3,284	3,413	3,810	2,938

Source: HM Treasury (2005, 2008)

Overall, the tables show expenditure per head for the major areas of social policy as mainly highest in Northern Ireland and lowest in England, with Scotland showing evidence of increased per capita expenditure during devolution. This pattern can be seen as generally responsive to the overview of need, with Northern Ireland displaying the highest needs in terms of poverty and fiscal exclusion, and Scotland with the highest health needs. Expenditure per capita in Wales may not always appear to reflect some of the evidence of major needs in Wales, particularly with older people. The data also raises the question of whether the countries with the highest levels of expenditure per head always have the best performance. If not, this might point to issues about the use of resources.

Comparison of data on aspects of provision

UK official statistical publications have increasingly provided data that provide a description of differences in provision between the four countries. The tables that follow provide information on education, health and social care.

Table 9.7: Pupil-teacher ratios and class size

	Scotland	Wales	Northern Ireland	England
Pupil-teacher: primary	16.3	19.9	20.8	21.8
Pupil-teacher: secondary	12.0	16.6	14.5	16.5
Class size primary	23.6	24.2	23.6	26.2
Percentage of key stage 2 classes with over 30 pupils	12.1	4.8	8.7	19.6

Source: ONS, Regional trends (2009)

Scotland has the lowest pupil–teacher ratio in both secondary and primary schools, and overall the lowest ratio of the four countries (see Table 9.7). There is little variability in class size at primary level, but more detailed statistical analysis shows considerable variation in the percentage of older primary classes with more than 30 pupils, with Wales having very few classes of this size compared with almost a fifth in England. England's lower position accords with its lowest per capita expenditure on education.

Table 9.8: Educational achievement and participation 2007

	Scotland	Wales	Northern Ireland	England
Percentage achieving 5 or more GCSEs A-C or equivalent	58.6	53.8	63.0	59.2
No graded GCSE	4.6	6.8	3.1	2.2
16-year-olds in education/training	78	80	91	82
17-year-olds in education/training	49	68	83	71
Percentage population with degree	18.5	17.2	17.5	19.9
With GCSE level	27.7	24.0	24.0	22.4
No qualifications	12.9	15.0	21.7	13.2

Source: ONS, Regional trends (2009)

Over three fifths of pupils in Northern Ireland achieved five or more GCSE grades A–C grades, the highest proportion of any country, reflecting policies on academic selection (see Table 9.8). Wales had the lowest percentage achieved for five or more GCSE grades A–C and also the highest proportion with no graded result. The proportion of 16- and 17-year-olds participating in full-time compulsory education and government-sponsored training do not vary greatly. In Northern Ireland the figure for 16-year-olds is very high; it is also high for 17-year-olds. Scotland presents a low figure for 17-year-olds, but this does include 12% of 17-year-olds who attend university (ONS, 2008, p 100). In 2007, England had the highest working-age population with a degree, although the percentage is quite similar across the UK as a whole. Scotland has the highest proportion with a GCSE or equivalent qualification. The outstanding distinct figure is that Northern Ireland has by far the highest proportion of its working-age population with no qualifications, at 22%, and this again is a clear reflection of a school system based on academic selection.

Table 9.9: Health activity 2005–06

	Scotland	Wales	Northern Ireland	England
Average daily beds per 1,000	3.4	4.7	4.8	3.5
Admissions per bed	49	36	42	43
Admissions per 1,000 population	150	170	199	170
Average length of stay-days	6.1	8.3	6.4	–
Average GP list size	1,310	1,643	1,631	1,610
Cervical screening percentage	83.8	75.4	71.5	79.5
Breast screening percentage	76.4	74.9	71.2	69.9

Source: ONS (2008b)

The average number of daily available beds are higher in Wales and Northern Ireland (see Table 9.9). Scotland has the highest rate of admissions per bed. Northern Ireland has the highest rate of hospital admissions per 1,000 population while Wales has the longest average length of stay. List sizes show a strong similarity with the exception of Scotland, which has by far the lowest ratio. Scotland also has the highest ratio for screening – in 2006 almost 84% of women aged 20-60 were screened. The rates for Scotland and Wales are higher than Northern Ireland, and this may reflect a higher commitment given to public health, particularly in Scotland.

Table 9.10: Time waiting for selected procedures 2006-07 (days)

	Scotland	Wales	Northern Ireland	England
Hip replacement	221	367	337	223
By-pass surgery	122	203	191	112
Hernia	179	315	241	187
Cataract surgery	146	125	172	116
Tonsillectomy	168	343	267	188

Source: ONS (2008b)

Waiting times for hospital admissions has been widely regarded by the populations and commentators as one of the main tests of the performance of devolution. Table 9.10 details waiting times for five of the most common procedures, and the data is based on coverage of 90% of the population. Wales has the longest waiting times for four of the five procedures, and for three of them it is over 300 days (WAG, 2008g). Scotland has the lowest waiting list for three procedures and the profile is not so different from England, which has the first or second lowest waiting time for all five procedures

Table 9.11: Children in poverty 2006-07

	Scotland	Wales	Northern Ireland	England
Percentage of children in poverty before housing costs	22	24	25	22
Percentage of children in poverty after housing costs	25	28	27	29

Source: NIA (2008)

Looking at Table 9.11, there is a difference depending on whether child poverty is measured using the 60% median threshold before or after housing costs. Using the after housing costs measure, England and Wales have the highest rates. Scotland is at the lowest rate on both measures, but the same as England for the before housing costs. Using a before housing costs calculation has a major effect on Northern Ireland's position.

Data for indicators of children's needs and services, a number of which are set out in Table 9.12 below, demonstrates wider gaps between Scotland, England and Wales and Northern Ireland than the poverty measure in Table 9.11, indicating wider dimensions to deprivation.

Having established Northern Ireland's weaker position, followed by Scotland, the report from ERINI and IFS (2007) then examined children's services expenditure between the four countries (see Table 9.13).

Table 9.12: Indicators of child needs in the UK

	Scotland	Wales	Northern Ireland	England
% living in workless households	16.5	14.3	18.3	16.3
Proportion of lone-parent households	7.3	7.0	8.8	7.2
% eligible free school meals	18.5	17	19.9	16.9
% special educational needs	4.0	3.3	2.7	3.0
Rate per 10,000 on child protection register	20	33	31	24

Source: ERINI and IFS (2007)

Table 9.13: Personal and social services (PSS) expenditure on children 2004-05

	Scotland	Wales	Northern Ireland	England
Per capita on children	513	429	287	402
Expenditure as % of total PSS expenditure	20.7	26.1	14.1	24.0

Source: ERINI and IFS (2007, p 51)

Further calculations showed that Northern Ireland was spending approximately 28.6% less compared with England, 33% less than Wales, and 44% less than Scotland.

Comparing changes in provision over time

It is possible to analyse statistics for some aspects of provision over the period of the operation of devolution. Statistics are normally available for the years 2000-06, but care has to be taken in attributing reasons for changes to devolution.

England had the lowest percentage with no qualifications but the figure for Scotland and Wales has reduced by 3% or more during devolution, with Scotland's rate coming down to equal England. Northern Ireland has by far the highest proportion without a qualification, although the proportion has also dropped. This can be interpreted as a consequence of Northern Ireland's different system of academic selection. The proportion who achieve five grades GCSE A-C has actually declined in each country other than England, while the proportion of pupils who achieved no graded GCSEs declined in Scotland and Northern Ireland but increased in Wales and England (see Table 9.14). Wales is the only country where the proportion with GCE A levels has actually increased. All four countries have increased the

Table 9.14: Qualifications: percentage of working age

	No qualifications		GCE A levels or equivalent		Degree or equivalent	
	2000	2005	2000	2005	2000	2005
Scotland	18.1	14.8	30.4	28.6	12.9	17.8
Wales	19.7	16.7	20.9	22.8	12.1	15.3
Northern Ireland	26.1	23.7	24.4	24.9	12.5	14.8
England	15.7	14.8	23.5	22.5	15.3	18.9

	5 or more Grades A-C		No graded GCSE	
	2000	2007	2000	2007
Scotland	63.6	58.6	5.0	4.6
Wales	54.9	53.8	6.4	6.8
Northern Ireland	65.4	63.0	4.6	3.1
England	54.6	59.2	1.9	2.2

Source: ONS (2008a)

Table 9.15: Health improvement 2001-06

		Scotland	Wales	Northern Ireland	England
Life expectancy	Male	+ 3.2	+ 3.5	+ 0.9	+ 3.8
	Female	+ 0.8	+ 0.9	+ 0.9	+ 0.9
Death rate coronary heart disease per 100,000	Male	– 76	– 67	– 96	– 63
	Female	–34	– 29	– 30	–24

Source: ONS (2008a)

percentage of degree holders – Scotland has had the highest increase although England remains with the highest proportion.

There has been a positive change in life expectancy for men in England as well as Scotland and Wales but the increase has been significantly less in Northern Ireland (see Table 9.15). The increase is more or less the same throughout the UK for females. Life expectancy rates have been increasing significantly since 1981, but it would be difficult to cite devolved policies as having a special impact. Despite changes, life expectancy remains the lowest for men and women in Scotland. Northern Ireland has had the highest reduction in coronary heart disease for men, and Scotland the highest reduction for women.

All four countries have reported achieving their recent set targets for reducing waiting times (see Table 9.16). However, the targets in England and Northern Ireland were more stringent than those applying in Scotland and Wales, where waiting times still have to be reduced to match England. The 'competition' to reduce waiting times may imply

Table 9.16: Outpatient waiting times

	Time target	Achievement
Scotland	18 weeks by December 2007 15 weeks by March 2009	18 weeks achieved
Wales	22 weeks by March 2008	22 weeks achieved
Northern Ireland	13 weeks by March 2008	13 weeks achieved
England	13 weeks by December 2005	13 weeks achieved

Source: NIAO (2008)

some redirection of resources to this activity or even demonstrate the lack of a punitive regime for those who miss targets (McEwen, 2008). The Welsh targets in particular have to be valued against the lengthy waiting times shown in Table 9.10.

Table 9.17: Hospital activity

	Average daily available beds		Admissions per 1000 population		Average length of stay		Cases treated per bed	
	1999	2006	1999	2006	1999	2006	1999	2006
Scotland	6.8	5.4	257	135	7.5	7.4	28	48
Wales	5.0	4.7	176	170	6.7	6.9	35	36
Northern Ireland	5.1	4.7	267	205	5.7	5.6	38	42
England	3.7	3.8	225	160	6.0	6.8	46	49

Source: ONS (2008a)

England had by far the lowest daily available bed numbers. The admissions rate dropped most dramatically in Scotland, and can be seen as reflecting the strategy of Scottish ministers moving to community-based care. Northern Ireland and England display the same trend, and only in Wales has there been no significant change, although Northern Ireland remains with the highest admissions rate. The average length of

Table 9.18: NHS staffing

	% Nurses, midwives, health visitors		Average size GP Lists	
	2000	2006	2000	2006
Scotland	48	44	1,426	1,310
Wales	44	40	1,695	1,650
Northern Ireland	40	30	1,673	1,631
England	46	32	1,853	1,610

Source: ONS (2008b)

stay has decreased in Scotland, as in England, but lengths of stay have increased in Wales between 2000 and 2006.

The percentage of NHS staff who are nurses, midwives and health visitors has dropped, but the reduction is much greater in Northern Ireland and England, and the lower reductions in Scotland and Wales may directly reflect devolved ministerial decisions. The reduction in the average size of GP lists has been much greater in England, with action also taken in Scotland to reduce the ratio. Little seems to have been done in Wales and Northern Ireland to change the ratio.

Table 9.19: Care homes places (%)

	Local authority		Voluntary sector		Other (private)	
	2000	2006	2000	2006	2000	2006
Scotland	32	14	44	17	25	68
Wales	29	–	11	–	60	–
Northern Ireland	36	34	25	26	39	40
England	16	7	19	14	65	79

Source: ONS (2008b)

The change in the use of care homes for both older people and children shows some major shifts in patterns. There has been a significant decline in the local authority and voluntary sector provision in Scotland. By 2000 the role of these sectors in England had already declined sharply. Table 9.19 does not provide evidence that the Scottish administration's declared preference for direct public provision has operated in this area. It is actually in Northern Ireland that the public sector still has a significant direct role, accounting for a third of places in 2006. Voluntary sector provision also still plays a significant role in Northern Ireland and private provision is at the lowest, demonstrating a mixed economy of care. Figures are not available for Wales, but the local authority and voluntary sector proportions would have declined.

A series of studies from the New Policy Institute (2008) has monitored indicators of poverty and social exclusion in the four countries and has been published in a series from the Joseph Rowntree Foundation. The separate country reports have noted similarities and changes and then identified more distinctive indicators and the reasons for them. The reports make some but rather limited comments on the role of devolution. Overall, there were similarities in the disadvantaged position of people with disabilities and there had been similar reductions in child poverty and pensioner income poverty. Despite the number of indicators of disadvantage for Northern Ireland, this study found income poverty, both overall and for particular groups, only around the Great Britain average (Kenway et al, 2006). The reasons for income poverty rates not being higher were lower housing costs, high rates of recipients of tax credits and recipients of out-of-work benefits and non-means-tested benefits. Northern Ireland also had a fall in those without paid work and a growth in job numbers. The report for Scotland found substantial problems remaining with ill health, low educational achievement by many children and low pay, but Scotland had met the target for reducing child poverty in contrast with Great Britain as a whole, where the target was missed (Palmer et al, 2006). Most of the fall in child poverty was found to be due to the reduced poverty risks for both working and workless families rather than a shift into work. The report in Wales found steady falls in the proportion of people of all ages living in low-income households and in levels of unemployment. Wales, however, stood out for the high prevalence of working-age ill health and low educational achievement, and worklessness was the most important reason for poverty (Kenway et al, 2005). Updates to the Scottish and Welsh poverty and social exclusion studies (Kenway et al, 2007; Kenway and Palmer, 2008) give some indication of changes since the late 1990s and found the following:

Child poverty: by 2007, 25% of all children in Scotland were living in low-income households and since 1999 child poverty has fallen further in Scotland than in Britain as a whole. Child poverty in Wales was around a quarter lower than in the late 1990s, although progress has slowed in the last two years and remained at 28%. Northern Ireland has also made progress, leaving England with the highest rate by 2007.

Pensions: the number of pensioners in poverty in Scotland has come down by more than 100,000 since the late 1990s, and the pensioner poverty rate has reduced from 31% to 16%, and in Wales from 26% to 20%.

Family poverty: in Scotland the number of working adults with children in low-income households has also fallen from the 1990s, both for those in working families and those in non-working families. In Wales, the fall in the number of working-age adults in poverty has been concentrated among those who are neither lone parents nor in a household where one adult has a disability. The number of lone parents in poverty has changed little. The overall study (Palmer et al, 2008) has noted that between 1997 and 2002/03, 30 out of 56 statistical indicators of poverty and social exclusion monitored had improved; by contrast, from 2003 to 2007, 14 had improved while 15 worsened. It was noted in these studies that some aspects of poverty and social exclusion were driven by the UK–wide tax and benefits system.

Assessments by the devolved administrations

In 2007, the Scottish Government developed 45 national indicators to enable it to track progress towards the achievement of its national outcomes (Scottish Government, 2008h). It is accepted that they do not provide a comprehensive measurement of every activity, largely drawing on existing targets. Of the 45 national indicators, about half relate to social policy topics. The assessment of progress makes a finding of performance improving, performance maintaining, performance worsening or data still being collected. Normally, if not always, the measurement of progress refers back to 2000 (see Table 9.20).

Table 9.20: National indicators for performance

- Reduce inpatient or daycare waiting times
- Reduce mortality from coronary heart disease in deprived areas
- Increase percentage of people over 65 with high core needs who are cared for at home
- All unintentionally homeless households will be entitled to settled accommodation by 2012
- Decrease number of problem drug users by 2011
- Reduce the number of working age people with literacy and numeracy problems
- Increase proportion of school leavers in positive and sustained destination

Source: Scottish Government (2008h)

The reduction in waiting times has emerged as a litmus test of achievements of devolved government. In 2002, there were over 20,000 patients waiting for over 18 weeks for inpatient or daycare hospital admission. At the end of 2007 there were no patients waiting. In 2004, 70,000 patients were waiting for 18 weeks for first patient appointments. In 2007, this had reduced to zero (Scottish Government, 2008h). A national indicator has now been established to achieve annual milestones, culminating in the delivery of an 18-week referral to treatment for 2011. A key milestone is achieving a 15-week maximum wait for both outpatient consultations and hospital admissions by March 2009. As Table 9.10 indicates, however, waiting times for hospital admissions can still be lengthy. There has been a steady increase in the proportion of people aged 65 and over with high levels of care needs who are cared for at home. The figure for 2007 of 29.5% shows an increase from 20.1% in 2001. The rates of premature mortality from coronary heart disease among the under-75s have shown a downward trend since 2000, both for the most deprived areas and the whole of Scotland. Scotland has a disproportionately serious problem with drug misuse, and the assessment of performance is fairly confident that there has been a reduction in the estimated levels since 2000. In education, a reduction is claimed in the proportion of working-age people with severe literacy and numeracy problems. Scottish governments have stressed the importance of their homelessness policy and this has meant changes in the criteria used and the percentage of homeless households in priority need has increased each year, from 60% in 2000 to 80% in 2007/08 (Scottish Government, 2008i).

The measurement of performance also showed areas where national indicators had not been achieved, which included:

- increasing the rate of new house building;
- a reduction in the proportion aged 65 and over admitted as emergency inpatients two or more times in a single year;
- reducing the percentage of the adult population who smoke to 22% by 2010; and
- reducing alcohol-related hospital admissions.

A number of other indicators are assessed to be in a steady state, the most important of which is:

- decreasing the proportion of individuals living in poverty.

This objective has been a core element of the Scottish administration's programme for government and their social justice programme. A 1% reduction to 17% for those living in relative poverty before housing costs was seen as relatively unchanged, although since 2000 the percentage has reduced from 21%. As discussed, many drivers of poverty are outside devolved government control (see also Chapters Five, Six and Seven). Sufficient information was not yet available for a number of other national indicators: mental health, school inspections, child protection inspections and the quality of healthcare experience.

Outside of the national indicators, the Scottish Government has produced other statistical evidence to support achievements. Between 2000 and 2007 there has been a significant increase in qualified clinical staff in the health workforce. The number of nurses has increased by 9%, consultants by 27%, dental practitioners by 37% and GPs by 3%

(Scottish Government, 2008h). Since 2002, the number receiving FPNC at home has risen to 42,000, with 73,000 older people in total receiving FPNC. Evidence of a successful programme was also claimed for the *Same as you* strategy for learning disability (Scottish Executive, 2007b), implemented between 2000 and 2007. A marked increase in personal life plans was reported from 4,000 in 2003 to 7,300 in 2007. Independent advocacy has also increased, from 1,550 in 2003 to 2,750 in 2007. More people were living in their own tenancies with less use of traditional day services, and overall fundamental changes in the way services were delivered were reported. At the same time it was noted that the delivery of some services had not achieved expectations.

Wales does not produce such integrated performance documentation as Scotland, but has continued a process of publishing statistical releases, headlines and bulletins updating key data and often referring to increased or worse performance or the need for more improvements. These have, on occasions, been backed up by ministerial statements. Assessments are often based on targets and the message on the key area of hospital waiting lists is largely positive. The Welsh devolved administration presented a detailed breakdown of its improved performance of the area (WAG, 2008f) (see Table 9.21).

Table 9.21: Waiting lists in Wales

	2003	2004	2005	2006	2007	2008
Inpatient						
Waiting more than 6 months	27,541	26,316	16,363	14,705	4,925	0
Waiting more than 12 months	11,831	8,457	840	0	0	0
Waiting more than 18 months	5,238	1,401	16	0	0	0
Outpatients						
Waiting more than 6 months	70,120	68,845	63,057	40,333	10,293	0
Waiting more than 12 months	24,606	21,626	13,860	15	0	0
Waiting more than 18 months	8,361	6,204	28	10	0	0

Source: WAG (2008f)

The statistics on NHS waiting lists show in December 2008 the number waiting over 22 weeks on the inpatient/day case list as 460 and the number waiting over 22 weeks on the outpatient list as only 13. The target for 2009 is to reduce the maximum waiting time for inpatient or day case treatment to 14 weeks, and in April 2009 the number waiting 14 to 22 weeks was 1,051 (WAG, 2009b). While the reduction to 22 weeks for a first outpatient appointment was achieved, an even more ambitious target of 10 weeks has been set for 2009.

Other performances quoted referred to aspects of education and social care. An evaluation of assessment and examination performance was compared with England, and was less positive. While pupils in Wales performed better at key stage 2, the proportion achieving the expected level was mainly lower than in England for key stages 1, 3 and 4. An evaluation of standards and training in Wales found that the rate of improvement was slowing down (Estyn, 2008). For 2007/08 absenteeism from secondary schools was at a lower rate than in the previous decade, although the percentage was still higher than in England, 9.4 compared with 7.9. Improvements in social care were marginal: an increase in social work staff; a reduction in the number of children starting to be looked after; an increase in the number of social services assessments from 81,190 in 2005/06 to 87,455 in 2007/08; and an increase in the number of direct payments. In other areas little change was noted. The numbers of delayed discharges had declined slowly, from 679 in 2007 to 548 in 2008, although this represented a small proportion of all discharges. It was recognised that more needed to be done in mental health services to improve access and quality of services and action was promised to put palliative care in voluntary hospices on a more secure financial basis. While progress was reported with child poverty, a range of stronger measures was proposed including, from 2009, monitoring data and research evidence, producing an improvement tool on children's well-being, formal agreements with all public bodies to help eradicate child poverty and a pilot to support local authorities to prioritise child poverty (Gibbons, 2008).

National audit office evaluations of performance

The audit offices of Scotland, Wales and Northern Ireland provide a more independent evaluation of the performance of devolved administrations. They are concerned with analysing statistical and financial evidence to judge efficiency and effectiveness, and many of the comments in their reports relate to performance in achieving targets or improving services. Their reports cover a wide range of public services, and in each country there is a different focus. Audit Scotland has a major interest in auditing best value and community planning in local government. The Wales Audit Office has spent considerable time on housing and RSLs, while the Northern Ireland Audit Office (NIAO) has concentrated more on fewer in-depth reports. Overall, health performance has been a topic in all three countries.

Audit reports on performance tend towards 'could do better' evaluations. An Audit Scotland report on day surgery identified steady progress in carrying out more surgical procedures, but Scotland continued to have lower rates of day surgery than in England (Audit Scotland, 2008b). The report found that performing more day surgery could free up about £8 million a year and would also benefit patients in providing a more speedy recovery. Audit Scotland also reported that access to good palliative care needed to improve and that specialist care mainly focused on people with cancer. Audit Scotland and the Wales Audit Office both reviewed the new General Medical Services contract, introduced in 2006. Both reviews found evidence of some improvement in patient care, which included better monitoring of long-term conditions, flexibility in planning local care and increased income for GP practices. The new contracts allayed the widespread concerns among GPs about workload, pay and the sustainability of services. The Wales Audit Office did, however, find some problems with checking the points awarded to each GP practice. Both reports made recommendations to guide further improvements and to develop the potential of the GP contracts. Audit Scotland found the potential to deliver better outcomes to move services from hospital to the community in line with Scotland's health policy. Waiting lists were examined in Wales and Northern Ireland. The Wales Audit Office reported considerable progress in reducing long waiting times (Wales Audit Office, 2006). NIAO found that there had been a steady decline in the number of people waiting to be admitted to hospital as inpatients or outpatients, the reduction for targets on inpatients had been met, and it was hoped this level of performance would be maintained. The Northern Ireland analysis was part of a larger report into the overall performance of the health service (NIAO, 2008), which reported marked improvements in quality and outcomes in many areas. It traced the health improvements to the first NIE's *Investing for health* strategy in 2000 that reflected health improvement as one of the Executive's five main priorities. However, it also noted some areas where progress may be falling short of initial expectations, particularly in relation to public health issues. Audit Scotland (2007) produced a report on NHS financial and performance management that identified improving performance against key targets, including waiting times. It noted that Scotland's health was improving, with longer life expectancy and lower mortality rates for key diseases. The NIAO report had similarly reported on a positive change in life expectancy, with fewer people dying from the most common conditions (NIAO, 2008, p 7). As in the Northern Ireland report, Audit Scotland reported concern about public health issues such as drugs, alcohol and obesity. A further 'could do better' report noted that while the care given to people with chronic illnesses was improving, the Scottish Executive could do more to build a joined-up system of care, with further development of community-based services.

Some health reports have been more sharply critical. The Wales Audit Office identified weaknesses in NHS financial management, particularly in local health boards, and the auditor-general recommended better financial planning, reviewing and monitoring to support forthcoming changes (Wales Audit Office, 2008). A Wales Audit Office report also found that adult mental health services were in danger of not meeting key standards and targets, and there were significant gaps in community-based services that could provide an alternative to hospital admission. This finding was of some significance, given that standards of mental health are one of the Welsh administration's health priorities. The Wales Audit Office also had a major role in recommending change to the operation of the Wales Ambulance Services Trust after there had been widespread criticisms (Colman, 2007). Reports on other aspects of social provision were more infrequent. A report on delayed discharge in Wales was critical that the independence of vulnerable people was being compromised, and identified the continuing weakness of patient transfers between health and social care. Recommendations were made for further improvement through partnerships in health and social care. The Audit Scotland report on free personal care policy was somewhat cautious, noting some variation and ambiguity in implementation, and a need for better planning and funding. In Northern Ireland a report on older people and domiciliary care found that while domiciliary care was increasing, there continued to be a relatively high dependence on institutional forms of care. The number receiving less complex services such as home help had fallen, and there remained a constant level of unmet need.

Housing attracts attention from the Wales Audit Office as it is responsible for carrying out the inspection of housing associations and rating their services – housing management, rents, housing provision or maintenance. A specific investigation of the national homelessness strategy in Wales found an apparent but not conclusive downward trend in homelessness, but a lack of quantifiable targets and a need to improve the coordination of local prevention services. An earlier audit report, *Housing the homeless* (NIAO, 2002), in Northern Ireland during the time of the first Executive had identified the statutory homeless population as proportionally the highest in the UK and recommended a formal prevention strategy.

Education reports in Scotland have been fairly specific: highlighting the progress made by the Scottish Qualifications Authority since 2000 when there had been problems in processing examination results; examining the state of higher education buildings; and an assessment of the impact of the Scottish teachers' 23% pay award in 2006. A highly critical education report (NIAO, 2006) was published in Northern Ireland on literacy and numeracy in schools, noting that none of the department's targets had been met, that some targets had been lowered and that the timescale for their achievement had been extended. In assessing special needs education, the NIAO report was similar to a Wales Audit Office report in referring to problems in collecting data.

Conclusion

While it is advisable to be cautious in drawing conclusions from statistical comparisons and rather fragmented evidence, it is possible to attempt a broad snapshot of indicators of need and a socio-economic profile, to detail per capita expenditure over the duration of devolution, and to examine internal and external performance assessments.

It is not possible to ascribe causation to devolution but in Scotland health indicators and performance have been improving, and per capita expenditure is now the highest in the UK. This does correspond with extensive and detailed strategy/action plans produced by Scottish administrations particularly in health, social care, education and social exclusion. Wales has improved waiting times and some health indicators. There is evidence of success in tackling child poverty but there is still evidence of poor performance in education. Despite higher proportional expenditure in most areas, Northern Ireland has shown less success in reducing some indicators of social need or improving its position in comparison with the other three countries.

TEN

Conclusion

This conclusion, while acknowledging some difficulties with comparative evidence, examines the impact of devolution on social policy from four different perspectives as well. The concluding comments address some wider consequences of devolution and social policy: the UK citizenship debate, devolved models of social policy and finally the future development of devolution and the future of devolved social policy.

A number of factors can be identified as constraining the evaluation of the impact of devolution on social policy. First, some believe that it is too early to make a judgement. Fawcett (2003), for example, thought it too early to answer whether devolution had produced welfare state divergence. Three years on, Schmuecker and Adams (2006, p 33) thought it was still difficult to discern the extent of divergence in the UK, and Wincott (2006b, p 175) also stated that it was too early for the impact of devolution on social citizenship to be judged definitively. Second, it is always difficult to control for influences on social policy developments other than devolution. Third, some differences in social policy that did exist in the three countries prior to devolution have attracted more focused attention since. The early experience has also been affected by differences in the operation of devolution, with less extensive legislative powers for Wales and the political disruptions in Northern Ireland; since 2007, however, these factors have lost some of their significance. A final factor has increased in influence – the financial pressures that can operate to limit radical departures in social policy between the four countries of the UK.

Assessments of the impact of devolution on social policy

An assessment of the impact of devolution on social policy can relate to four domains: first, a comprehensive overall assessment covering all three countries and the whole field of social policy; second, an assessment of the impact of devolution on social policy in the individual countries; third, a comparative assessment of the impact of devolution on different areas of social policy; and fourth, apart from these more comparative assessments, it is also possible to identify the more isolated impact of a distinctive component of a policy, found in only one country.

Comprehensive overall assessment

Opinions remain divided in making overall general assessments, and they tend to be fairly cautious. McEwen and Parry (2005, p 54) believe that the degree of divergence should not be exaggerated, and apart from high profile cases there has been considerable convergence in social policy. Keating (2007b, p 9) suggests that since devolution there has been a disappointing absence of policy debate and policy innovation. Trench and Jarman (2007) find a general trend that the devolved administrations have sought to do things differently, and many of these policy areas have related to social policy. Greer (2007) sees the greatest impact of devolution as its generation of policy divergence. Williams and Mooney (2008, p 498) still identify considerable disagreement as to the extent to which devolution represents a significant departure in terms of policy making. Ten years on it is possible to acknowledge the wide area of discretion that the devolved administrations have in which to take initiatives in social policy, through strategies, action plans, allocation of finance, administrative structures and through secondary legislation, not just through primary legislation. Wales was able to develop policy and provision despite the lack of primary powers. Over time the ability of the devolved administrations to formulate, shape and implement their own policies has substantially increased through building and focusing their policy capacity. They have established devolved government control over the machinery of local government, non-departmental public bodies and the voluntary sector. The devolved governments, parliaments and assemblies have also established themselves as the institutions that determine provision in main areas of social policy. This means that they have increasingly become the focus for pressure group activity, advisory bodies' recommendations, policy networks, research bodies and media and public attention. The policy-making capacity of the civil service has also increased, with a stronger focus on policies to suit each country. The creation of a significant area of policy difference has been enhanced by the changes in government following the 2007 elections, which has added a further impetus to more autonomy in decision making, to more initiatives to meet current needs and to more diversity in policy approaches. There are also still strong counter pressures promoting convergence in social policy and these are twofold. One set of pressure comes from membership of the UK and the fact that the devolved institutions are subordinate in power to the UK Parliament. In terms of intergovernmental relations the UK Government has accepted the need to make devolution work and has been largely non-interventionist (Trench, 2007, p 279), even if it may not have been happy with some policies introduced in Scotland, for example, free personal care. The other set of pressures relate to circumstances where the devolved administrations actually decide to maintain or pursue convergence, as that aligns with their perception of the best policy option.

While assessment of the general impact of devolution on social policy may have been dominated by the divergence–convergence debate since 1999, there is now evidence for the scope and importance of collaboration in areas of social policy, that are either devolved or non-devolved, but impinge on each other or intertwine with each other. This has created a need for cooperation and comparison of strategies, for example in relation to child poverty, social inclusion, regulation of health professions and welfare to work. At the same time, there has had to be an increasing awareness of demarcation lines, especially in Whitehall. It has become common for UK Government strategies to acknowledge that the departmental documents in health, social care, education, social inclusion, housing, benefit take-up and children's services apply only to England, or include a statement that cooperation with the devolved administrations will be necessary. Similarly Westminster select committees are clarifying that their inquiries on social policy topics cover only England.

The early years of devolution were marked by statements for Scotland and Wales that social policy was the dominant policy area. Education and health and social services account for about 60% of expenditure and 40% of the aims and programmes of the administrations throughout devolution. Some questions can be raised about the current validity of that view, even if one adds other aspects of social policy in the more peripheral areas of criminal justice, planning, arts and leisure or areas relevant to social policy where the devolved administrations have input into non-devolved subjects. Expressions of the dominance of social policy rather overlook the salience of the environment, agriculture, transport and economic developments as devolved responsibilities, and any assessment of the general impact of social policy, has to be made in this context.

Country-specific assessments

Some of the earlier assessments of the impact of devolution on social policy in Scotland also varied. Stewart, writing in 2004, put the rhetorical question 'has devolution made a difference to Scottish welfare?', and stated that the answer is unequivocally 'yes'. Scott and Mooney (2005, p 266) provided a five-year report card on the Scottish Parliament and pointed to gradual and incremental changes rather than radical differences to address inequalities in Scotland. Mooney and Poole (2004) assessed that a distinctive social policy had not yet emerged in post-devolution Scotland, while between 1999 and 2007 McGarvey and Cairney (2008) identify an overall picture of limited legislative divergence, although mainly occurring in social policy. The same authors have described policy change as significant in Scotland, given some implementation difficulties (McGarvey and Cairney, 2008, p 217). Scotland clearly has formulated and implemented distinctive social policies and developed coherent underpinning narratives. It has developed the capacity for policy analysis, shaping policies to match what are defined as Scotland's needs and engaging the public in policy formulation and implementation. Policy innovations have proved popular with the public and the Scottish polity has moved on to hold a debate on extending governmental powers and fiscal autonomy, which would lead to more control over social policy and more differences between Scotland and the rest of the UK.

Devolution started in Wales with modest hopes and limited confidence of making a difference in such areas as social policy (Drakeford, 2005). Expectations were raised by Rhodri Morgan's aspiration in 2002 to create 'clear red water' between Wales and UK policies, and to encourage an agenda that would differ from the UK Government even if it was also a Labour Government. As in Scotland, there were doubts about the timing of assessments. There were comments that 'despite devolution addressing hardship and unfairness it is too early to say if devolution will make a difference to people's lives' (Bransbury, 2004, p 180), and that 'although it is possible to identify divergence from England in key areas of social policy it is too early to judge the policy outcomes' (Chaney and Drakeford, 2004, p 136). Since that time the scope and extent of initiatives in social policy has increased, and WAG found ways of compensating for the lack of primary legislative powers through 'the imaginative use of instruments and levers at its disposal' (Drakeford, 2007b, p 5). Views suggesting limited development are still being expressed. D. Hill (2008, p 5), for example, notes that for every Children's Commissioner Act, many organisations voiced disappointment that their distinctive policy hopes were not expressed in legislation. The value of devolution lies not just in the policy outcomes and differences but in what Kay (2003) determines as 'the intrinsic value of devolution'. The Welsh Executive and Assembly are able to formulate policies, strategies and actions, whether different or not from the other UK countries, determined in Wales by elected representatives and aligned to the needs of the Welsh people.

The devolution of social policy in Northern Ireland has a long history, but policy making has been subject to political disruption in both periods of devolution since 1999. The arrangements for major legislation also require cross-community, that is, cross-party support. An evaluation of the impact of the first period of devolution on social policy identified limited policy divergence and a dominant value of deserving social groups (McLaughlin, 2005). Social policy issues do not dominate political party agendas even if the population view health and education issues as important. The nature of political debates has stymied policy formulation and led to a lack of appreciation of the crisis in the health service (Jervis, 2008, p 20) and inhibited social policy debates. The outcome has been threefold. First, there has been a lack of innovation in social policy and delays in introducing new policies and practices from Great Britain, for example in integrated children's services and early years provision. Second, significant differences with the other three countries do exist in policies, provision and particularly delivery structures. Part of this divergence is a consequence of the conflict and divided society and post-conflict transformation, for example the equality agenda and integrated schools. Some differences reflect more practical policy decisions, for example the integration of health and social care and the absorption of the Child Support Agency into a government department. Third, there is a predominantly conservative approach to social policy, very much in contrast to Scotland and Wales. This is reflected in the views of the NIA on such issues as academic selection, abortion, streamlining delivery mechanisms, less priority for social care and early years, a role for PPPs and the lack of structures for public involvement. Somewhat paradoxically, the historic absence of ideological debates or clearly articulated party political positions has also left Northern Ireland without a significant private sector in social services provision, demonstrated by the complete absence of fee-paying private schools and a very small private health sector. Since devolution the relative lack of ideological debates on social policy issues has facilitated some policy copying from Scotland and Wales, as with free prescriptions.

Comparing areas of social policy across countries

'As devolution evolves it seems increasingly necessary to speak of the UK's national health services rather than of its NHS' (Woods, 2002, p 55). Health has a claim to be the area of social policy where devolution has had the most impact. Early signs indicated that policy in Scotland was branching off in a different direction from England (Tannahill, 2005, p 199). Distinctive health policies and approaches were also emerging in Wales, although Drakeford (2006, p 558) alluded to some difficulties in implementation. A review of health provision in Northern Ireland (Appleby, 2005) identified significant differences in acute provision with England. By the time of the election of new governments the divergence between all four countries was seen as striking by Greer (2005), who has traced the pattern of growing differences, driven by separate agendas and policy-making processes. This dynamic of health divergence has been seen as set to continue, with each of the four countries furthering their own policy directions 'employing entirely different levers and philosophies' (Smith and Babbington, 2006, p 2). A study by the Nuffield Trust concluded that there are some real policy differences but still forces for convergence, although the report states 'we now need to talk about the four health systems of the United Kingdom, rather than a unitary NHS' (Jervis, 2008, p 127). A rather dissenting note in relation to a key aspect of health policy is made by Harrington et al (2009), who suggest that claims about the extent of health policy divergence may be exaggerated and that while Scotland, Wales and England have taken different approaches to performance assessment and the setting of targets, policy approaches to health inequalities appear to have been remarkably similar. It is possible to identify the main forms of divergence as covering structures, commissioning, integration with social care and aspects of mental health, local community involvement and public participation. More policy divergence has continued with decisions on prescriptions, hospital car parking and approval of drugs.

Social care provides a more fragmented profile in making an assessment of the impact of devolution. Social work services have continued to display a not dissimilar pattern of concerns and responses to similar challenges. Wales may have a stronger rights-based ethos, Scotland more integration with criminal justice and Northern Ireland more integration with health services, but these distinguishing features existed prior to devolution and have largely just been continued by devolution. Differences can be identified over direct payments, attitudes to personalisation, user participation, collaborative working and community development approaches. Scourfield et al (2008) suggest the similarities between social work in Wales and England are very obviously so much greater than what separates them, and Scotland and Northern Ireland could be added to this assessment.

Early years provision has been the subject of initiatives by the devolved administrations, with Wales originally setting the lead through some groundbreaking schemes. Wales made full use of its powers in relation to early childhood education and care and, it has been argued, achieved more than Scotland (Wincott, 2006a, p 295). Early years provision may have been more at the centre of devolution during the first period of WAG, but Scotland and England were to introduce similar schemes and some innovations of their own. Northern Ireland has lagged behind in terms of expanding provision, adopting new initiatives and in levels of expenditure. Children's services in general again display many similarities, and Scotland and Wales have largely followed the *Every Child Matters* agenda. Again Northern Ireland has not adopted the policy of integrated children's services and expenditure on children's services is lower. Wales (Williamson, 2007) and Northern Ireland also lag behind in new practices and structures for youth policy.

Housing policy and provision no longer occupies such a central role in social policy and divergence in housing policies and strategies is limited. The room for discretion and the scope for radical innovations is restricted by national market and fiscal policies and similar systems of social housing management, housing finance and dependence on similar social housing institutions. Thus housing policy in Scotland, Wales and Northern Ireland has continued with very little that is distinctive from other parts of the UK (Murie, 2004, p 16). This is not to ignore some specific housing problems that have led to some variety in responses by the devolved administrations: in strategies on homelessness, the Right to Buy, affordable housing and stock transfer.

Education is notable for the existence of significant differences in policy pre-devolution. Devolution has enabled Scotland and Wales to build on their existing traditions. The overall scenario shows some significantly different policies emerging under devolution, the Welsh Baccalaureate, structural integration of schools and childcare in England, testing and curriculum development, differences over special schools and the dominance of the debate over academic selection in Northern Ireland. All the devolved administrations have acted on curriculum reform and to counter low levels of educational achievement, to improve literacy and numeracy and develop the skills basis.

An assessment of the impact of devolution on social policy must take into account the impact that the devolved administrations have been able to make to services where the main responsibility lies with the UK Government. Child poverty is an area where Scotland and Wales have made major contributions through devolved actions, and gender and disability initiatives have been taken in all three devolved administrations.

Devolved government activity to help people into employment and initiatives for lone parents and to assist rural communities can also be quoted. Fuel poverty is another area of overlapping responsibility that has received priority attention from all three governments, and Scotland and Wales have turned their attention to identifying ways in which they can assist with financial inclusion and indebtedness. Cooperation with UK Government departments is also more likely to result in generally similar schemes in each country.

Innovations in one country

The fourth category of assessment is the more individual social policy introduced in one country as simply a component of the main social policy areas. One factor in considering this category is that some such initiatives have not remained as isolated unique policies but have been copied by the other countries, as was the case with free prescriptions for Scotland, Wales and Northern Ireland, and children's commissioners in all four countries. A second factor to take into account is that the unique policy may have originated before devolution, but has so far been endorsed by the devolved governments. Examples are the children's hearing system in Scotland or the maintenance of academic selection in Northern Ireland or community health councils in Wales. In this context there are relatively few examples of major innovation and unique features of social policy initiatives determining in one country only. Generally, listings of totally unique policies are not extensive. For Scotland such a list would be:

- free personal and nursing care
- student fees
- free bus travel for older people
- free eye and dental checks
- free pre-school places for all three- and four-year-olds
- community schools

The list for Wales could include:

- commissioner for older people
- prescription charges
- free car parking at hospitals
- free swimming for those aged 60 plus

- primary schools free breakfast initiative
- Welsh Baccalaureate qualification
- foundation phase curriculum
- Flying Start children 0-3 in deprived communities
- integrated children's centres
- student support

Northern Ireland can provide few unique examples to date; some that can be identified reflect a more selective approach to social policy provision and Direct Rule ministers put some initiatives in place during 2002–07:

- abolition of 11 plus transfer test
- free prescriptions
- specialist public health agency
- free train and bus travel for people aged 60 plus
- fully integrated structure of health and social care
- childcare expenses for lone parents to family members

A focus on initiatives which diverge from England and from each other can also lead to neglect of the extensive impact of low-level differences made in implementing common general policies and of cooperation with the UK department on anti-poverty and social inclusion policies. However, any assessment of the impact of devolution would also include reference to setting and meeting many detailed commitments and targets within social policy provision. Scotland can include: increases in young people entering full-time higher education; more investment in colleges and universities; helping to increase employment rates; a fall in pupil–teacher ratios; lifting children out of poverty; affordable housing measures; and a programme for multiple and complex needs. Wales can include: improvement in workforce skills; a rise in employment; childcare for hard-to-reach groups; Want 2 Work for people claiming incapacity benefit; affordable housing measures; community regeneration; lifting children out of poverty; school-based counselling; distinctive health service frameworks; and a children and well-being monitor for Wales. Northern Ireland can include: assistance with increasing employment; reducing child poverty; maintaining equality of opportunity and anti-discrimination measures; high levels of educational achievement and widening participation in higher education; freezing local council rates; maintaining high standards of housing fitness and social housing management; and continuing community development approaches.

UK social citizenship debate

Assessment of the impact of devolution on social policy has increasingly been placed in the context of what can be called the 'UK social citizenship debate'. This is the view that the welfare state has developed throughout the UK as a national UK welfare state (Clarke, 2005). The UK's comprehensive system of social welfare is seen as contributing to identification with and belonging to the UK state, with the British welfare state (McEwen, 2002, p 86) guarantor of social and economic services. Thus the welfare state promoted the idea of a national community sharing burdens, risks and security (McEwen and Parry, 2005, p 45), and a system of national rights embodying 'nationalised social citizenship' (Wincott, 2006b, p176). This position owes its origins in part to an interpretation of T.H. Marshall's writings on social citizenship that added uniform national social rights to civil and political rights (Marshall, 1950 [1992]). However, in this analysis Marshall made no reference to Scotland, Wales or Northern Ireland, nor does he in his later book, *Social policy in the twentieth century* (Marshall, 1975), instead referring only to social policy in the UK or Britain. The implications of relating UK social citizenship to the welfare state for devolution were spelt out by Bogdanor (1999), who noted welfare should depend on need not geography, and suggested that the devolution of social policy implied different standards of social welfare in different parts of the country which therefore threatened the very foundations of the welfare state. The existence of devolved sub-states within the state makes it more difficult to enforce a uniformity of social rights and policy provision: 'the core fields of social citizenship can in principle vary' (Jeffery, 2006a, p 67). Support for the UK welfare state and the social solidarity implied by shared citizenship came from the Calman Commission (2008a, p 35), which saw devolution as allowing radical differences between the rest of the UK and Scotland in areas where common UK citizenship might suggest greater uniformity. Calman raised the question of how uniform or integrated a welfare state the UK should be, and stated that there may be a case for a broadly common social citizenship across the UK.

This position can be challenged on a number of grounds. Historically, aspects of the welfare state were always different, particularly in Scotland and Northern Ireland and not just through administrative differences. Wincott (2006b, p 181) points out that 'need not geography' has never determined the practice of the British welfare state. The education and legal systems in Scotland and Northern Ireland have had historic differences from England and Wales. Since Mrs Thatcher's government, there has also been a drawing back from the welfare state, which meant that the UK Government was not delivering the kind of social citizenship that Scots expected (Jeffery, 2006b, p 84). In practice, to date, the UK welfare state has not been subject to massive fragmentation because of devolution. Schmuecker and Adams (2006, p 7) note that the early experience of devolution has not produced a fundamental divergence in the quality of social citizenship.

There can also be a dispute about what the term 'social citizenship' implies. Is it only very basic principles, covering core health services free at the point of access and free state education? What other welfare provision would meet the social citizenship criteria? This also raises the issue of setting or enforcing minimum standards of welfare. Would central government have an enforcement role that could undermine or destabilise devolution, or would these minimum standards be legislated for in a new Bill of Rights? The Northern Ireland Human Rights Commission has actually called for measures in a Bill of Rights along these lines (NIHRC, 2008). In practice the devolved administrations have not shown any intention to reduce welfare provision but have a rather more developed social citizenship than England. Only in Northern Ireland has there been less demand for an expansion in social provision and a switch to support for the economy. However, the main criticism of the argument for uniform national social citizenship centres on which nation 'national' refers to. As discussed in Chapter Eight, the devolved countries can also develop welfare systems to build identity, citizenship and solidarity. The reality is that the contribution of the UK and devolved governments to social citizenship can be complementary and coexist. Ultimately devolution must result in some significant social policy divergence; and consequently some imbalance in social citizenship, and that is the inevitable and desirable outcome of devolution.

Devolved models of social policy

Is there now a Scottish social policy, a Welsh social policy and a Northern Ireland social policy? Writing more broadly, Greer (2007, p 137) states 'we are seeing the progressive construction of models of the public sector and the public services'. In one sense there are Scottish, Welsh and Northern Irish systems, as devolution means a major component of social policies in Scotland, Wales and Northern Ireland is determined by their own government and parliament/assemblies. What are the characteristics that would identify separate systems of models of social policy? Key elements can be seen as occupying a continuum, as set out in Table 10.1.

Table 10.1: Components of models of social policy

Principle of allocation	Universalism	Selectivity
Delivery mechanism	State	Voluntary and private sectors
Choice of providers	Uniformity	Choice
Commissioner-provider split	None	Complete use
Public involvement	Extensive	Limited
Underpinning values	Social justice	Less emphasis on social justice
	Equality	Equality of opportunity
	Collectivism	Individualism
	Social rights	Liberal rights

Scotland and Wales occupy a common position at one end of this spectrum, with a preference for universalism and state provision, against choice and competition, for public and user involvement, and underpinned by the values of social justice, equality and collectivism. These principles and values are not to be found in all social policies and strategies, and are most evident in health, social care, education and treatment of offenders and in relation to poverty, social inclusion and employment, as far as devolved powers allow. The prospects for a fundamentally different social policy in Scotland and Wales from England and Northern Ireland lie mainly in health and education. Northern Ireland is different in not having coherent government statements concerning social policies, principles or values. Conservative social values tend to predominate in terms of individual responsibility, traditional family values and a preference for selectivity and against universalism. Yet Northern Ireland also has a tradition of extensive state provision with little private sector involvement in health, education or social care, and there have been 'populist' decisions by government to copy Scotland and Wales at times. These perspectives raise the question of how different the three devolved systems are from England. Under New Labour there has been less of a preference for the principles of universalism and state provision and more of a preference for choice and competition, although commitments to public and user involvement and improved public services are very similar. Narratives in England would also not differ so much in commitments to social justice, equality and improving services and well-being.

Future development of devolution

The immediate future of devolution will be determined by developments in three main areas: the prospects for fiscal autonomy and the influence of the financial and economic crisis; the likelihood of an increase in devolved powers; and the future political context of devolution.

Financial and economic factors

Scotland, in particular, has been keen to pursue greater fiscal autonomy. SNP preference for independence would lead to total fiscal autonomy, but short of that the Scottish Government has made strong representations to have powers to borrow that would provide greater control over capital expenditure and enable it to act in times of economic need. The Holtham Independent Commission on funding and finance for Wales will make recommendations in relation to the Barnett formula and needs in 2010. The Northern Ireland Government has been seeking unsuccessfully a differential rate of corporation tax. The Calman Commission has considered views on funding principles, funding mechanisms and financial accountability for the future. The context for greater fiscal economy and for the immediate future of devolution is the global economic and financial crisis. This has seen the devolved administrations look inventively at how devolved powers can assist in tackling recession and helping with economic recovery. Devolved administrations have taken action to lessen the impact on home owners and business, for example through freezes on local taxation, reshaping capital spending plans and focused expenditure on affordable housing, fuel poverty, schools and health. Some of this activity has required closer working with the UK departments in Scotland and to provide a seamless service for those made redundant between Jobcentre Plus and Skills Development Scotland. Of more immediate concern have been the cuts in public expenditure across the devolved administrations proposed by the UK Government of £1 billion in Scotland for two years from 2010/11 and of more than £500 million for Wales and £200 million in Northern Ireland, described by the Treasury Minister as 'efficiency cuts'. The extent to which UK decisions control the budgetary position and overall fiscal freedom of the devolved governments is unlikely to shift dramatically. Short-term pressures on finance and the economy may have more effect as major changes in financing devolution appear unlikely.

Powers of the devolved governments

This is again an area of some uncertainty, but the options and choices are quite clearly mapped out. Scotland has the most uncertain future, with two contrasting constitutional options with implications for social policy. The most radical development would be progress towards independence for Scotland that would entail the replacement of devolved government by an independent parliament and government with sovereign powers. In the event of failure to gain popular support in a referendum, the SNP will at least campaign for enhanced devolved powers with new responsibilities for taxation, broadcasting, the civil service, benefits, energy, transport, aspects of asylum and immigration and employment (Scottish Executive, 2007a). The Calman Commission made recommendations on how devolution might be adjusted, with a case for additional responsibilities in the areas of broadcasting, elections, misuse of drugs, road safety, animal health, marine planning and new funding mechanisms (Calman, 2009).

Northern Ireland presents quite a clear picture for the future development of powers, with the devolution of law and order pending. This will involve a new devolved justice department and a new justice and policing minister. UK legislation also allows some executive functions in the justice field to be transferred to the Executive, even where the legislative competence remains reserved (House of Commons, 2009). When justice powers are devolved, it will impact on some joined-up legislation in social policy areas, and should, in theory, facilitate a more joined-up approach in a wholly devolved setting.

Wales also presents a degree of uncertainty as it progresses towards a referendum on fully devolved legislative powers. The procedure was specified in the 2006 Government of Wales Act. An All Wales Convention has been set up to facilitate a participative consultation on the issue of giving NAW primary law-making power (All Wales Convention, 2009), to assess the level of public support and to make recommendations on holding a referendum. In the interim or without endorsement by a referendum, WAG will continue to acquire, on a case-by-case basis, the legislative competence from Westminster to make its own laws through measures in devolved fields, and new fields or policy areas can be devolved when Welsh ministers acquire new functions.

Cairney, P. (2006) 'Venue shift following devolution: when reserved meets devolved in Scotland', *Regional Federal Studies*, vol 16, no 4, pp 429-45.

Cairney, P. (2007) 'Using devolution to set the agenda? Venue shift and the smoking ban in Scotland', *British Journal of Politics and International Relations,* vol 9, no 1, pp 73-89.

Cairney, P. (2009) *Scotland devolution monitoring report. January 2009* (www.ucl.ac.uk/constitution-unit/files/research/devolution/dmr/Scotland_Jan09.pdf).

Calman, K. (2008a) *The future of Scottish devolution within the Union. A first report*, Edinburgh: Commission on Scottish Devolution.

Calman, K. (2008b) *Serving Scotland better*, Edinburgh: Commission on Scottish Devolution.

Campbell, H. (2007) '"Nothing about me, without me": NHS values past and future in Northern Ireland', in S.L. Green and P. Rowland (eds) *Devolving policy, diverging values*, London: The Nuffield Trust.

Carmichael, P. and Osborne, R. (2003) 'The Northern Ireland Civil Service under direct rule and devolution', *International Review of Administrative Sciences*, vol 69, no 2, pp 205-17.

Chaney, P. (2006) 'A case of institutional decoupling: equality and public policy in post devolution Wales', *Scottish Affairs*, no 56, Summer, pp 22-34.

Chaney, P. and Drakeford, M. (2004) 'The primacy of ideology: social policy and the first term of the National Assembly for Wales', in N. Ellison, L. Bauld and M. Powell (eds) *Social Policy Review 16*, Bristol: The Policy Press.

Chaney, P. and Fevre, R. (2002) *An absolute duty: Equal opportunities and the manpower assembly for Wales*, Cardiff: Institute of Welsh Affairs.

Cheetham, J. (2001) 'New Labour, welfare and social work and devolution: a view from Scotland', *British Journal of Social Work*, vol 31, pp 625-8.

Children in Wales (2007) *A Wales fit for children and young people* (www.childreninwales.org.uk).

Clarke, C. (2006) 'Scottish education in the 21st century: a story of tradition, myth, conflict and progress', in G. Mooney, T. Sweeney and A. Law (eds) *Social care, health and welfare in contemporary Scotland*, Paisley: Kynoch and Blaney.

Clarke, J. (2005) 'Welfare states as nation states: some conceptual reflections', *Social Policy and Society*, vol 4, no 4, pp 407-15.

Cohen, B., Moss, P., Petrie, P. and Wallace, J. (2004) *A New Deal for children*, Bristol: The Policy Press.

Collins, S., James, A., Lynn, E. and Williams, C. (1997) 'Welsh language developments on a social work course: the Bangor case', *Social Work Education*, vol 16, no 1, pp 80-100.

Colman, J. (2007) 'A case study from Wales', in M. Lavender (ed) *Watchdogs straining at the leash*, London: Public Management and Policy Association.

Committee of OFMDFM (Office of the First Minister and Deputy First Minister) (2007) *Interim report on the Committee's inquiry into child poverty in Northern Ireland*, Belfast: Northern Ireland Assembly.

Cook, A., Petch, A., Glendinning, C. and Glasby, J. (2007) 'Building capacity in health and social care partnerships: key messages for a multi-shareholder', *Journal of Integrated Care*, vol 18, no 4, pp 3-10.

COSLA (Confederation of Scottish Local Authorities) (2008) *Relationships between local authorities and the third sector* (www.cosla.gov.uk).

Cowell, R. (2004) 'Community planning: fostering participation in the congested state?', *Local Government Studies*, vol 30, no 4, pp 497-518.

Cuthbert, M. and Cuthbert, J. (2007) 'Free personal care for the elderly: the monitoring of the cost of the policy', *Scottish Affairs*, no 59, Spring, pp 49-67.

Daly, G., Mooney, G., Poole, L. and Davis, H. (2005) 'Housing stock transfer in Birmingham and Glasgow: the contrasting experiences of two UK cities', *European Journal of Housing Policy*, vol 5, no 3, pp 327-41.

Day, G. (2009) 'The independence of the voluntary sector in Wales', in M. Smerdon (ed) *The first principle of voluntary action*, London: Baring Foundation.

Dear, J., O'Dowd, C., Timoney, A., Paterson, K.R., Walker, A. and Webb, D.J. (2007) 'Scottish medicines consortium: an overview of rapid new drug assessment in Scotland', *Scottish Medical Journal*, vol 52, no 3, pp 20-6.

Deloitte (2007) *Examining the case for a commissioner for older people: Report*, Belfast: OFMDFM.

DFP (Department of Finance and Personnel) (2007) *Outcome of Northern Ireland Executives 2007 review of domestic rating system*, Belfast: DFP.

DH (Department of Health) (2006a) *Cross-border emergency treatment: Agreement between England, Scotland, Wales and Northern Ireland* (www. dh.gov.uk/en/publicationsandstatistics/publications).

DH (2006b) *Concluding the review of patient and public involvement* (www.dh.gov. uk/en/Managingyourorganisation/PatientAndPublicinvolvement/index. htm).

DH (2007) *Trust, assurance and safety – the regulation of health professionals in the 21st century*, Cm 7030, London: The Stationery Office.

DHSSPS (Department of Health, Social Services and Public Safety) (1999) *Children first: The Northern Ireland childcare strategy* (www.dhsspsni.gov. uk/cfcontents.pdf).

DHSSPS (2000) *Building the way forward in primary care: A consultation paper*, Belfast: DHSSPS.

DHSSPS (2002a) *Developing better services, modernising hospitals and reforming structure*, Belfast: DHSSPS.

DHSSPS (2002b) *Health and well-being in Northern Ireland: Developing a regional strategy for the health and personal social services 2002-2022*, Belfast: DHSSPS.

DHSSPS (2002c) *Investing for health: Report 2002*, Belfast: DHSSPS.

DHSSPS (2003) *Investing for health: Promoting mental health strategy and action plan*, Belfast: DHSSPS.

DHSSPS (2005a) *A healthier future: A 20 year vision for health and well-being in Northern Ireland 2003-2025*, Belfast: DHSSPS.

DHSSPS (2005b) *Review of Children First: Final report* (www.dhsspsni.gov.uk/publications).

DHSSPS (2008a) *Proposals for health and social care reform* (www.dhsspsni.gov.uk).

DHSSPS (2008b) *Delivering the Bamford vision* (www.dhsspsni.gov.uk).

Dickenson, H. Glasby, J. Forder, J. and Beesley, L (2007) 'Free personal care in Scotland: a narrative review', *British Journal of Social Work*, vol 37, no 3, pp 459-474.

Dickson, B. (2005) *The legal system of Northern Ireland*, Belfast: SLS Legal Publications.

Dickson, B. and Osborne, R. (2007) 'Equality and human rights since the Belfast Agreement' in P. Carmichael, C. Knox and R. Osborne (eds) *Devolution and constitutional change in Northern Ireland*, Manchester: Manchester University Press.

Ditch, J. (1988) *Social policy in Northern Ireland between 1939-1950*, Aldershot: Avebury.

Dixon, J. (2009) 'Devolution and divergence in UK health policies', Seminar at Institute for Public Policy Research, 2 February (www.ippr.org.uk).

Donnelly, C. and Osborne, R. (2005) 'Devolution, social policy and education: some observations from Northern Ireland', *Social Policy and Society*, vol 4, no 2, pp 147-56.

Downe, J. and Martin, S. (2006) 'Joined up policy in practice? The coherence and impacts of the local government modernization agenda', *Local Government Studies*, vol 32, no 4, pp 465-88.

Drakeford, M. (2005) 'Wales and a third term of New Labour: devolution and the development of difference', *Critical Social Policy*, vol 25, no 4, pp 497-506.

Drakeford, M. (2006) 'Health policy in Wales: making a difference in conditions of difficulty', *Critical Social Policy*, vol 26, no 3, pp 543-61.

Drakeford, M. (2007a) 'Social justice in a devolved Wales', *Benefits*, vol 15, no 2, pp 171-8.

Drakeford, M. (2007b) 'Progressive universalism', *Agenda, Institute of Welsh Affairs*, Winter, pp 4-7.

DSD (Department for Social Development) (2007) *Review into affordable housing* (Semple Review) (www.dsdni.gov.uk).

DWP (Department for Work and Pensions) (1999) *Concordat between the Department of Social Security and the Scottish Executive.* (www.dwp.gov.uk/resourcecentre/archive/policy_strategy_publications.asp).

DWP (2003a) *Report of the Quinquennial Review of the Social Security Committee*, Cm 6189, London: The Stationery Office.

DWP (2003b) *United Kingdom national action plan on social inclusion 2003-05* (www.dwp.gov.uk/publications/dwp/2003/nap).

DWP (2005) *Opportunity age: Meeting the challenges of ageing in the 21st century* (www.dwp.gov.uk/opportunity_age).

DWP (2006) *A New Deal for welfare: Empowering people to work*, Cm 6730, London: The Stationery Office.

DWP (2007a) *Working for children*, Cm 7067, London: The Stationery Office.

DWP (2007b) *Ready for work: Full employment in our generation*, Cm 7290, London: The Stationery Office.

DWP (2007c) *Wales – Towards full employment: Joint strategy with Welsh Assembly Government* (www.dwp.gov.uk).

DWP (2007d) *Reducing dependency, increasing opportunity* (www.dwp.gov.uk/mediacentre/pressreleases/2007/mar/emp017-050307.asp).

DWP (2008a) *DWP commissioning strategy*, Cm 7330, London: The Stationery Office.

DWP (2008b) *UK national report on strategies for social protection and social inclusion* (www.dwp.gov.uk/publications/dwp/2008/socialprotection).

Edwards, J. (1995) *Affirmative action in a sectarian society*, Aldershot: Avebury.

Egan, D. (2008) 'School effectiveness', *Agenda, Institute of Welsh Affairs*, Summer, pp 40-2.

EHRC (Equality and Human Rights Commission) (2008a) *About the Equality Commission and Human Rights Commission in Scotland* (www.equalityhumanrights.com/en/scotland).

EHRC (2008b) *Wales programme 2008/9: Bringing people together* (www.equalityhumanrights.com/en/wales/publications/pages/walesprogramme).

Ellison, N. and Ellison, S. (2006) 'Creating opportunity for all? New labour, new localism and the opportunity society', *Social policy and society*, vol 5, no 3 pp 337-48.

Equality Commission for Northern Ireland (2007) *Section 75: Keeping it effective*, Belfast: Equality Commission for Northern Ireland.

ERINI (Economic Research Institute for Northern Ireland) and IFS (Institute of Fiscal Studies) (2007) *An analysis of public expenditure on children in Northern Ireland*, Belfast: ERINI.

Essex, S (2008) *Affordable housing in Wales: An independent report to the Minister for Housing*, Cardiff: WAG.

Estyn (2008) Annual report of HM Chief Inspector of Education and Training in Wales 2007-07 (www.estyn.gov.uk/home.asp).

Evans, D. and Forbes, T. (2009) 'Partnership in health and social care', *Public Policy and Administration*, vol 24, no 1, pp 67-83.

Evason, E. (2006) *Digest of Northern Ireland law: A short guide to social security law in Northern Ireland*, Belfast: SLS Legal Publications.

Fahey, T. and McLaughlin, E. (1999) 'Family and state, north and south', in A.F. Heath, R. Breen and C.T. Whelan (eds) *Ireland North and South: Perspectives from social science*, Oxford: Oxford University Press.

Farren, S. (2004) 'Barnett formula must go', Press release (www.sdlp.ie).

Fawcett, H. (2003) 'Social inclusion policy-making in Scotland: assessing the capability–expectations gap', *Political Quarterly*, vol 74, no 2, pp 429-39.

Fawcett, H. (2004) 'The making of social justice policy in Scotland: devolution and social exclusion', in A. Trench (ed) *Has devolution made a difference? The state of the nations 2004*, Exeter: Imprint Academic.

Fitzpatrick, B. (2006) *Article 24 of the Commissioner for Children and Young People (Northern Ireland) Order 2003 – The review of the office of the commissioner* (www.niccy.org).

Fitzpatrick, S. (2004) 'Homelessness policy in Scotland', in D. Sim (ed) *Housing and public policy in post-devolution Scotland*, Coventry: Chartered Institute of Housing.

Flint, T (2008) 'Governing sectarianism in Scotland', *Scottish Affairs*, no 63, Spring.

Foster, A. (2008) 'Foster announces functions for new councils', Department of the Environment press release, 31 March (www.northernireland.gov. uk/news-doe/news-doe-march-2008).

Freeman, I. and Moore, K. (2008) 'Community health (and care) partnerships in Scotland', *Journal of Integrated Care*, vol 16, no 3, pp 38-47.

Fyfe, N., Timbrell, H. and Smith F.M. (2006) 'The third sector in a devolved Scotland: from policy to evidence', *Critical Social Policy*, vol 26, no 3, pp 630-41.

Gallagher, J. (2006) 'The impact of devolution on education policy: two case studies', in C. Donnelly, R. Osborne and P. McKeown (eds) *Devolution and pluralism in education in Northern Ireland*, Manchester: Manchester University Press.

Gallagher, J. and Raffe, D. (2008) 'Difference and divergence within the UK', Seminar on *Higher education across national boundaries: The impact of Europe and devolution*, Langbank.

General Social Care Council (2008) *Social work at its best: A statement of social work roles and tasks for the 21st century* (www.gscc.org.uk).

Georghiou, N. and Kidner, C. (2007) 'Equal opportunities subject profile', Scottish Parliament Information Centre briefing 07/50 (www.scottish.parliament.uk).

Gibb, K. (2003) 'Transferring Glasgow's council housing: Financial, urban and housing policy implications', *European Journal of Housing Policy*, vol 3, no 1, pp 89-114.

Gibbons, G. (2008) 'Child poverty', written statement (http://new.wales.gov.uk/about/cabinet/cabinetstatements/?lang=en).

Government Equality Office (2008) *Framework for a fairer future – The Equality Bill*, Cm 7431, London: The Stationery Office.

Gray, A.M. and Carragher, L. (2008) *Lone parents speaking out*, Belfast: Gingerbread NI.

Greer, S.L. (2004) *Territorial politics and health policy*, Manchester: Manchester University Press.

Greer, S.L. (2005) 'Becoming European: devolution, Europe and health policy-making', in A. Trench (ed) *The dynamics of devolution*, Exeter: Imprint Academic.

Greer, S.L. (2007) 'The fragile divergence machine: citizenship, policy divergence and devolution', in A. Trench (ed) *Devolution and power*, Manchester: Manchester University Press.

Greer, S.L. and Trench, A. (eds) (2008) *Health and inter-governmental relations in the devolved United Kingdom*, London: The Nuffield Trust.

Hallowell, M., Price, D. and Pollock, A (2008) *The use of private finance initiative (PFI) and public, private partnerships in Northern Ireland*, Belfast: Northern Ireland Public Service Alliance.

Halpern, D. (2009) 'Devolution and life changes', Seminar at Institute for Public Policy Research, 2 February (www.ippr.org.uk).

Harrington, B., Smith, N., Hunter, D., Marks, L., Blackman T., McKee, L., Greene, A., Elliot, E. and Williams, G. (2009) 'Health inequalities in England, Scotland and Wales: stakeholders', accounts and policy compared', *Public Health*, vol 123, no 1, pp 24-8.

Harvey, C. (2001) 'Human rights and equality in Northern Ireland', in C. Harvey (ed) *Human rights, equality and democratic renewal in Northern Ireland*, Oxford: Hart Publishing.

Heald, D. (2003) *Funding the Northern Ireland Assembly: Assessing the options*, Research Monograph 10, Belfast: Northern Ireland Economic Council.

Heald, D. (2008) *Response to the Holtham Commission's five broad questions* (www.davidheald.com/publications.htm).

Heald, D. and McLeod, A. (2005) 'Embeddedness of UK devolution finance within the public expenditure system', *Regional Studies*, vol 39, no 4, pp 495-518.

Heenan, D. and Birrell, D. (2006) The integration of health and social care: the lessons from Northern Ireland', *Social Policy and Administration*, vol 40, no 1, pp 47-66.

Hexagon (2007) *Evaluation of free pensioner care: Research findings No 55*, Hexagon Research and Consultation (www.hexagonresearch.co.uk/).

Hill, D. (2008) *21 years of children and young people policy in Wales*, London: Action for Children.

Hill, M. (2008) *21 years of children's policy in Scotland*, London: Action for Children.

HMI (Her Majesty's Inspectorate) (2006) *The sum of its parts: The development of integrated community schools in Scotland* (www.hmie.gov.uk/documents/publication/dicss-02.html).

HMI (Her Majesty's Inspectorate) for Education and Training in Wales (2007) *The foundation phase pilots, August* (www.estyn.gov.uk).

HM Treasury (2004) *Choice for parents: The best start for children* (www.hm-treasury.gov.uk/prebud_pbr04_adchildcare.htm).

HM Treasury (2006) *Leitch review of skills* (www.hm-treasury.gov.uk/leitch).

HM Treasury (2007) *Funding the Scottish Parliament, National Assembly for Wales and Northern Ireland Assembly: Statement of funding policy* (www.hm-treasury.gov.uk/3765) (www.hm-treasury.gov.uk/pbr_csr07_statement_of_funding_policy.htm).

HM Treasury. (2008) *Public expenditure statistical analysis of public expenditure by country and region*, London: The Stationery Office.

Horgan, G. (2006) 'Devolution, direct rule and neo-liberal reconstruction in Northern Ireland', *Critical Social Policy*, vol 26, no 3, pp 656-88.

House of Commons (2006) *The Northern Ireland (St Andrews Agreement) Bill 2006-7,* House of Commons Research Paper 06/56, London.

House of Commons (2009) *The Northern Ireland Bill 2009,* House of Commons Research Paper 09/18, London.

Hudson, R. (2007) 'Partnering through networks: can Scotland crack it?', *Journal of Integrated Care*, vol 15, no 1, pp 3-13.

Hughes, J., Campbell, A., Hewstone, M. and Cairns (2007) 'Segregation in Northern Ireland', *Policy Studies*, vol 28, no 1, pp33-53.

Humes, W.M. and Bryce, T.G.K. (2003) 'The distinctiveness of Scottish education', in T.G.K. Bryce and W.M. Humes (eds) *Scottish education second edition post-devolution*, Edinburgh: Edinburgh University Press.

Hutton, J (2007) 'The future of welfare: tackling poverty and worklessness in Scotland', Speech at John Wheatley College, Glasgow, 27 January (www.dwp.gov.uk/aboutus/2007/26-01-07.asp).

IWA (Institute of Welsh Affairs) (2006) *Future of social housing in Wales*, Cardiff: IWA.

Jarrett, T. (2006) *Commissioner for Older People Wales Bill*, House of Commons Research Paper 06/33, London: House of Commons Library.

Jeffery, C. (2006a) 'Devolution and local government', *Publius: The Journal of Federalism*, vol 36, no 1, pp 57-73.

Jeffery, C. (2006b) 'Devolution and social citizenship: which society, whose citizenship?', in S.L. Greer (ed) *Territory, democracy and justice*, Basingstoke: Palgrave Macmillan.

Jenkins, S. (2008) *Extension of the New Deal Plus for lone parents pilot to Scotland and Wales: Qualitative evaluation*, Research Report No 499, London: Department for Work and Pensions.

Jervis, P. (2008) *Devolution and health*, London: The Nuffield Trust.

Joint Committee on Human Rights (2007) *The work of the children's commissioners*, HL24/HC1672, London: The Stationery Office.

Jones, C. (2004) 'Reforming the right to buy', in D. Sim (ed) *Housing and public policy in post-devolution Scotland*, Coventry: Chartered Institute of Housing.

Kay, A. (2003) 'Evaluating devolution in Wales', *Political Studies*, vol 51, no 1, pp 51-66.

Keating, M. (2005) *The government of Scotland: Public policy making after devolution*, Edinburgh: Edinburgh University Press.

Keating, M. (ed) (2007a) *Scottish social democracy, progressive ideas for public policy*, Brussels: Peter Lang.

Keating, M. (2007b) 'Public services: renewal and reform', in M. Keating (ed) *Scottish social democracy: Progressive ideas for public policy*, Brussels: Peter Lang.

Keating, M., Stevenson, L., Cairney, P. and Taylor, K. (2003) 'Does devolution make a difference? Legislative output and policy divergence in Scotland', *Journal of Legislative Studies*, vol 9, no 3, pp 110-39.

Kenway, P. and Palmer, G. (2007) *Monitoring poverty and social exclusion in Wales*, York: Joseph Rowntree Foundation.

Kenway, P., MacInnes, T. and Palmer, G. (2008) *Monitoring poverty and social exclusion in Scotland*, York: Joseph Rowntree Foundation.

Kenway, P., MacInnes, T., Kelly, A. and Palmer, G. (2006) *Monitoring poverty and social exclusion in Northern Ireland*, York: Joseph Rowntree Foundation.

Kenway, P., Parsons, N., Carr, J. and Palmer, G. (2005) *Monitoring poverty and social exclusion in Wales*, York: Joseph Rowntree Foundation.

Kerr, D. and Feeley, D. (2007) 'Collectivism and collaboration in NHS Scotland', in S.L. Greer and D. Rowland (eds) *Devolving policy, diverging values?*, London: The Nuffield Trust.

Kidner, C. (2007) *Children's services*, Scottish Parliament Information Centre Briefing 07/40 (www.scottish.parliament.uk).

Kintrea, K. (2006) 'Having it all? Housing reform under devolution', *Housing Studies*, vol 21, no 2, pp 187-207.

Knox, C. (2008) 'Policy making in Northern Ireland: ignoring the evidence', *Policy & Politics*, vol 36, no 3, pp 343-59.

Laffin, M. (2002) *The National Assembly for Wales and local government* (www.jrf.org.uk).

Lister, R. (2007) 'Social justice: meanings and politics', *Benefits*, vol 15, no 2, pp 113-25.

Lloyd, G. (2000) 'Quasi government in Scotland: a challenge for devolution and the renewal of democracy', in A. Wright (ed) *Scotland: The challenge of devolution*, Aldershot: Ashgate Press.

Local Government and Communities Committee (2008) *Schemes to tackle fuel poverty: Evidence* (www.scottish.parliament.uk/s3/committees/lgc/inquiries/fuelpoverty).

Local Government Data Unit – Wales (2009) *Welsh annual housing statistics 2008* (www.dataunitwales.gov.uk).

Lyons, M. (2007) *Lyons inquiry into local government* (www.communities.gov.uk/localgovernment/localgovernmentfinance/lyonsinquiryinto/).

MacLeavy, J. and Gay, O. (2005) *The quango debate*, House of Commons Research Paper 05/30, London: House of Commons Library.

Maclennan, D. and O'Sullivan, T. (2008) *Housing policies for Scotland: Chances and challenges*, York: Joseph Rowntree Foundation.

Marshall, T.H. (1950 [1992]) *Citizenship and social class*, London: Pluto Press.

Marshall, T.H. (1975) *Social policy in the twentieth century*, London: Hutchinson.

Martin, P. (2007) 'The times they are a changing: the challenges facing social work in Northern Ireland', *Child Care in Practice*, vol 13, no 3, pp 261-9.

Martin, S. and Webb, A (2009) 'Citizen-centred 'public services: contestability without consumer-driven competition?' *Public Money and Management*, vol 29, no 2, pp 123-30.

Maxwell, S. (2007) 'The voluntary sector and social democracy in devolved Scotland', in M. Keating (ed) *Scottish social democracy: Progressive ideas for public policy*, Brussels: Peter Lang.

McAteer, M. and Bennett, M. (2005) 'Devolution and local government: evidence from Scotland', *Local Government Studies*, vol 31, no 3, pp 285-306.

McCafferty, P. (2006) 'Safe in their hands? Understanding health and health policy in the devolved Scotland', in G. Mooney, R. Sweeney and A. Law (eds) *Social care health and welfare in contemporary Scotland*, Glasgow: Kynoch and Blaney.

McClelland, R. (2007) Letter to OFMDFM from Board for Mental Health and Learning Disability, 21 December (*www.pfgbudgetni.gov.uk/boardformentalhealthandlearningdisability.pdf*).

McClelland, S. (2007) 'The reconfiguration debate challenging "group think"', in *The Welsh Health Battleground* , Cardiff: Institute of Welsh Affairs.

McConnell, A. (2004) *Scottish local government*, Edinburgh: Edinburgh University Press.

McConnell, A. (2006) 'Central–local government relations in Scotland', *International Review of Administrative Sciences*, vol 72, no 1, pp 73-84.

McCready, S. (2000) *Empowering people: Community development and conflict*, Belfast: The Stationery Office.

McCrudden, C. (2001) 'Equality', in C. Harvey (ed) *Human rights, equality and democratic renewal in Northern Ireland*, Oxford: Hart Publishing.

McEwen, N. (2002) 'State welfare nationalism: the territorial impact of welfare state development in Scotland', *Regional and Federal Studies*, vol 12, no 1, pp 66-90.

McEwen, N. (ed) (2008) *Scotland devolution monitoring report*, May (www.ucl.ac.uk/constitution-unit/files/research/devolution).

McEwen, N. and Parry, R. (2005) 'Devolution and the preservation of the United Kingdom welfare state', in N. McEwen and L. Moreno (eds) *The territorial politics of welfare*, London: Routledge.

McGarvey, N. (2002) 'Intergovernmental relations in Scotland post-devolution', *Local Government Studies*, vol 28, no 3, pp 29-48.

McGarvey, N. and Cairney, P. (2008) *Scottish politics*, Basingstoke: Palgrave.

McIver, I. (2006) *Future structural fund programmes in Scotland 2007-2013*, Scottish Parliament Information Centre Briefing 06/45 (www.scottish.parliament.uk/business/research/briefings-06/SB06-45.pdf).

McKay, A. and Gillespie, M. (2007) 'Gender mainstreaming or mainstreaming gender? A question of delivering on gender equality in the new Scotland' in M. Keating (ed) *Scottish social democracy: Progressive ideas for public policy*, Brussels, Peter Lang.

McKee, K. (2007) 'Community ownership in Glasgow: the devolution of ownership and control, or a centralizing process?', *European Journal of Housing Policy*, vol 7, no 3, pp 319-36.

McLaughlin, E. (2005) 'Governance and social policy in Northern Ireland (1999-2004): the devolution years and postscript', in M. Powell, K. Clarke and L. Bauld (eds) *Social Policy Review 17*, Bristol: The Policy Press.

McLaughlin, E. (2007) 'From negative to positive equality duties: the development and constitutionalisation of equality provisions in the UK', *Social Policy and Society*, vol 6, no 1, pp 111-21.

McLean, I., Lodge, G. and Schmuecker, K. (2008) *Fair shares? Barnett and the politics of public expenditure*, London: Institute for Public Policy Research.

Meehan, E. (2006) 'The experience of a single equality commission in Northern Ireland', *Scottish Affairs*, no 56, Summer, pp 35-56.

Michael, P. and Tanner, D. (2007) 'Values *v* policy in NHS Wales', in S.L. Greer and D. Rowland (eds) *Devolving policy, diverging values?*, London: The Nuffield Trust.

Mitchell, J. et al (2001) 'Scotland: maturing devolution', in A. Trench (ed) *The state of the nations 2001*, Exeter: Imprint Academic.

Mooney, G. and Poole, L. (2004) '"A land of milk and honey"? Social policy in Scotland after devolution', *Critical Social Policy*, vol 24, no 4, pp 458-83.

Mooney, G. and Williams, C. (2006) 'Forging new "ways of life"? Social policy and nation building in devolved Scotland and Wales', *Critical Social Policy*, vol 26, no 3, pp 608-29.

Mooney, G., Scott, G. and Williams, C. (2006) 'Rethinking social policy through devolution', *Critical Social Policy*, vol 26, no 3, pp 483-97.

Morgan, R. (2005) 'Working together', *Agenda, Institute of Welsh Affairs*, Winter, pp 29-32.

Mullins, E. and Murie, A. (2006) *Housing policy in the UK*, Basingstoke: Palgrave Macmillan.

Murie, A. (2004) 'Scottish housing: the context', in D. Sim (ed) *Housing and public policy in post-devolution Scotland*, Coventry: Chartered Institute of Housing.

Navarro, M. and Lambert, D. (2005) *The nature and scope of the legislative powers of the National Assembly for Wales*, Devolution Briefing no 13, Devolution and Constitutional Change, Swindon: Economic and Social Research Council.

NAW (National Assembly for Wales) (2001) *The learning country: A comprehensive education and lifelong learning programme to 2010 in Wales*, Consultation document, Cardiff: NAW.

NAW (2005) *Report of review of the interface between health and social care*, Cardiff: NAW (www.assemblywales.org/).

NAW (2008a) *Guide to the legislative process* (www.assemblywales.org/bu-home/bus-legislation-guidance.htm).

NAW (2008b) *Affordable housing – legislative competence order.* Memorandum, (www.assemblywales.org/lco-ld6897-em-e.pdf).

Needham, C. (2007) 'Realising the potential of co-production: negotiating improvements in public services', *Social Policy and Society*, vol 7, no 2, pp 221-31.

New Policy Institute (2008) *Annual monitoring poverty and social exclusion reports* (www.npi.org.uk).

NIA (2007) *Policies targeting child and older citizen/pensioner poverty*, Department for Social Development Research Paper 03/07, Belfast: NIA.

NIA (2008a) *The Children and Young Persons' Commissioner for Northern Ireland*, Research Paper 54/08, Belfast: NIA.

NIA (2008b) *Childcare provision in the UK and Republic of Ireland*, Research Paper 16/08 (www.niassembly.gov.uk/io/research_link_08.htm).

NIA (2008c) *Comparing child poverty in Northern Ireland with other regions*, Briefing Note 23/08, Belfast: NIA.

NIA (2008d) *Final report into child poverty in Northern Ireland*, Committee for the Office of the First Minister and Deputy First Minister (www.niassembly.gov.uk).

NIA Social Development Committee (2002) *Homelessness* (www.niassembly.org.uk).

NIAO (Northern Ireland Audit Office) (2002) *Housing the homeless* (www.niauditoffice.gov.uk/pubs).

NIAO (2006) *Improving literacy and numeracy in schools*, HC 953, Belfast: NIAO.

NIAO (2008) *The performance of the health service in Northern Ireland*, NIA18/08-09, Belfast: NIAO.

NICE (National Institute for Health and Clinical Excellence (2009) *NICE and the NHS* (www.nice.org.uk).

NIE (Northern Ireland Executive) (2001) *Programme for government: Making a difference*, Belfast: Office of the First Minister and Deputy First Minister.

NIE (2008a) *Building a better future: Draft programme for government 2008-11*, Belfast: Office of the First Minister and Deputy First Minister.

NIE (2008b) *Building a better future: Draft budget 2008-11*, Belfast: Office of the First Minister and Deputy First Minister.

NIHE (Northern Ireland Housing Executive) (2002) *The homelessness strategy* (www.nihe.gov.uk/index/foi_publications/homelessness-5.htm).

NIHE (2009) *Northern Ireland housing market review and prospectus 2009-2012*, Belfast: NIHE.

NIHRC (Northern Ireland Human Rights Commission) (2008) *A bill of rights for Northern Ireland*, Belfast: NIHRC.

NIO (Northern Ireland Office) (1998) *Northern Ireland Act 1998*, London: The Stationery Office.

NIO (2005) *Statement by the Secretary of State for Northern Ireland on the outcome of the Review of Public Administration 22 November 2005*, Belfast: The Stationery Office.

NIO (2006) *Devolving policing and justice in Northern Ireland: A discussion paper*, London: The Stationery Office.

OFMDFM (Office of the First Minister and the Deputy First Minister) (2005) *A shared future: A consultation paper on improving relations in Northern Ireland*, Belfast: OFMDFM.

OFMDFM (2006) *Lifetime opportunities: Government's anti-poverty and social inclusion strategy for Northern Ireland*, Belfast: OFMDFM.

OFMDFM (2007) *Promoting social inclusion: Homelessness action plan* (www.ofmdfm.gov.uk).

ONS (Office for National Statistics) (2008a) *Regional trends 40*, Basingstoke: Palgrave Macmillan.

ONS (2008b) *United Kingdom health statistics No 3*, Basingstoke: Palgrave Macmillan.

OPSI (Office of Public Sector Information) (2008a) *Acts of the Scottish Parliament and explanatory notes* (www.opsi.gov.uk/legislation/scotland/s-acts.htm).

OPSI (2008b) *Northern Ireland Legislation* (www.opsi.gov.uk/legislation/northernireland/ni_legislation.htm).

OPSI (2008c) *Graduate Endowment Abolition (Scotland) Bill*, Policy memorandum (www.opsi.gov.uk/legislation/scotland/acts2008/pdf/asp_20080003_en.pdf).

Osborne, R.D. (2003) 'Progressing the equality agenda in Northern Ireland', *Journal of Social Policy*, vol 32, no 3, pp 339-60.

Osborne, R.D. (2007) '"Evidence" and equality in Northern Ireland', *Evidence and Policy*, vol 3, no 1, pp 79-97.

Osborne, R.D. (2008) 'Emerging equality policy in Britain in comparative context: a missed opportunity?', *Public Money and Management*, vol 28, no 5, pp 305-12.

Osmond, J. (2004) 'Nation building and the Assembly', in A. Trench (ed) *Has devolution made a difference?*, Exeter: Imprint Academic.

Owen, J.W. (2007) 'Legislation for the health of the people', in *The Welsh Health Battleground*, Cardiff: Institute of Welsh Affairs.

Page, A (2005) 'A parliament that is different? Law making in the Scottish Parliament' in R. Hazel and R. Rawlings (eds) *Devolution, law making and the constitution*, Exeter: Imprint Academic.

Page, A. and Batey, A. (2002) 'Scotland's other parliament: Westminster legislation about devolved matters in Scotland since devolution', *Public Law*, Autumn, pp 501-23.

Palmer, G., MacInnes, T. and Kenway, P. (2006) *Monitoring poverty and social exclusion in Scotland 2006*, York: Joseph Rowntree Foundation.

Palmer, G., MacInnes, T. and Kenway, P. (2008) *Monitoring poverty and social exclusion 2008*, York: Joseph Rowntree Foundation.

Paris, C. (2008) 'The changing housing system in Northern Ireland 1998-2007', *Ethnopolitics*, vol 7, no 1, pp 119-36.

Parry, R. (1997) 'The Scottish Parliament and social policy'. *Scottish Affairs*, no 20, pp 34-46.

Parry, R. (2004) 'Devolution and social security in Scotland', *Benefits*, vol 41, no 12, pp169-74.

Parry, R. (2005) 'The civil service response to modernization in the devolved administrations', *Financial Accountability and Management*, vol 21, no 1, pp 57-74.

Parry, R. (2007) 'Public service reform and the efficiency agenda', in M. Keating (ed) *Scottish social democracy: Progressive ideas for public policy*, Brussels: Peter Lang.

Patchett, K. (2005) 'Principle or pragmatism? Legislating for Wales', in R. Hazell and R. Rawlings (eds) *Devolution, law making and the constitution*, Exeter: Imprint Academic.

Paterson, L. (2002) 'Scottish social democracy and Blairism: difference, diversity and community', in G. Hassan and C. Warhurst (eds) *Tomorrow's Scotland*, London: Lawrence and Wishart.

Pawson, H. and Davidson, E. (2008) 'Radically divergent? Homelessness policy and practice in post-devolution Scotland', *European Journal of Housing Policy*, vol 8, no 1, pp 39-60.

Payne, J. (2007) *Mental health services in Scotland*, Scottish Parliament Information Centre Briefing 07/39 (www.scottish.parliament.uk).

PDP (Possibilities Development Partnership) (2007) *Equalities of opportunity for lone parents*, Belfast: Northern Ireland Executive.

Pearson, C. (2004) 'Keeping the cash under control: what's the problem with direct payments in Scotland?', *Disability and Society*, vol 19, no 1, pp 3-14.

Pearson, C. (ed) (2006) *Direct payments and personalisation of care*, Edinburgh: Dunedin Academic Press.

Pemberton, S. and Lloyd, G. (2008) 'Devolution, community planning and institutional decongestion?', *Local Government Studies*, vol 34, no 4, pp 437-51.

Pidgeon, C. (2009) *The Barnett formula*, Research paper, Belfast: Northern Ireland Assembly.

Pilgrim, D. (2007) 'New "mental health" legislation for England and Wales: some aspects of consensus and conflict', *Journal of Social Policy*, vol 36, no 1, pp 79-95.

Pinkerton, J. (2008) *Children's policy in Northern Ireland 1987-2008: Progress and prospects*, London: Action for Children.

Platt, D. (2007) *The status of social care – A review 2007* (www.dh.gov.uk/en/ Publicationsandstatistics/Publications/PublicationsPolicyAndGuidance/ DH_074217).

Ponton, M. (2008) 'Priorities for the incoming government', in (Academy Health Wales) *The Welsh health battleground*, Cardiff: Institute of Welsh Affairs.

Poole, L. and Mooney, G. (2005) 'Governance and social policy in the devolved Scotland', in G. Mooney and J. Scott (eds) *Exploring social policy in the 'new' Scotland*, Bristol: The Policy Press.

Poole, L. and Mooney, G. (2006) 'Privatizing education in Scotland? New Labour, modernization and "public" services', *Critical Social Policy*, vol 26, no 3, pp 562-86.

Pratchett, L. (2004) 'Local autonomy, local democracy and the new localism', *Political Studies*, vol 52, no 2, pp 358-75.

Quirke, P. and McLaughlin, E. (1996) 'Targeting social need', in E. McLaughlin and P. Quirke (eds) *Policy aspects of employment equality in Northern Ireland*, Belfast: Standing Advisory Commission on Human Rights.

Raffe, D. (2006) 'Devolution and divergence in education policy', in J. Adams and K. Schmuacker (eds) *Devolution in practice 2006*, London: Institute for Public Policy Research.

Raffe, D. and Croxford, L. (2000) *The education and training systems of the UK: Convergence on divergence*, Edinburgh: Edinburgh University Press.

Rawlings, R. (2003) *Delineating Wales: Constitutional legal and administrating aspects of national revolution*, Cardiff: University of Wales Press.

Rees, G. (2007) 'The impacts of parliamentary devolution on education policy in Wales', *Welsh Journal of Education*, vol 14, no 1, pp 8-20.

Reynolds, P. (2002) 'Developing differently: educational policy in England, Wales, Scotland and Northern Ireland', in J. Adams and P. Robinson (eds) *Devolution in practice*, London: Institute for Public Policy Research.

Richard, (Lord) I. (2004) *Report of the Richard Commission on the powers and electoral arrangements of the National Assembly for Wales*, Cardiff: The Stationery Office.

Riddell, S., Pearson, C., Barnes, C., Jolly, D., Morgan, G. and Priestly, M. (2005) 'The development of direct payments in the UK: implications for social justice', *Social Policy and Society*, vol 4, no 1, pp 75-85.

Riddell, S., Priestly, M., Pearson, C., Morgan, G., Barnes, C., Jolly, D. and Williams, V. (2006) *Disabled people and direct payments: A UK comparative study*, Swindon: Economic and Social Research Council Report.

Robson, K. (2007) *The National Health Service in Scotland*, Scottish Parliament Information Centre Briefing 07/32 (www.scottish.parliament.uk).

Robson, K and Payne, J. (2005) *The national framework for service change in the NHS in Scotland (The Kerr Report)*, Scottish Parliament Information Briefing 03/62 (www.scottish.parliament.uk).

Roy, E. (2008) *The private finance initiative and public private partnerships*, Paper No 08/005, Cardiff: National Assembly for Wales Commission (www.assemblywales.org/bus-home/bus-guide-docs-pub/bus-assembly-publications-research).

RPA (Review of Public Administration) (2003) *The Review of Public Administration in Northern Ireland*, Belfast: RPANI.

RPA (2005) *The Review of Public Administration in Northern Ireland: A further consultation*, Belfast: RPANI.

RPA (2006) *Better government for Northern Ireland*, Belfast: RPANI.

Salmond, A. (2008) 'Delivering more effective government', Speech by First Minister, 30 January (www.scotland.gov.uk/news).

Save the Children (2008) *Children in severe poverty in Wales: An agenda for action*, Cardiff (www.savethechildren.org.uk/en/54_5056.htm).

Schmuecker, K. and Adams, J. (2006) 'Divergence in priorities, perceived policy failure and pressure for convergence', in J. Adams and K. Schmuecker (eds) *Devolution in practice*, London: Institute for Public Policy Research.

Scott, G. and Mooney, G. (2005) 'Social policy in Scotland: imagining a different future?', in G. Mooney and G. Scott (eds) *Exploring social policy in the 'new' Scotland*, Bristol: The Policy Press.

Scott, G. and Mooney, G. (2009) 'Poverty and social justice in the devolved Scotland: neoliberlism meets social democracy?', *Social Policy and Society*, vol 8, no 3, pp 379–90.

Scottish Affairs Committee (2006) *The Sewel Convention: The Westminster perspective, Hc983* (www.publications.parliament.uk/pa/cm200506/cmselect/cmscotaf/1634/1634.pdf).

Scottish Affairs Committee (2007) *Second Report: Poverty in Scotland, Hc128* (www.publications.parliament.uk/pa/cm200708/cmselect/cmscotaf/128/12802.htm).

Scottish Affairs Committee (2008a) *Third Report: Child poverty in Scotland, Hc277* (www.publications.parliament.uk/pa/cm200809/cmselect/cmscotaf/55/5504.htm).

Scottish Affairs Committee (2008b) *Poverty in Scotland and child poverty in Scotland: Responses by the Government and the Scottish Executive to the Committee's Second and Third Reports of Session 2007-8 Hc525* (www.publications.parliament.uk/pa/cm200708/cmselect/cmscotaf/525/525.pdf).

Scottish Executive (1999a) *Making it work together: A programme for government.* (www.scotland.gov.uk/Resource/Doc/158140/0042788.pdf).

Scottish Executive (1999b) *Social justice, a Scotland where everyone matters: Milestone sources and definitions.* (www.scotland.gov.uk/Publications/1999/11/SocialJustice)

Scottish Executive (2000) *Report of the joint future group.* (www.scotland.gov.uk/library3/social/rjfg).

Scottish Executive (2001a) *New directions: Response on the review of the Mental Health (Scotland) Act 1984* (www.scotland.gov.uk/health/mentalhealthlaw/millan/Report/rnhs.pdf).

Scottish Executive (2001b) *Patient focus and public involvement* (www.scotland.gov.uk/publications/2001/12/10431).

Scottish Executive (2001c) *For Scotland's children report* (www.scotland.gov.uk/library3/education).

Scottish Executive (2001d) *Public bodies proposals for change*, Edinburgh: Scottish Executive.

Scottish Executive (2002) *Closing the opportunity gap*, Scottish Budget for 2003-06 (www.scotland.gov.uk/publications/2002/10/15579).

Scottish Executive (2003a) *A partnership for a better Scotland: Partnership agreement* (www.scotland.gov.uk/publications/2003).

Scottish Executive (2003b) *Partnership for care: Scotland's Health White Paper* (www.scotland.gov.uk/Publications/2003/02/16476/18730).

Scottish Executive (2004a) *Ambitious excellent schools – Our agenda for action* (www.scotland.gov.uk/Publications/2004/11/20176/45853).

Scottish Executive (2004b) *A curriculum for excellence*, The Curriculum Review Group (www.scotland.gov.uk/Publications/2004/11/20178/45862).

Scottish Executive (2005a) *Building a health service fit for the future* (www.scotland.gov.uk/publications/2005).

Scottish Executive (2005b) *The mental health of children and young people: A framework for promotion, prevention and care* (www.scotland.gov.uk/publications/2005).

Scottish Executive (2005c) *Delivering for health* (www.scotland.gov.uk/publications/2005).

Scottish Executive (2005d) *Homes for Scotland's people: A Scottish housing policy statement* (www.scotland.gov.uk/publications/2005).

Scottish Executive (2006a) *Delivering for mental health* (www.scotland.gov.uk/publications/2006).

Scottish Executive (2006b) *Getting it right for every child*, Implementation plan (www.scotland.gov.uk/Publications/2006/06/22092413/1).

Scottish Executive (2006c) *Changing lives: Report of the 21st century social work review* (www.scotland.gov.uk/publications/2006).

Scottish Executive (2006d) *Workforce plus – An employment framework for Scotland* (www.scotland.gov.uk/publications/2006).

Scottish Executive (2006e) *Transforming public services: The next phase of reform* (www.scotland.gov.uk/publications/2006).

Scottish Executive (2006f) *People and place: Regeneration policy statement.* (www.scotland.gov.uk/publications/2006).

Scottish Executive (2007a) *Choosing Scotland's future: A national conversation: Independence and responsibility in the modern world* (www.scotland.gov.uk/publications/2007/08).

Scottish Executive (2007b) *Adults with learning disabilities implementation of 'The same as you', Scotland, 2006* (www.scotland.gov.uk/publications/2007).

Scottish Fuel Poverty Forum (2008) *Towards 2016: The future of fuel poverty policy in Scotland* (www.scotland.gov.uk/Publications/2008/10/09155649/0).

Scottish Government (2007a) *Principles and priorities: The government's programme for Scotland* (www.scotland.gov.uk/publications/2007).

Scottish Government (2007b) *All our futures: Planning for a Scotland with an ageing population* (www.scotland.gov.uk/publications/2007).

Scottish Government (2007c) *Better health, better care: Action plan* (www.scotland.gov.uk/publications/2007).

Scottish Government (2007d) *Firm foundations: The future of housing in Scotland: A discussion document* (www.scotland.gov.uk/publications/2007).

Scottish Government (2007e) Consultation Document. Abolition of the graduate endowment fee. (www.scotland.gov.uk/publications/2007/07).

Scottish Government (2007f) Government economic strategy, Edinburgh: Scottish Government.

Scottish Government (2008a) *Moving Scotland forward: The government's programme for Scotland 2008/9* (www.scotland.gov.uk/publications/2008/09).

Scottish Government (2008b) *Gender equality scheme 2008-11* (www.scotland.gov.uk/publications/2008).

Scottish Government (2008c) *Disability equality scheme 2008-11* (www.scotland.gov.uk/publications/2008).

Scottish Government (2008d) *Statistics modern curriculum – Gaelic* (www.scotland.gov.uk/topics/statistics).

Scottish Government (2008e) *Closing the opportunity gap programme: Phase 1 evaluation* (www.scotland.gov.uk/publications/2008).

Scottish Government (2008f) *Taking forward the economic strategy: A discussion paper on tacking poverty, inequality and deprivation in Scotland* (www.scotland.gov.uk/publications/2008).

Scottish Government (2008g) *Early years and early intervention: A joint Scottish Government and COSLA policy statement* (www.scotland.gov.uk/publications/2008/03).

Scottish Government (2008h) *Scotland performs. National indicators* (www.scotland.gov.uk/about/scotperforms/performance).

Scottish Government (2008i) *Responding to the changing economic climate – Further action on housing* (www.scotland.gov.uk/publications/2008).

Scottish Parliament (2008a) *The licensing of medicines in the UK and their use in the NHS*, Scottish Parliament Information Centre Briefing 08/17 (www.scottish.parliament.uk/business/research).

Scottish Parliament (2008b) *An inquiry into the transposition of EU directives*, European and External Relations Committee Report (www.scottish.parliament.uk/nmCentre/news/news-comm-07/ceu07-s3-002.htm) 07 report,

Scottish Parliament Education Committee (2006) *Early years inquiry* (www.scottish.parliament.uk/business/committees).

Scourfield, J., Holland, S. and Young, C. (2008) 'Social work in Wales since democratic devolution', *Australian Social Work*, vol 61, no 1, pp 42-56.

Simeon, R. (2003) 'Free personal care: policy divergence and social citizenship', in R. Hazell (ed) *The state of the nations 2003*, Exeter: Imprint Academic.

Sinclair, S. (2008) 'Dilemmas of community planning: lessons from Scotland: *Public Policy and Administration*, vol 23, no 4, pp 453–70.

Smith, C. (2006) *Commissioner for Older People (Scotland) Bill*, Scottish Parliament Information Centre Briefing, 06/07 (www.scottish.parliament.uk/business/bills/71-CommOldPeople/71-CommissionerforOlderPeopleBillsummary.pdf).

Smith, C. and Babbington, E. (2006) 'Devolution: a map of divergence in the NHS', *Health Policy Review*, issue 2, Summer, pp 1-12.

Smith, R. (2006) 'Devolution and divergence in social housing policy in Britain', in J. Adams and K. Schmuecker (eds) *Devolution in practice 2006*, London: Institute for Public Policy Research.

Social Services Improvement Agency (2005) *Social work in Wales: A profession to value* (www.wlga.gov.uk/english/meeting-documents).

SSAC (Social Security Advisory Committee) (2000) *Thirteenth report 1999-2000* (www.ssac.org.uk).

Stewart, J. (2004a) *Taking stock: Scottish social welfare after devolution*, Bristol: The Policy Press.

Stewart, J. (2004b) 'Scottish solutions to Scottish problems? Social welfare in Scotland since devolution', in N. Ellison, L. Bauld and M. Powell (eds) *Social Policy Review 16*, Bristol: The Policy Press.

Stoker, G. (2004) *Transforming local governance from Thatcherism to New Labour*, Basingstoke: Palgrave Macmillan.

Stokes, R. (2008) *European structural and cohesion funds 2007-2013*, National Assembly for Wales, Members' Research Service Briefing.

Sturgeon, N. (2007) 'Firm foundations – the future for housing in Scotland', Statement (www.scotland.gov.uk/news/releases/2007).

Sturgeon, N. (2008) *Future of the NHS in Scotland* (www.scotland.gov. uk/news/releases/2008).

Sullivan, M. (2005) 'Wales, devolution and health policy: policy experimentation and differentiation to improve health', *Contemporary Wales*, vol 17, no1, pp 44-65.

Sutherland, (Lord) S. (1999) *With respect to old age: Long-term care – Rights and responsibility*, Cm 4192, London: The Stationery Office.

Sutherland, (Lord) S. (2008) *Independent review of free personal and nursing care in Scotland*, Edinburgh: Scottish Government Publications.

Talbot-Smith, A. and Pollock, A. (2006) *The new NHS: A guide*, London: Routledge.

Tannahill, C. (2005) 'Health and health policy', in G. Mooney and G. Scott (eds) *Exploring social policy in the 'new' Scotland*, Bristol: The Policy Press.

Thomas, A. (2004) *The reform of assembly sponsored public bodies*, Cardiff: National Assembly for Wales.

Thompson, W., Parry, J. and Walker, R. (2006) *National Report: United Kingdom mainstreaming social inclusion* (www.europemsi.org/media/findings/uk.pdf).

Tomlinson, M. (2000) 'Targeting social need, social exclusion and social security statistics', in N. Yeates and E. McLaughlin (eds) *Measuring social exclusion and poverty*, Belfast: Department for Social Development.

Trench, A. (2004) 'The more things change the more they stay the same. Intergovernmental relations four years on', in A. Trench (ed) *Has devolution made a difference?*, Exeter: Imprint Academic.

Trench, A. (2007) 'Washing dirty linen in private: the processes of intergovernmental relations and the resolution of disputes', in A. Trench (ed) *Devolution and power in the United Kingdom*, Manchester: Manchester University Press.

Trench, A. (2008) *Devolution and higher education: Impact and future trends. Research report*, London: Universities UK.

Trench, A. and Jarman, H. (2007) 'The practical outcomes of devolution: policy-making across the UK', in A Trench (ed) *Devolution and power in the United Kingdom*, Manchester: Manchester University Press.

Trench, A. and Jeffery, G. (2007) *Older people and public policy: The impact of devolution*, London: Age Concern.

UK Government (1998) *The agreement: The agreement reached in the multi-party negotiations*, Cmnd 3883, London: The Stationery Office.

UK Government (2007) The consolidated 3rd and 4th periodic report to the UN Committee on The Rights of the Child. (www.everychildmatters. gov.uk/strategy/uncrc/ukreport)

WAG (Welsh Assembly Government) (2000) *A better Wales*, Cardiff: WAG.

WAG (2001a) *Adult mental health services for Wales: Equity, empowerment, effectiveness, efficiency*, Strategy document (www.wales.nhs.uk/publications/ adult-health-e.pdf).

WAG (2001b) *Child and adolescent mental health services: Everybody's business*, Strategy document (www.nhs.wales.nhs.uk/publications).

WAG (2001c) *Improving health in Wales* (www.wales.nhs.gov.uk).

WAG (2002) *Well-being in Wales*, Consultation document, Cardiff: WAG (www.wales.nhs.uk.gov.uk.about/strategy/publications).

WAG (2003a) *Wales: A better country: The strategic agenda of the Welsh Assembly Government*, Cardiff: WAG.

WAG (2003b) *Strategy for older people in Wales* (www.wales.gov.uk/topics/ olderpeople/publications).

WAG (2003c) *Wanless review of health and social care in Wales* (www.wales. gov.uk/dhss/publications/health/reports/wanlessreview/wanlessreviewe. pdf?lang=en).

WAG (2004a) *An independent commission to review the voluntary sector* (www. wales.gov.uk/topics/housingandcommunity).

WAG (2004b) *Making the connections: Delivering better services for Wales* (www. new.wales.gov.uk/about/strategy/makingtheconnections/?lang=en).

WAG (2004c) *Mainstreaming equality: A strategy by the Welsh Assembly* (http:// wales.gov.uk/topics/housingandcommunity/communitycohesion/ publications/mainstreamingequality/?lang=en).

WAG (2005a) *Designed for life: Creating world-class health and social care for Wales in the 21st century* (www.new.wales.gov.uk/strategy/strategies/ designedforlife/strategye.pdf?lang=en).

WAG (2005b) *A fair future for our children* (www.new.wales.gov.uk/dsjlg/ publications/childrenyoung/fairfuture/strategye?lang=en).

WAG (2005c) *Childcare is for children* (www.new.wales.gov.uk/news/ archivepress/healthpress/healthpress2005/708551/?lang=en).

WAG (2005d) *Cymorth. A review* (www.new.wales.gov.uk/topics/childrenandyoungpeople/cymorth).

WAG (2005e) *Tackling domestic abuse: The All Wales national strategy* (www.new.wales.gov.uk/?view=Search+results&lang=en).

WAG (2005f) *Social justice report 2005* (www.new.wales.gov.uk/dsjlg/publications/socialjustice/report2005) (www.new.wales.gov.uk/topics/socialjustice/publications/sjreport05/?lang=en).

WAG (2005g) *Raising the standard: The revised adult mental health national service framework and an action plan for Wales* (www.wales.nhs.uk/documents).

WAG (2006a) *Mental health promotion action plan for Wales* (www.new.wales.gov.uk/hcwsubsite/healthchallenge/news/mental-health-action-plan1?lang=en).

WAG (2006b) *Child poverty implementation plan* (www.new.wales.gov.uk/dsjlg/publications/childrenyoung/implementplanphase1/report?lang=en).

WAG (2006c) *National homelessness strategy for Wales 2006-2008* (www.new.wales.gov.uk/desh/publications/housing/homelessnessstrategy/strategye.pdf?lang=en).

WAG (2006d) *Social justice report 2006* (www.new.wales.gov.uk/dsjlg/publications/socialjustice/report2006/summarye.pdf?lang=en).

WAG (2006e) *Delivering beyond boundaries: Transforming public services in Wales* (www.wales.gov.uk/topics/improvingservices/strategy).

WAG (2007a) *One Wales: A progressive agenda for the government of Wales* (www.wales.gov.uk/about/strategy/publications/onewales/?lang=en).

WAG (2007b) *Eighth annual report on work to promote equality and diversity for 2006-2007* (www.wales.gov.uk/topics/equality/publications).

WAG (2007c) *Voluntary sector scheme, Annual report 2006-07* (www.swanseasthirdsector.com/wag).

WAG (2007d) *Fulfilled lives, supportive communities: A strategy for social services in Wales over the next decade* (www.wales.gov.uk/about/strategy/publications).

WAG (2007e) *Communities First guidance 2007* (www.wales.gov.uk/topics/housingandcommunity/regeneration/publications/cfguidance2007/?lang=en).

WAG (2008a) *Draft budget main expenditure group allocations* (http://new.wales.gov.uk/about/finance/assemblybudgets/currentbudgetindex/draftbudgetoctober2008/?lang=en).

WAG (2008b) *The strategy for older people in Wales 2008-2013* (www.new.wales.gov.uk/about/strategy/publications/olderpeople/olderphase2/?lang=en).

WAG (2008c) *Iaith Pawb and Welsh Language Scheme, Annual Report 2007-08* (www.new.wales.gov.uk/topics/welshlanguage/publications/iaithannual0708/?lang=en).

WAG (2008d) *Proposals to change the structure of the NHS in Wales: Proposed new planning system* (www.new.wales.gov.uk/consultations/closedconsultations/healthsocialcare/nhswales/?lang=en).

WAG (2008e) *The third dimension: A strategy action plan for the voluntary sector* (www.new.wales.gov.uk/topics/housingandcommunity/voluntarysector/publications/thethirddimension/?lang=en).

WAG (2008f) *Health statistics Wales 2008* (www.new.wales.gov.uk/topics/statistics/publications/hsw2008/?lang=en).

WAG (2009a) *Unification of public health services in Wales,* Consultation paper (www.wales.nhs.uk/sites3/page.cfm?orgid=811&pid=35647).

WAG (2009b) *NHS waiting times: At end April 2009* (www.wales.gov.uk/topics/statistics/headlines/health2009/hdw200905272/?lang=en).

Wakefield, S. (2008) *Child poverty,* Scottish Parliament Information Centre, 08/05 (www.scottish.parliament.uk/business/research/briefings-08/SB08-05.pdf).

Wales Audit Office (2006) *NHS waiting times: Follow-up report* (www.wales.nhs.uk/documents/NHS_waiting_times_update.pdf).

Wales Audit Office (2008) *Are the devolved financial management arrangements in the NHS Wales effective?* (www.wao.gov.uk/assets/englishdocuments/NHS_Finances_2008_eng.pdf).

Wales Centre for Health (2008) *Doing it differently in Wales* (www.wch.wales.nhs.uk).

Wales Office (2005) *Better governance for Wales,* Cm 6582, London: The Stationery Office.

Wales Office (2008) 'Joint Ministerial Committee: Murphy meets Salmond', Press release (www.walesoffice.gov.uk/2008/04/16).

Watkins, P. and Pearce, A. (2004) *Assembly sponsored public bodies,* Cardiff: National Assembly for Wales.

Welsh Affairs Committee (2008a) *Legislative competence orders-in-council, Hc 175,* London: The Stationery Office.

Welsh Affairs Committee (2008b) *The provision of cross-border health services for Wales, Hc 870* (www.publications.parliament.uk).

Welsh Affairs Committee (2009) *Cross-border provision of public services for Wales: Further and higher* (www.publications.parliament.uk/pa/cm200809/cmselect/cmwelaf/57/57.pdf).

Wilcox, S. (2008) *UK housing review 2007/2008,* Coventry: Chartered Institute of Housing.

Williams, C. and Mooney, G. (2008) 'Decentring social policy? Devolution and the discipline of social policy: a commentary', *Journal of Social Policy*, vol 37, no 3, pp 489-507.

Williams, M. (2008) *A well-being and mental health service fit for Wales* (www.gwalia.com/main.cfm).

Williamson, H. (2007) 'Youth policy in Wales since devolution: from vision to vacuum', *Contemporary Wales*, vol 19, no 1, pp 198-216.

Wilson, R. (2007) 'Rhetoric meets reality: Northern Ireland's equality agenda', *Benefits*, vol 15, no 2, pp 151-62.

Wincott, D. (2005) 'Reshaping public space? Devolution and policy change in British early childhood education and care', *Regional and Federal Studies*, vol 15, no 5, pp 453-70.

Wincott, D. (2006a) 'Paradoxes of New Labour social policy: toward universal child care in Europe's "most liberal" welfare regime?', *Social Politics*, vol 13, no 2, pp 286-312.

Wincott, D. (2006b) 'Social policy and social citizenship: Britain's welfare states', *Publius: The Journal of Federalism*, vol 36, no 1, pp 169-88.

Windle, G. and Porter, A. (2008) 'Policy for older people in Wales', in T. Maltby, P. Kennett and K. Rummery (eds) *Social Policy Review 20*, Bristol: The Policy Press.

Winetrobe, B. (2005) 'A partnership of the parliaments? Scottish law-making under the Sewell convention at Westminster and Holyrood', in R. Hazell and R. Rawlings (eds) *Devolution, law making and the constitution*, Exeter: Imprint Academic.

Woods, K. (2002) 'Health policy and the NHS in the UK', in J. Adams and P. Robinson (eds) *Devolution in practice*, London: Institute for Public Policy Research.

Woods, K. (2004) 'Political devolution and the health services in Great Britain', *International Journal of Health Services*, vol 34, no 2, pp 323-39.

Wyn Jones, R. and Scully, R. (eds) (2009) *Welsh devolution monitoring report, January 2009* (www.ucl.ac.uk/constitution-unit).

Index